"Somehow, Daniel Leader, long a pioneer in the American baking world, finds a way to blaze a new path in his excellent new book with precision and passion. *Living Bread* guides you around the world to make breads that will entice your nose, your mouth, and your heart."

—NANCY SILVERTON, author of *The Mozza Cookbook*

"Daniel Leader's journey with bread began with the spirit of curiosity and inquiry, which led him to founding the iconic bakery Bread Alone. And now we have his new book, *Living Bread*, which is both a warm reflection on his own place within the long tradition of bread-making and a charming collection of stories about the people who have enriched his own experiences and skills, along with many of their delicious recipes."

—NATHAN MYHRVOLD,
co-author of *Modernist Cuisine* and founder of Modernist Cuisine

"This is the book all of us sleepless bread makers have been waiting for. It is a visually stunning homage to land, grain, history, craft, tradition, and travel, and, at its essence, the story of a lifelong love affair with bread. Humble. Passionate. Honest. Inspiring."

—ZACHARY GOLPER, chef and owner of Bien Cuit

"Dan has been a colleague and mentor to me for over thirty years, since I first met him at Bread Alone just a little while after we had both opened our bakeries. He has always been deeply and comfortably curious about everything to do with bread and baking and unfailingly generous with his knowledge and advice. This gorgeous book translates Dan's curiosity and wisdom into a rich and valuable tool for thoughtful and inquisitive bakers."

—STEVE SULLIVAN, co-founder of Acme Bread

"Finally . . . a beautiful cookbook worth reading (and savoring). It's almost as delicious to page through as Daniel's bread is to eat."

—SETH GODIN, author of *This Is Marketing*

"This book is a gold mine for lovers of real bread and the future generation of bread bakers."

—ANDRÉ SOLTNER, author of *The Lutèce Cookbook*

LIVING BREAD

DANIEL LEADER

WITH LAUREN CHATTMAN
TECHNICAL ADVISOR DIDIER ROSADA

LIVING BREAD

Tradition and Innovation in Artisan Bread Making

AVERY
an imprint of Penguin Random House
New York

AVERY

an imprint of Penguin Random House LLC
penguinrandomhouse.com

Most Avery books are available at special quantity discounts for bulk purchase for sales promotions, premiums, fund-raising, and educational needs. Special books or book excerpts also can be created to fit specific needs. For details, write SpecialMarkets@penguinrandomhouse.com.

Library of Congress Cataloging-in-Publication Data

Names: Leader, Daniel, author. | Chattman, Lauren, author.
Title: Living bread : tradition and innovation in artisan bread making / Daniel Leader with Lauren Chattman.
Description: New York : Avery, an imprint of Penguin Random House, [2019] | Includes bibliographical references and index.
Identifiers: LCCN 2019015854| ISBN 9780735213838 (hardcover : alk. paper) | ISBN 9780735213845 (ebook)
Subjects: LCSH: Bread. | LCGFT: Cookbooks.
Classification: LCC TX769 .L3736 2019 | DDC 641.81/5—dc23
LC record available at https://lccn.loc.gov/2019015854
p.   cm.

Printed in China
10 9 8 7 3 6 5 4 3 2 1

Book design by Ashley Tucker

IN LOVING MEMORY
OF BENNETT LEADER
AND ALAN WEISBERG

CONTENTS

NOS PLATS A LA CARTE

- Cuisse de Canard Confit   16,30
- Poulet Fermier Roti Du Jour   14,70
- Cuisse poule confite   14,70
- Risotto au chorizo, courgettes   14,90
  et pignons croquants   16,70
- Tartare De Saumon
- Bavette D'Irlande à l'échalote   15,—
  (150gr)
- Belle ENTrecôte grillée   22,80
  (Sauce au choix)
- Cheese Burger Steack Haché 13,5
  Frais 150gr
- Tartare De Boeuf   13,70
  Faite Salade
- Tartare De Boeuf à l'italienne   16,70
- Tagiatelle au Saumon   15,30
  capelette et ciboulette
- Sauce au choix   1,80

AN ACCIDENTAL BAKER

Paris, 1978

I'm 22, a recent graduate of the Culinary Institute of America, a fledgling restaurant cook, and in Paris for the first time in my life. I've just finished my first year cooking in New York, at Le Veau d'Or, the oldest and most traditional French bistro in the city, and then at The Palace, the most expensive restaurant of the day. While I learned to make a few classics like *blanquette de veau* and *tarte tatin* that year, I mostly spent the time learning what it meant to be the newest member of the brigade and on the lowest rung of the ladder in a tough French kitchen. To get away and broaden my horizons, I've flown from New York to Amsterdam, taken a train to the Gare du Nord, checked into a little hotel near the Place de la Sorbonne, and set my travel alarm clock for 5 a.m. I have a list of Michelin 3-star restaurants I plan to visit in France and Switzerland, including Fernand Point's La Pyramide and Frédy Girardet's eponymous place, at that moment considered the greatest restaurant in the world. In those days, great

chefs were regularly in their kitchens and accessible to those who dared to knock on the door. But today I'm determined that my first food experience in Paris will be an early morning stroll through the nearby Marché Mouffetard, an ancient and expansive outdoor food market I had originally read about in Ernest Hemingway's *A Moveable Feast*.

With a 22-year-old's energy, I'm practically sprinting from my hotel along the narrow cobblestone streets in the direction of the market, from the Pantheon to the Rue Mouffetard, stopping short at every corner to take in the ornately carved doorways and small shops, and regularly unfolding and checking my map, which I have carefully marked with culinary destinations around the city. It's a warm August morning. The sky is brightening to a grayish blue and this quiet Parisian neighborhood is just waking up. Street cleaners in their uniforms are already at work washing the sidewalks and sweeping up debris with their long-handled brooms. At the Cafe Le Mouffetard, the staff is neatly arranging outdoor tables and red and white rattan chairs. Burly workmen are standing at the bar and chatting in small groups, downing small cups of espresso with shots of golden liquor.

Just short of the cafe, I'm bewitched by the perfume of fresh bread that pulls me to a doorway between a *fromagerie* and an *epicerie*. Under a stone archway, the bakery door is open, a pounding afro beat mingles with the scent of the bread, and through a suspended haze of flour and steam I see a guy in his fortiess, in worn cream-colored cotton shorts, sandals, and a frayed white T-shirt printed with the image of a wind-powered flour mill. He is standing next to an enormous mixer, its wide forked arm turning the bowl slowly. Smokey puffs of flour erupt from the bowl each time it makes a revolution. I smell the warm, earthy aroma of fresh bread. A lanky kid, maybe 16, his hair, eyebrows, eyelashes, and arms coated with a dusting of flour,

stands to the baker's right, dressed in an equally worn and frayed outfit. He is pushing a long conveyor on a rolling stand, neatly lined with unbaked baguettes, into the multitiered oven. He pulls a lever on the conveyor after pushing it into the oven and I'm astonished when it emerges empty. He presses a silver button on the front of the oven and there is a loud groan and a strong whoosh of steam out the oven door followed by a lingering whistle. The baker leaves the mixer churning, goes to a work table, casually throws a large tub of soft dough on the table, and starts dividing it into small chunks with a wood-handled scraper, weighing each piece with a quick flick of his wrist on an old brass balance scale, and then nonchalantly placing pieces, neatly lined up like soldiers, on the linen-lined wooden shelves below the table as he goes. He sees me, walks over with a stern expression, and, just when I expect him to throw me out, asks, *"Voulez-vous une baguette chaude, Monsieur?"*

Having been coached before dinner service by my French colleagues at The Palace, I recite the introduction I have memorized: "I'm an American cook on my first trip to Paris. Is it okay if I come in to watch?" And then I ad-lib, "Today is actually my first day in France." I'm astonished when he commands "*Entrez!*" He welcomes me in with a warm, flour-encrusted handshake and swift pat on the back, creating a cloud of flour by the side of my face. I sheepishly walk into the oven room and hit an invisible wall of heat. I have experienced hot kitchens, but this is different—thick, moist heat that you could cut with a knife. The baker gives me a detailed tour of the small room starting with the *pétrin* (fork mixer), explaining that the very slow revolutions of the fork mimic hand-kneading. He tells me that he examines every batch of dough as it is mixing and checks it regularly, and explains why being in touch with the dough is a baker's job. "You know the dough is alive and changes every day." He places a piece of dough, rounded like a golf ball, in my hand and tells me to look at it. I look and then look up at him. He admonishes me, "No, you have to really look at it." He shows me how to stretch it so it looks like a transparent window, which determines the strength of the dough. At least, his dough is stretched to a transparent sheet. Mine, not so much.

Two hours later he is showing me how to score my first baguette. When the breads are in the oven, he instructs me to hold down the steam button until the oven rattles. The three of us take a break, and they show me how to slice the long bread horizontally to examine the *alvéolage* (the French term for a bread's inner structure of holes and bubbles). He points out the cuts on another dark, gnarly bread and then breaks it along the cuts with quick movements. Using the bench knife, he smooths a layer of sweet yellow butter onto the bread, and then some chunky red strawberry jam made by his wife. I eat my first tartine. I am now thoroughly dusted with flour, only slightly cleaner than the two of them, and

intoxicated and possessed by my first Parisian food experience. I don't know it yet, but I just finished my first class at the Backdoor School of Baking.

The Backdoor School of Baking

Fearlessness when it comes to introducing myself and asking questions has been the constant of my career. My formal training in bread baking consisted of a two-week stint in the Culinary Institute of America (CIA) Hyde Park bake shop, located in the basement of what had been an old monastery building and put together with used and surplus baking equipment, haphazardly arranged. Meyer Zwerdling, the Eastern European bread shop instructor, used to say that as long as he could heat an oven to 350 degrees, he could make good bread. While we were learning the basics, we were also a production engine, baking hard and soft rolls to serve to hundreds of students for breakfast, lunch, and dinner. If we had time, our teacher would lead us through the recipe for his classic Jewish rye bread—a large deli-style loaf scented with caraway seeds made with Chef Zwerdling's bubbling rye starter, which he kept in a special clay crock on his desk. We all knew never to touch the sourdough, but we would sneak large chunks of rye bread into the dining room.

What a difference a few decades make. Today, there is a brand-new baking and pastry building on the CIA campus, equipped with German proof boxes and hearth ovens, where students can work toward bachelor's degrees in subjects like baking science. Every student makes sourdough from scratch, and organic and specialty flours are standard.

Everything else I've learned about bread and baking has been through encounters with people who were living it. Bakers in France, Italy, Germany, Austria, Latvia, Slovenia, Czech Republic, Holland,

Belgium, South Africa, and the U.S. generously shared their experiences, techniques, and stories with me. They introduced me to their customers and families, invited me into their homes and favorite restaurants, cooked for me and shared their homemade wines and spirits. They introduced me to their millers, who introduced me to farmers, who walked their fields with me, showing me the wheat varieties they grew. Thirty-five years after opening my own bakery, I'm still meeting people devoted to their craft. I remain passionately curious about the unique ways they produce delicious breads to feed their communities.

A year after my first trip to Paris I returned with another list of restaurants as well as an article torn from the *New York Times,* written by Patricia Wells, about the ten best bakeries in the city. My French had improved after working in the all-French kitchen at La Grenouille and my confidence in knocking on the back doors of bakeries was stronger as well. For four weeks, I immersed myself in Parisian bakery culture, visiting different bakeries at different times of day, watching the staff set up displays, introducing myself to dozens of bakers, listening as discriminating customers chose one bread instead of another. I hadn't consciously decided to leave the restaurant world, but unconsciously I was moving toward baking.

I visited Poilâne for the first time. The long line of customers at the bakery reminded me of my recent visit to the United Nations. People of all shapes sizes, colors, speaking a multitude of languages, all patiently waiting to buy the world-famous bread. There was an elderly man, a beret neatly angled on his forehead, at the door directing the crowd. I introduced myself and was stunned to find out he was Pierre Poilâne. He personally guided me through the shop and down the well-worn stone stairs to get my first glance of the famed Poilâne oven. The Poilâne miches cooling on a wooden rolling rack looked like volcanic mounds compared to the re-

fined breads I had just seen in the windows of other boulangeries. The flour in the mixing bowl was dark and flecked with bran, Monsieur Poilâne scooped up a large handful, placed it in my hand, and said, *"Jeune homme, c'est le vrai or de la France."* Young man, this is the real gold of France.

I met with Bernard Ganachaud on the same fateful trip. The very first baker to be awarded the Meilleur Ouvrier de France for excellence in his craft, he told me that becoming a master baker requires a focus that not everyone possesses. With tense, dark, serious eyes, he asked me, "Do you have, yes or no, the vocation to suffer?" I didn't think he was trying to scare me off, but to convey that the profession demanded dedication and perseverance. The son of a baker, he had spent a lifetime refining his baguette recipe, and was proud to tell me: "I use what my father taught me. I don't have a miracle recipe; I just take the best of tradition and improve it."

I got a taste of the suffering Bernard had described soon after, when I spent my first night at Basile Kamir's subterranean workroom. Basile was becoming well-known for helping to revive exclusively levain-raised breads, which were on the brink of extinction in Paris at the time. When I first met him at his bakery, Moulin de la Vierge, he looked me up and down skeptically, doubting my interest and commitment. As a test, he instructed me to return to the bakery at midnight on the dot.

Basile's mentor and head baker, Jean LeFleur, dressed in shorts and an open frayed shirt over an equally frayed tank top, let me in the back door, barely shrugging to let me know that I was annoying, like a pesky insect. He led me down a steep, creaky wooden staircase into the workroom, and then uncovered the flour that he had preweighed the day before in Basile's prized yellow forked arm mixer. He threw in a couple of scoops of salt, a tub of thick, earthy, and sour-smelling levain from the cooler, and three buckets of water and turned on the slow-churning machine. At one end of the 12- by 15-foot room was the massive wood-fired oven. Opening the firebox with a dangerous-looking long iron hook, he crumpled a couple of empty flour bags inside, and then grabbed some skinny sticks of dried wood from the pile at the side of the oven and tossed them on top of the bags, igniting the wood, and then slammed the firebox door shut with a swift, hard kick. There was a roar as the heat from the fire rose and the smoke was drawn through the open dampers in the rear of the oven, up through the basement and four stories of the building to the roof. Embers and ashes fell into the water troth under the firebox with loud hisses. The fire's roar would be the background noise for most of the night, as Jean used a cast-iron flame thrower (called a *gueulard*), placed on the oven floor, to direct the flames, and fed the hungry beast with armloads of wood as necessary.

Together, we mixed a second batch of dough. He ordered me to pick up and then empty a 25-kilo sack of flour into the mixing bowl and fetch a tub of firm levain from the refrigerator on the other side of the room. He put the levain on the worktable and tore off a handful, examining the texture and showing me the elastic spider-web-like structure, flecked with bran. He put it up to my nose and had me smell and taste the earthy sourdough. "This is where the soul of *pain au levain* is born." He watched as I dumped levain into the mixer along with buckets of water and gray sea salt. He turned the mixer on, turning it off every two minutes to show me how the dough developed over time. Using a sharp dough knife, he cut the dough into 1-kilo pieces at lightning speed and gently rounded them on a floured worktable, arranging them so there was a small space in the middle of the table where he continued to work. Then he placed the first preshaped round in this center space and shaped it into a tighter boule, gently tossing it into a floured banneton and placing the banneton on a dolly next to the worktable. He continued until all of the breads were shaped and a tower of large baskets was care-

fully balanced on the dolly, which we then pushed near the warmth of the oven to proof.

By now, it was 2:30 in the morning and the first of the breads were ready for the oven. As if on cue, two more bakers leapt down the squeaky staircase and immediately went to work. One used the iron hook to grab the glowing red flamethrower and place it underneath the firebox. The other swept the debris from the oven floor with a long broom, and then swished and twirled a 4-foot-long wet cloth attached to a long stick to mop up. They then cranked up the radio, first arguing and cursing at one another and then agreeing on a station. Spurred on by some R&B rhythms, they began loading the bread onto a 14-foot-long oven peel, a couple loaves at a time, in sync with the music. One baker flipped the large baskets quickly on the peel head. Immediately the other baker reached deep into the oven and with a sharp pull of the peel left the loaves in place. The floor of the oven immediately started to smoke and flicker from bits of dough and flour that fell off the loaves. After 15 minutes the oven was filled with bread and the two bakers were slick with sweat. The door was closed and Jean filled a little copper reservoir, built into the oven, with water. A valve controlled a steady drip of water into a cast-iron tray, creating a steamy environment for the bread.

By 6 a.m., when a clerk arrived to unlock the upstairs bakery doors and began to set up for business, there were hundreds of breads baked and ready to sell. Several large willow panniers on wheels were now filled and then pulled along a motorized track up the stairs. At least we didn't have to carry the breads ourselves. By the end of the night my body understood with pinches, aches, burns, and bruises what a tremendously physical grind it was. I was shellacked with sweat, soot, and flour dust as I devoured my morning tartine, this one made with *pain au levain*. Jean glanced over at me with a nod and a half smile. I was for that moment a baker.

Good Bread

When I wrote my first book in 1993, I was young and relatively inexperienced. I had a limited definition of good bread that I shared with my readers. Good bread was made in small batches from organic grain, preferably with a natural starter, well hydrated, kneaded well to encourage good structure, fermented long enough to develop great flavor, and baked in a wood-fired hearth oven for a dark and rugged crust.

Today, after I've seen how bread is made by so many different craftspeople in so many different locations and with so many different results, my definition is more complex and subtle. It is still true that some of the best bread in the world comes from tiny bakeries, like the *pane nero di Castelvetrano* that Maurizio Spinello makes in his little shop in a half-abandoned hill town in Sicily. But the thousands of fragrant rye loaves produced every day by Josef Hinkel in his highly efficient, well-organized Dusseldorf *bäckerei*, raised with a two-stage 100-percent rye sourdough starter, are a less romantic but just as delicious example.

When I talk to bakers now, I don't simply ask them if they are using organic flour. I want to know where the grain was grown; is it a single variety or is it a mixture of varieties blended at the mill? I ask about their relationships with their millers and whether the grain is stone- or roller-milled. Or I ask them why they have chosen to mill their flour in-house.

I'm deeply interested in how bakers cultivate their sourdoughs. Is it a method that is traditional to the area and if so, what is the history behind it? What is the hydration? What is the feeding schedule? Do they use a timed and temperature-controlled sourdough tank, for more flexible baking? Do they know what lactobacilli they are cultivating? How do they manage their soakers and sponges and pre-ferments?

Kneading used to be a simple topic, but today there are so many ways to mix and knead dough. At Forno Campo de' Fiori, the bubbly Roman pizza dough is kneaded on a very high speed for a very long time. There is a renewed interest in old-style two-armed mixers, especially in France, Italy, and Spain. In Germany, many bakers have returned to using diving arm mixers for delicate rye doughs. Home bakers are using KitchenAid mixers and getting great results but are also buying professional-style spiral mixers that can handle the softest doughs with ease. While testing recipes for this book, I had great results using the Häussler spiral mixer for both soft and firm doughs.

Baking bread in a traditional wood-fired hearth oven is incredibly evocative of the artisan past, and present also. But I've tasted more good bread from modern deck ovens than from wood-fired ovens. They're easier to operate, more consistent, and more environmentally friendly than wood-fired ovens. Most people would be surprised that Jochen Gaues's dark and crusty loaves don't come from a wood-fired oven. But his Heuft thermal oil-heated oven is considered by many bakers, including me, to be the finest in the world.

Today I believe that bread should be discussed with a consciousness and language similar to that used for wine. So much goes into producing an outstanding bottle. Wine writers can go on for pages about the land, weather, fertilization, grape varieties, fermentation, sugar, color, bottling, and aging. They compare old-world wines with rich pedigrees from Italy and France to new world wines from Australia, South Africa, and the U.S. Why not evaluate bread by considering the farming and milling practices that produced the flour, by discussing the type of sourdough that was used to raise and flavor it, by understanding the mechanics and technology of mixing it, with the same curiosity and depth?

Professional artisan baking has dramatically evolved since Poilâne was the epitome, influenced by advances in milling, farming, and baking sci-

ence. But so has home bread baking. When Bernard Clayton's book, *The Breads of France: And How to Bake Them in Your Own Oven*, came out in 1978, he was introducing artisan bread to a U.S. audience entirely unfamiliar with the subject. Forty years later, home baking enthusiasts are participating in online debates about whether or not a 36-hour cold fermentation is too long and sharing their recipes for sourdoughs made with rose petals. The recipes in *Living Bread* were collected with the latter audience in mind.

Breaking Bread

Since my first book, *Bread Alone*, came out 25 years ago, many wonderful books by my colleagues in both the U.S. and Europe have been published. In my office at the bakery I have a 200-volume, ever-expanding library on baking that I reference every day. There's a lot of overlap in the recipes, of course, but I'm always interested in the different ways that these authors define good bread. It is the little things that bakers do differently that distinguish and differentiate their loaves. One of the reasons I wrote my second book, *Local Breads*, in 2007 was to document the people, local traditions, ingredients, and techniques that make bread in certain places—the Auvergne in France, Altamura in Italy—exceptional and unique.

In the years since *Local Breads*, I have continued to travel extensively through Europe and the U.S., visiting mills, farms, university grain research centers and labs, sourdough conferences, and bakery equipment exhibitions and manufacturers as well as bakeries. I even went to Malta to visit a bakery with a large enough solar array to heat all of their water and to air-condition the whole place with absorption coolers. That experience inspired my son Nels to put a 664-panel solar array on Bread Alone's roof, with the intention to reach net zero energy use as quickly as we can.

Every encounter led to another. I met master miller Bertrand Girardeau through Basile Kamir. Through Bertrand, I met the mill's test baker Fabrice Guéry. My friend Didier Rosada introduced me to Hubert Chiron, who is the pilot bakery director of INRA, the biggest agricultural research center in Europe. Hubert pointed me in the direction of Richard Ruan, who used to do a job like Hubert's, and now runs a tiny three-man shop in Angers. Baking alongside Florian Domberger in Berlin, I met his mentor, Bavarian baker Björn Meadow. My circle of baking colleagues and friends continues to widen as each experience opens doors to new people and breads. In addition to learning about old ways, I met a new generation of bakers who are putting their own fingerprint on traditional breads. In Avignon, the partners at Bella Ciao Boulangerie Utopiste demonstrated their stripped down, simplified *pain de campagne*, which wasn't even shaped before it was tossed into the oven. At Boulangerie Utopie in Paris (it is funny how the young bakers chose similar names for their businesses), the baguette is traditional except for a small amount of activated charcoal powder that turns the dough a deep black. Denise Pölzelbauer has transformed her grandfather's traditional bakery, making breads with grape seed flour as well as wheat.

My friend Jean-Philippe de Tonnac, the author of the *Dictionnaire Universel du Pain*, introduced me to his friend Joerg Lehmann, a gifted food photographer with a passion for bread. (At the time, Joerg was living in an apartment in Paris above one of Rodolphe Landemaine's bakeries, so I met Rodolphe through Joerg.) I saw work that Joerg had already done to document the lives of bakers, farmers, and millers, and realized I had found a partner in telling the rich stories of the places I have visited and the people I have met, all of whom are living to bake good bread. Only someone as passionate and driven as Joerg would be willing to crisscross Europe by air, train, and Volkswagen Beetle to get every picture necessary. With him and his wife, Lisa, who traveled with us and worked tirelessly as Joerg's creative partner, I returned to some of my favorite places, and together we discovered new ones. As I took notes and recorded conversations, Joerg took thousands of pictures.

Writing a new book about my own bread wasn't at all interesting to me. I've been lucky to be a witness to the work of so many talented and dedicated craftspeople, an incredible cast of characters. I wanted to write a book about the larger community of which I'm proud to be a small part. The people I write about in the pages that follow are all very passionate and very idiosyncratic when it comes to their vocation. They take what they do, whether it is baking, milling, farming, or studying the science of bread, very seriously and believe in its importance. My own baking has changed for the better because of what I've learned from them. It is with gratitude and humility that I share with you their stories, their recipes, and their ideas about bread today.

Petits pains

* tradition   0,30€
* Sarrazin   0,40€
* Maïs   0,60€
* graines   0,40€
* Fruits   0,90€
* Ficelle   0,55€

THE BAKER ON THE RUE DU CHERCHE-MIDI

APOLLONIA POILÂNE, POILÂNE, PARIS, FRANCE

Reconnecting with Apollonia Poilâne vividly reminded me of the early days of my enchantment with bread. It brought back memories of my first trip to Paris in the late 1970s, when her grandfather Pierre guided me through his Rue du Cherche-Midi shop, down the semi-circular stone staircase, and into the tiny oven room. He showed me the iconic single-speed Mahot mixer (I ordered one for Bread Alone on his recommendation) and instructed me to touch

the dough in the mixing bowl to get a sense of its slightly gritty texture, typical of dough made with Type 85 flour, to open the door of his brick oven to feel its dense radiant heat, and to see what the vaulted interior looked like. A decade later, when I recognized her father, Lionel, at a nearby bistro, he too invited me back to the shop, which hadn't changed. The commitment of both Poilânes to this timeless craft struck me then and has stayed with me.

A slender woman with intense eyes and a sheet of shiny auburn hair, Apollonia dresses simply, in dark dresses and black tights, when she is not wearing a blue cotton workman's jacket, like her father's trademark uniform, during her frequent forays into the workroom. Lionel Poilâne and his wife, Irena, died tragically in a helicopter accident on their way to their vacation home in Brittany in 2002, when Apollonia was just 18 and her sister Athena was 16. About to begin her freshman year at Harvard, she persisted in her educational plans while simultaneously taking control of the family business. Because of her astute management and an earnest belief that bread bridges differences and brings people together, she has brought a renewed vitality to the family business.

Apollonia's childhood memories are centered on the bakery. Before she was tall enough to reach the worktable, she would stand on a special bench built just for her and shape dough alongside the bakers at the original Rue

profile continues

profile continued from previous page

du Cherche-Midi shop. Although her hands were too small to handle the 2-kilo pieces, she mimicked the bakers' movements, making tiny boules to match their larger Poilâne miches. She'd watch from her regular spot while they loaded the large proofed rounds onto a 14-foot-long baker's peel and quickly pushed them into the brick oven. She learned to count by bagging *sables* and making change for customers. Under her grandfather Pierre's watchful eye, she always added an extra cookie, "to express generosity." She'd sit with her father, Lionel, in his small office behind the bakery counter, surrounded by paintings of bread, and observe the long line of locals and bread lovers from around the world who waited patiently for their miches and apple tarts. Comfort in the bakery is what she knows and lives.

Poilâne was founded in 1932 by Pierre Poilâne, the son of a farmer from Normandy. Pierre's idea was to bake the type of country bread he had eaten as a child, a large sourdough round that stayed fresh for days and could be sliced and toasted to make tartines, the open-faced sandwiches that became popular at 1930s cafes and bistros. The famous Poilâne miche is impressively simple. Made with just four ingredients—flour, salt, water, and levain from a previous batch—it is mixed on low speed for 15 to 18 minutes, fermented in wooden tubs, weighed on a vintage balance scale, loosely shaped, proofed in linen-lined bannetons, and scored with an elegant cursive "P." The loaves bake for close to an hour. The crusts are dark brown and chewy, the crumb is dense and moist in the extreme, but with some lightness from the small bubbles produced during natural fermentation. It was Pierre's son Lionel, a would-be intellectual and initially reluctant baker, who

built the business into a multi-million-dollar, worldwide enterprise. As he learned about the history of bread and its place in society, he came to see the bakery as an important part of French culture. Amassing a 2,000-volume library of bread books, he became an authority as well as an artisan. A famous dandy and man-about-town, Lionel mingled with actors and artists, baking a bread bird cage for one of Salvador Dalí's installations, and a bread chandelier for another. He also built relationships with chefs, elevating the importance of good bread at a time when general bread quality was deteriorating. His most forward-thinking innovation was to build a "manufactory" near a freight airport outside of Paris, with an all-manual production line and 24 ovens, for turning out loaves that could be shipped to destinations far and wide as soon as they were cool enough to handle.

Since taking the reins, Apollonia has expanded Poilâne's U.K. business, making deals with the upscale supermarket chain Waitrose, supplying bread to luxury department stores including Harrods, and opening Comptoir Poilane near Sloane Square. Her plan to become an integral part of Britain's bread scene is not simply about making more money. It is an extension of her father's philosophy of using bread to connect people and cultures. She says it's a lesson that was reinforced at Harvard. "When I went to Harvard, my hope was to get an education in economics that would help me run my family's business. But I was also able to do more with what my parents had taught me about having an open mind and about the connections between bread and the world. I forged fantastic friendships, developed wonderful partnerships with people and companies." Although she runs an empire, she speaks like a small artisan. "It's part of my job as a baker to continually define what is good bread." The Poilânes, across generations, have not been interested in what is new or trendy. Pierre found success in reviving a type of whole wheat sourdough country loaf that had fallen out of fashion after World War II. Lionel worked to promote its virtues worldwide. Apollonia is focused on maintaining the integrity of the simple loaves that bear her name.

She emphasizes that Pain Poilâne will always be made the same way, by hand and with flour from stone mills that the Poilâne family has been associated with for 80 years. And she has deep respect for craft, inherited from her father, who wrote a book about the survival of traditional French trades (The Poilâne Guide to Living Commercial Traditions). "What I like the most about our baking method is the use of our five senses to feel the right balance in proportions, textures, and times. This is what is exciting about showing people the bakehouse,

seeing them understand how fine the balances are."

Because the business is so sprawling, she doesn't have a typical day. But she does have daily rituals that keep her focused on the bread. Each morning she eats breakfast—sourdough toast—with her team. She speaks with her production managers about the previous night's bake and checks on the quality of the bread. Her tone lightens and her words become more playful when she talks about her favorite time, Saturday morning at the bakery, when she works in the bakehouse. "It reminds me of my apprenticeship," she says. "It is a chance to practice my craft, and test bake with my team." She is passionate about the importance of the baker's job, especially because baking has not received the respect she believes it deserves. "It is a tough craft," she says. "Baking is still a profession that people don't regard highly." Finding bakers with Poilâne-level passion, "is always a quest, and our door will always be open to new talent."

LIVING BREAD 24/7 AT BREAD ALONE

Some type of work is going on every minute of every day at Bread Alone. Daily logs help us keep track of the temperature and pH of our doughs and sourdoughs as they ferment. Our bakers taste the doughs and sourdoughs throughout the day. No two days are exactly alike. We get frantically busy before holidays (last Thanksgiving we baked over 13,000 pies). Mondays we typically bake 8,000 to 10,000 kilos of bread. On Fridays that number jumps to 17,000 kilos. We bake 30,000 pieces of pastry a week. Here's a timeline of a typical 24 hours, to give you an idea of how we live bread at the bakery.

4 A.M.–First customers receive deliveries; first mixer arrives

5 A.M.–Examining and testing pH of last night's sourdoughs; first feeding of the day's sourdoughs; cafes set up; Greenmarket set up

6 A.M.–Bread shapers begin shaping doughs that have been slowly fermenting for 12 hours overnight

7 A.M.–Cafes open for business

7 TO 9 A.M.–Mixing and shaping continues

8 A.M.–Office staff arrives

9 A.M.–Pastry staff arrives and begin shaping laminated doughs for croissants and Danish

10 A.M.–First breads, which have fermented for 12 hours, go into the ovens

11 A.M.–More mixing, shaping, and dough processing; daily inspection of delivery trucks

NOON–Second shift sourdough feeding

1 P.M.–Staff meeting to review the next day's orders; first distribution manager arrives and readies the packing department for today's production

2 P.M.–Final orders come in for next day's delivery; starter and production formulas for tomorrow's breads are adjusted

3 P.M.–Slicing team arrives to slice breads going to supermarkets

4 P.M.–Baguettes, ciabatta, levain (breads that are baked in the afternoon) shaped

5 P.M.–Cafes close; mixing doughs for tomorrow begins

6 TO 8 P.M.–Doughs are shaped for tomorrow and placed in retarder proofers

9 P.M.–Third shift sourdough feeding; baking continues

10 P.M.–Packing begins; trucks are loaded

11 P.M. TO MIDNIGHT–Pastries are baked and packed

MIDNIGHT TO 4 P.M.–Trucks leave the bakery every hour to destinations up and down the Hudson Valley and as far as New York City and Pennsylvania

1 A.M.–Cleaning crew arrives

2 TO 3 A.M.–Thousands of pounds of bread dough and sourdough continue to ferment overnight while cleaners, packers, and drivers go about their business

3 A.M.–Trucks arrive at Long Island City warehouse, where distributors receive breads for delivery across the tri-state area

4 A.M.–We start all over again

1
CHANGING
WHEAT
LANDSCAPES

Important Dates in the History of Wheat

10,500 BCE: The archaeological record shows evidence of spikelet forks of emmer and einkorn wheat in pre-pottery Neolithic villages in Southwest Asia, suggesting pre-domestication cultivation in advance of true agriculture.

9,600 BCE: The first definite signs of wheat domestication in the Fertile Crescent.

6,500 BCE: The cultivation of emmer wheat reaches Greece.

5,500 BCE: Millstones first used for grinding flour.

5,000 BCE: Spelt cultivation begins in the Middle East.

3,000 BCE: The Egyptians bake leavened breads, inventing bread molds and ovens.

3,000 BCE: Wheat reaches the British Isles and Scandinavia.

750 BCE: Spelt becomes a principal wheat species in southern Germany and Switzerland.

500 BC: Spelt is in common use in southern Britain.

200 BCE: The Romans use teams of animals or slaves to grind wheat in large quantities.

168 BCE: A Roman baker's guild, *Pistorum*, is created, making bread baking a recognized profession.

1500 AD: Wheat reaches the Americas after the early voyages of Columbus.

1701: Jethro Tull invents a simple seed drill based on organ pipes, which economically sows seeds in neat rows.

1831: Cyrus McCormick invents the mechanical reaper, allowing farmers to reap four times as much wheat in a day as they did by hand.

1842: The first grain elevator is built in Buffalo, New York.

1862-75: The change from hand power to horse power signals a shift in American agriculture.

1874: Turkey Red wheat arrives in North America with Russian Mennonite immigrants.

1882: The oldest continuously cultivated wheat field site used in wheat research, Plot 2 at North Dakota State University in Fargo, is established.

1884-90: The horse-drawn combine debuts.

1892: The first gasoline tractor is built.

1909: Nitrogen fertilizer is invented; chemically fertilizing the soil increases productivity of wheat farms.

1952: Norman Borlaug breeds a fungus-resistant wheat for a project funded by the Rockefeller Foundation.

1954: The number of tractors on farms exceeds the number of horses and mules for the first time.

1963: 95 percent of Mexico's wheat is Norman Borlaug's variety, and the country's wheat harvest is six times what it had been previously.

1970: Borlaug is awarded the Nobel Peace Prize for initiating the "green revolution."

1980: Recombinant DNA techniques are developed and work begins on creating the first transgenic wheat.

1988: The Grist Mill historic site in Keremeos, British Columbia, plants seven historical wheat varieties—Red Fife, Ladoga, Preston, Stanley, Hard Red Calcutta, Marquis, and Thatcher—in hopes of encouraging their re-commercialization in Canada.

*1996: The first reference to ancient grains as a health food appears in the New York *Daily News*.

*2014: General Mills debuts Ancient Grains Cheerios.

*2018: The First International Conference of Wheat Landraces is held in Bologna, Italy.

Back to Wheat's Beginnings

I heard about Sicilian grain long before I opened Bread Alone, when I was moonlighting as a baking apprentice at D&G Italian Bakery in Little Italy after my shift as a restaurant chef. My teacher, Tonnino, proclaimed Sicilian bread to be the best in Italy, and Sicilian wheat to be the best in the world. I was reminded of his words repeatedly over the years as I visited bakeries in Genzano, Altamura, Tuscany, and the Italian Alps because, invariably, Italian bakers would recommend visiting Sicily to sample unique flours that couldn't be found anywhere else.

I knew that wheat farming in Sicily goes back at least 2,000 years and that the region continues to produce much of the country's crop. Much of European bread history begins in this region, where wheat from North Africa and the Middle East was first imported before making its way north. Before my first visit to the region in 2017, I was expecting a farming culture steeped in thousand-year-old traditions, distant from modern technology and science. What I found was a much more complicated and dynamic system of farming, milling, and baking that points as much to the future as it does to the past.

My introduction to the contemporary Sicilian grain movement came from Silvia Siletti, who had taken over her father's farm in 2000 and was now exclusively growing organic wheat. Silvia's farm is

a two-hour drive from Palermo, outside the medieval town of Caltanissetta. This inland area has a distinctively variable landscape, with steep hills and small mountains, valleys, flat areas, and large rocky outcroppings. Patches of wheat grew in every possible location, not only in the rare flat areas, but climbing up 2,000-foot mountains. The colorful, hilly scene was completely different from the endless, flat fields of wheat I had seen in the United States. I thought, "How on earth do they harvest this wheat? No combine I know could do that." As I approached the farm, I saw the farmhouse, which sits atop a hill overlooking numerous valleys and other hills. Silvia's house was cradled by olive trees. Beyond the olive trees, every dip and swell of land in sight was planted with wheat.

Silvia Siletti greeting her crop of Senatore Capelli

I had planned my visit to coincide with the beginning of the harvest, so I could see and touch the wheat. There were strips of land where wheat had already been cut. Other strips were covered with plants in a range of colors. It was still morning, and drops of dew made the heads of the wheat glisten. What I saw here was stunning and completely new to me. Most wheat grown today is knee- to waist-high. Silvia's wheat, in contrast, appeared to be taller than I was, at least 6 feet. Because of their height, the stalks undulated in the brisk breeze. The motion was like waves hitting the beach. Every wave was different. As the air blew through these tall grasses, you could see the various colors of their heads—green, brown, gold—in various stages of ripening.

Silvia is a buoyant dark-haired woman, proud of her Sicilian roots and culture. She is very attached to the experience of growing wheat and speaks of it often and with great vigor. Everything about her daily thinking and conversation comes back to farming. She has vivid memories about growing up in this place and being with her father, the birds flying in and out of the fields. She is passionate about carrying on her father's wheat-growing tradition and determined to be part of the current renaissance in Sicilian wheat cultivation.

I asked her about this tremendously tall wheat and she explained that her farm wasn't simply organic, but dedicated to the organic cultivation of *grani antichi,* or old grains, and in particular a variety called Senatore Cappelli, named after an Italian politician who commissioned agronomist and plant breeder Nazareno Strampelli in the early 1900s to develop a hardy plant that could be grown all over the country to feed the nation. It was the wheat she knew from childhood. "My father used to plant these seeds, I grew up with this name in my head

Wildflowers bloom in Silvia's wheat field

in the 1960s. Back then, we needed something very tall to control the weeds. And at that time also we needed wheat that would produce a lot of dry grass for animal feed.

"In the 1970s, farmers around here started to focus on growing shorter wheat, so they would have less dried grass and their fields would be more productive. They started using strains crossbred in the laboratory that produced less grass and larger wheat heads." This legacy lingers today. Although dozens of old wheat varieties are grown in the region, over half of the 10 million tons of wheat grown in Sicily is of a single dwarf variety. While her husband practiced medicine in Palermo, Silvia maintained the family farm as a hobby. But eventually, she got more serious. "I wanted to plant the wheat my father planted, so I got some organic Senatore Cappelli seeds in Sardinia—which I'm told are the best in the world—from the same grower my father had dealt with. It was unusual back then, but now everybody around here wants Senatore Cappelli."

With a Little Help from Her University Friends

These days, Silvia is growing Senatore Cappelli and testing other varieties with the hope of finding one that grows well on her land and is marketable to bakers. She is part of a group of fifteen organic wheat farmers in the area, called ProBio, who share knowledge and experience with old wheat varieties. Since forming their organization, they have increased their output, these days selling 15,000 tons of organic wheat annually. The group regularly consults with Dr. Giuseppe Di Carlo, the head of Agriculture and Forestry Science at Palermo University, to diversify their wheat crops, increase the fertility of their soil, increase production, and learn more about growing a range of *grani antichi* successfully. I was fascinated to learn that Sicilian farmers with generations of wheat growing experience were col-

laborating with the university to grow old grain in larger quantities and with more success.

The next day, we drove to San Biagio Platani, about an hour away, to the university's test farm. This research center, a 680-acre parcel donated in 1972 by philanthropist Salvatore Lima Mancuso, began as a study center for Sicilian agriculture in general. Today it is ground zero for rediscovering old wheat varieties and getting them into the hands of farmers. Giuseppe is a sturdy and energetic guy with a full head of thick gray hair. He speaks in an earthy and richly colorful way that seemed to me to echo the rich and colorful wheat fields all around him. In November 2010, he became the general director of the center, and has focused on selectively breeding Sicilian *grani antichi*. He is very aware of the unique opportunity he has to reach back in time, explore old seed stock, and reintroduce old varieties to farmers today. Most grain scientists don't have the access he does to sophisticated small millers and farmers, who are located within an hour's drive of the center.

Giuseppe has been collecting and breeding wheat for 25 years, but has the passion and energy of an eager undergraduate. He calls Sicilian wheat the best in the world for its baking quality, flavor, and aroma. He also believes it to be free of vomitoxins (toxins produced by fungi that grow on wheat) that are present in newer varieties grown in other parts of the world. He put on his well-worn old straw hat, dented perfectly to fit his head, and we went out to the test plots. There was a bounce in his step. As we walked, he continually reached up or down low to touch the spikes atop the wheat stalks, pointing out their different colors, heights, and the size of the grains. He described specifically the characteristics of each variety, carefully breaking open a head of wheat as we passed what seemed like a hundred small test plots, showing me how to examine the head size, look at the color, taste the berries in the bright Sicilian sun. He constantly

Giuseppe shows me his seed bank and test plots

remarked on different wheats, how they baked, how they should be milled, which baker liked this one or that one. There were blue, black, red, golden, and brown-toned wheats. I had to reconsider what a wheat field could look like. There were varieties that had originated in North Africa and Turkey along with native Sicilian wheats and wheat varieties from France, Sardinia, and Puglia. Each one had a well-documented history.

I asked Giuseppe how he acquired the seeds for these rare breeds, and he told me that each one had a unique story. He pointed to a particular patch, called Scorsonera, as an example and explained:

For the last twenty years, I've toured Sicily from the coastline of Agrigento up to Nebrodi in the north and passing through the inner part of the island where the Sicanis first lived. In June 2007, my destination was Ragusa, at the extreme tip of Sicily. My dear friends Pippo and Gaetano, who know the province well, were my guides. I'll never forget the day. At 5 a.m., the sun was already hot and the farmers had already left the farms to look after the cattle. Out in the fields we met Salvatore, a breeder of Modician cattle, who spoke to us in his local dialect of the wheat he and his grandfather cultivated, not for the grain but for the straw that was good for the animals. We picked some of his plants and guessed from their red color that the wheat was Russello di Ible, a variant of the Russello that is grown for grain. Seeing our interest in the wheat's particular look, he recommended that we find U'zi Matteo, another cattle breeder on the opposite side of the hill. Salvatore remembered playing with his cousins in Matteo's field and noticing some oddly colored wheat. We got back into our truck and drove off, through brambles and weeds, until we saw a field of wheat. From a distance it seemed almost burnt. We immediately assumed a fungal disease, but as we got closer we

could see that the spikes themselves were black. I grabbed my copy of Ugo De Cillis's book, I Fruenti Siciliani (a catalog of pure Sicilian wheat varieties), which accompanies me on these trips, and paged through it to see if I could identify this variety. There it was, at the end: Scorsonera. I looked out at the black sea of plants swaying in the wind and heard a voice. "Ehhh you atri!" It was Matteo, a tiny elderly man who talked to us about planting the wheat with his father, and about the sweet and intensely aromatic bread his mother made with Scorsonera flour. Every time I see this wheat I think of the day I spent with Matteo, Gaetano, and Pippo.

The seed bank on the University's test farm is the secured vault of all this history. It had been established years ago in one of the older farm buildings, and today contains an amazing array of more than 1,000 varieties of seeds from around the world. A long-term storage area contains airtight cans of hundreds of seeds, not just wheat but other cereals and legumes so that they will be viable in 10 or 15 years or longer. In a short-term storage area, there were dozens of drawers filled with carefully marked containers of seeds ready for testing and growing in the near future. The state-of-the-art laboratory has high-tech equipment for performing genetic and quality testing on all of the wheat grown in the test plots. In addition, researchers are developing improved techniques for natural fertilization as well as studying cover crops and nitrogen fixing.

In keeping with the facility's emphasis on seed purity, the actual breeding practices are quite low-tech and often take place in the field. Researchers start by choosing a single exemplary stalk of wheat. From this stalk, a single row of spikes is grown. The line is observed up close. If a certain percentage of the new seeds display the desired characteristics of the variety, they are used to grow a bigger plot. If there is too much variation, the row is eliminated. The process is repeated in a larger test plot, to produce about 15 kilos of seeds, and then again to produce about 400 kilos. After three years' time, the center can produce 2 tons of seed, enough to plant 25 to 50 acres. When the carefully bred seeds are handed over to farmers, the cycle is completed. At the moment, only 25,000 of the 700,000 acres of wheat in Sicily are planted with old wheat. But Giuseppe estimates that every year will see an increase of 6,000 to 7,500 acres, and eventually these *grani antichi* will be a significant, if expensive, presence in the market. Silvia's cash crop right now is Senatore Cappelli, but she is also testing some of a less well-known variety of durum wheat, Trinachium, on Giuseppe's recommendation. Trinachium was a success at his test farm, and he and Silvia want to see if it might be a practical choice for local wheat farmers.

The Miller as Partner

This cooperation between researchers and farmers is completed by a partnership with small millers equally invested in bringing *grani antichi* to market. Silvia and many others who are growing Giuseppe's seeds rely on Molino Riggi, a family business run by three generations of millers, to buy and process their grain. The Riggi mill was founded in 1955 by Calogero Riggi. Ten years later he was joined by his son Cataldo. In 1995 they received their organic certification. Today grandsons Marco and Alessandro oversee sales and production.

The mill is built into a steep hillside on the outskirts of Caltanissetta. The entrance is on the top level of the building. The hallway and small front office are decorated with pictures of old mills. Every other room in the building is watched over by a portrait of a different saint. Before a truck is allowed to proceed down the steep driveway to the first floor of the mill to unload, someone from Riggi comes out,

takes a handful of grain, and throws it into an Inframatic Grain Analyzer sitting on the reception desk. It has a personal, neighborly feel. Everyone knows everyone else.

Riggi has staked a large part of their business on milling and marketing old Sicilian wheat. Using three stone mills from the 1800s, along with some older roller mills from the 1950s, they work closely with many of Giuseppe's farmers, accepting individual harvests of *grani antichi,* storing them in their segregated silos, choosing the best way to mill each type of grain, and packaging it so consumers can choose single-grain flours like Russello, Tumminia, Maiorca, and Senatore Cappelli. The Riggis are passionate about this local grain because of its history in the area, but also because of its distinctive and delicious flavor. I was thrilled to bring home some of their flour and share it with everyone at Bread Alone, and delighted to learn of their plans to sell it to consumers in the U.S. Test baking with their flour was a delight. Russello is a brilliant mix of yellow, soft orange, and rust. It produced a bread with a rich, buttery flavor and wheaty fragrance. Pizza and focaccia made with Perciasacchi was light but chewy with an herbaceous aroma.

Finally, the Bread

I often hear theoretical conversations about sustainability and grain diversity, but it was in Sicily where I witnessed, in the close cooperation between scientists, farmers, and millers, this idea becoming a reality. Among the bakers using *grani antichi* exclusively is Maurizio Spinelli, a Sicilian native as devoted as any farmer, scientist, or miller to keeping old traditions alive.

It's a tale that could only come from Sicily. Maurizio was born in tiny Santa Rita, a village built in the 1920s to house workers on a large estate. Santa Rita was virtually abandoned during the 1960s when jobs became scarce. Maurizio's fam-

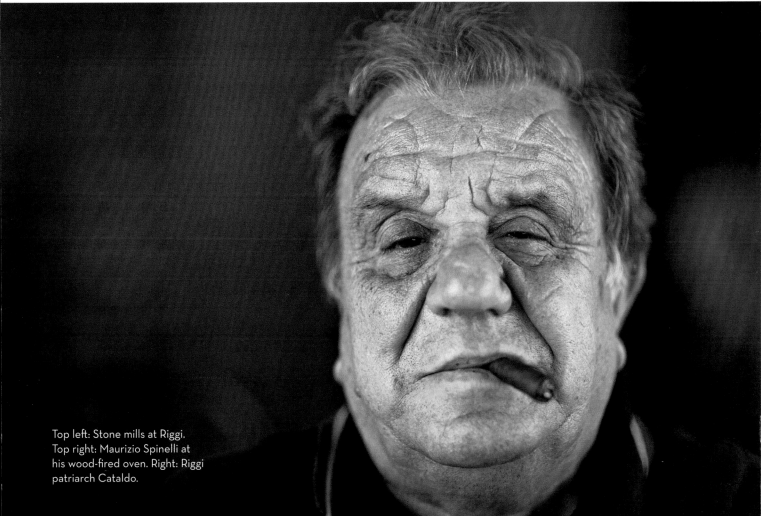

Top left: Stone mills at Riggi.
Top right: Maurizio Spinelli at
his wood-fired oven. Right: Riggi
patriarch Cataldo.

Brasetto rye growing in the Hurley Flats,
minutes from Bread Alone

ily stayed behind in this ghost town, looking after a herd of cows and baking bread to sell along with eggs and milk to anyone passing through. An idealistic banker put up the money for Maurizio to open a bakery in 1999 in this empty place, and with the help of his parents he began producing traditional Sicilian bread in a wood-fired oven, believing, like an Italian Kevin Costner, that if he baked it, customers would come. Fate cooperated, and he found plenty of restaurateurs and grocers to take his product. His staff has expanded to include refugees from war-torn Africa who he has trained in the ancient art of sourdough. His bakery is now a destination for tourists, and as a result of the publicity he's brought to Santa Rita, homesteaders have begun to repopulate the town.

I spent a day at Maurizio's bakery, helping him mix and shape his dough and load it into his ferociously hot oven. He was very particular about using skinny little olive branches, which exploded like firecrackers, to build his fire. The rustic torpedoes we produced, using Maurizio's perpetual sourdough and Senatore Cappelli flour milled nearby from local organic farmer Carla La Placa's grain, had their own particular aroma and flavor, barely musty with hints of earth, hay, and olive wood. Simple bread, with a timeless character but bound to the life of wheat farming in Sicily today.

Old Wheat Varieties in the United States

In Italy, France, and Germany, smaller farms are the norm, and old varieties of wheat have been grown continuously, albeit in smaller and smaller quantities, even after modern farming practices came to dominate the landscape.

In the U.S., grain scientists interested in older wheat have to search seed collections to find it. Dr. Mark Sorrells and his team at Cornell University is currently testing about 1,000 wheat varieties, including some that used to be grown in my part of Upstate New York but virtually disappeared when wheat farming became consolidated in the Midwest. Mark has sown experimental plots of landrace and modern wheats, including Fulcaster, Dawson Golden Chaff, Gold Coin, Pride of Genesee, and Rural New Yorker, that used to be grown locally. Ironically, he obtains the seeds for these experiments not from a local farmer, but from a germplasm collection in Aberdeen, Idaho. The process of identifying varieties good for local farmers is long and complicated, involving field trials to assess agronomic characteristics of the wheat and its ability to resist disease and then milling and baking trials to determine which of the wheats that grow well might also have potential for commercial use.

At Heartland Plant Innovations, a biotech research center in Manhattan, Kansas, Dr. Chris Miller cross-breeds all kinds of wheat in search of plants farmers and bakers will value. "We house one of the largest public collections of wild wheat varieties and related species. We have about three thousand genetically distinct lines of wild relatives of wheat. They're really weeds. These native grasses would have been the parents of wheat. They serve as a gene bank for our research and development."

Dr. Stephen Jones, of Washington State University's Bread Lab, emphasizes that it's not the lineage of the wheat, but its potential to grow well and make quality flour that is important. "Some heirloom varieties get a religious following. To me, I don't care if it's the exact variety that came from the Ukraine. I care if it tastes good and works for the farmers," says Stephen. "We do value tremendously the history and tradition. We have wheats from the 1500s in our fields. But you have to understand that even older Turkey wheat was a farmer selection from the Ukraine. And farmers have been crossing wheats since the 1700s." Purity isn't the be all and end all.

Finding or breeding grain that works for the farmer, miller, and baker is the goal.

Research scientists admit that growing wheat in places like the Northeast, where many modern varieties won't grow well and uncertain weather can destroy an entire crop, isn't easy. And yet, the desire to succeed is strong. Scientists want to preserve wheat's biodiversity. Consumers want more local foods. Farmers want to grow niche organic products to support their farms. Sharon Burns-Leader, our local grain and sustainability coordinator at the bakery, has been working with Mark Sorrells, test-baking with flour milled from their grain. Sharon delivered some of these baked goods to a harvest event at the Hudson Valley Farm Hub. Mark said it was the first time in his career that he tasted anything made from a wheat variety he had personally bred. When he described the experience, he dropped his scientific demeanor and radiated satisfaction.

In fact, some heritage wheat has already made its way to the market. Heartland Mill sells Turkey Red wheat flour, a variety brought to the U.S. in the late 1800s from the Ukraine. Grist & Toll in L.A. is experimenting with fine but exceptionally strong Star wheat, originally from Spain. Advocates like Amber Lambke of the Maine Grain Alliance have been connecting small Maine farmers with heritage seed providers. Until recently, says Amber, "We just bought grain as a medium for baking. But I think wheats will start to become known for their own unique flavors and colors and profiles."

Researchers are just beginning to identify varieties that will grow well and that have the characteristics that artisan bakers are looking for. Other steps in the process need more development. Getting farmers to buy in is a project in and of itself. Once they do, there's the difficulty of finding a mill. In Europe, small wheat farmers can choose from many specialty mills that welcome small loads and in fact encourage them. In North America, with a few exceptions including La Milanaise, these mills are almost nonexistent. This hole in the infrastructure is probably the most daunting challenge. Often, farmers turn to brewers and distilleries to sell their grain, and bakers miss out. Even with these challenges, this incipient movement is already influencing the marketplace.

The New York City Greenmarket now requires all participating bakers to use at least 25 percent locally grown grain. La Milanaise in Quebec, one of North America's leading processors of organic grain, has been working with Dr. Heather Darby, an agronomic and soils specialist at the University of Vermont, to test the baking qualities of the heritage grains, including Red Chief, Wasatch, Turkey Red, and Forward. The agronomists at La Milanaise then work with farmers to ensure a productive harvest. While right now logistics, baking quality, and sufficient availability present challenges, it it is their intention to encourage farmers to grow enough of these heritage varieties so they can mill and market them individually.

GRANI ANTICHI

The following grains are among the favorites of Sicily's artisan bakers and are increasingly available by mail in the U.S.:

MAIORCA: This wheat grows almost 2 meters tall and is identifiable by its red spikes and white grains. It makes a low-protein flour used in traditional Sicilian cakes and sweets. Also good for tender Neapolitan-style pizza crust.

PERCIASACCHI: The berries of this variety are sharp and pointed, thus its name, which translates as "pierce the sack," referring to the jute bags in which it was transported. Naturally drought-resistant, it grows well in Sicily without the aid of chemical fertilizers. Its chest-height stalks are also particularly weed-resistant, obviating the need for chemical herbicides. The flour itself is a beautiful pale yellow, and strong enough to make a satisfying focaccia or *pizza al taglio*.

RUSSELLO: Russello was a popular durum wheat variety in Sicily before World War II. It is genetically similar to wheat that was widespread in the Balkans, the Anatolian Peninsula, and North Dakota, where it arrived with Russian immigrants around 1900. The heads of the tall stalks are reddish in color, hence the name. With stalks that measure 1½ meters, Russello is difficult to harvest and produces more straw than seed, reasons why it fell out of favor with postwar farmers. Sicilian bakers are rediscovering the high-protein, low-gluten Russello flour, which works well in dense Sicilian pane *di casa*.

TUMMINIA: Grown on Sicily since Grecian times, Tumminia is a drought-resistant wheat planted in March (it's also known as *grano marzulo*). When milled it has a slightly gray color. Valued for the sweetness it imparts, it is used in combination with stronger Russello flour to make traditional *pane nero di Castelvetrano*, which has an even, moist crumb and an intense flavor.

"ANCIENT GRAINS," HEIRLOOM WHEAT, AND WHEAT SENSITIVITY

When you see the words "ancient grains" in relation to bread baking, they most likely refer to bread baked with flour milled from einkorn, emmer, spelt, or khorasan. These grains do indeed descend from ancient plants. They have never been crossed with other varieties, maintaining their ancient DNA. Einkorn, a diploid wheat, has two sets of chromosomes. Emmer, believed to be a cross between two wild grasses, has four sets and is tetraploid. Spelt, a cross of emmer and another diploid wild grass, is a hexaploid wheat with six sets of chromosomes. Today's hexaploid wheats (this category includes both common wheat and heritage varieties) evolved in farmers' fields through natural selection and intentional cross-breeding.

In recent years, my customers have increasingly asked me about the ailments associated with gluten, and whether or not bread made with ancient or heritage grain is healthier than bread baked with common wheat. Every baker I know gets the same questions. I'm not a scientist or nutritionist, so I rely on wheat researchers who have dedicated their careers to seeking the scientific truth for information and guidance on how to answer my customers' concerns.

Sensational reports have equated the ingestion of gluten with stomach upset, headache, fatigue, and more. According to Dr. Mark Sorrells of Cornell, "There's a lot of misinformation in the popular press that does a disservice to the public, spreading unscientific, unfounded claims." The truth is, wheat has been consumed by humans for at least 9,000 years and currently supplies about 20 percent of global dietary protein. According to Mark, today's wheat is, genetically speaking, 99.9 percent identical to old hexaploid wheat including spelt. In a paper he has authored with three of his students, *A Grounded Guide to Gluten*, to clarify and report accurately on the subject, Mark admits that there are thus far no definitive answers, but persuasively analyzes the evidence and hypothesizes that it is the processing of wheat and the increased consumption of processed foods made with vital wheat gluten that may account for the reported increase in wheat sensitivity. "In particular, certain modern processing practices used over the last century may have increased consumer exposure to components implicated in wheat sensitivity . . . (1) using ungerminated grain, (2) replacing long and diverse fermentation with fast-acting baker's yeast . . . , (3) using non-acidic dough, (4) adding extracted wheat proteins and inulin to food products, and (5) focusing on refined white flour."

I tell my customers that bread made with organic, whole grain flour with no additives and fermented slowly with a sourdough starter is a different kind of food. The bread I make at Bread Alone, and the bread that my artisan colleagues are making, is not in any way comparable to bread made with ultra-refined flour milled from wheat grown with pesticides, herbicides, and fungicides and processed with a high percentage of commercial yeast, dough conditioners, preservatives, and additives. It is neither logical nor fair to lump together all wheat products, when some are manufactured industrially and others are made by hand, when some are adulterated and others are pure. The jury is out on the question of whether or not heritage and ancient grains are inherently healthier than common wheat. No matter what the chromosomal makeup or variety of the grain, there is no question that if it hasn't been treated with dangerous pesticides and herbicides, if it hasn't been bleached, bromated, or otherwise treated with additives, it is less likely to cause harm.

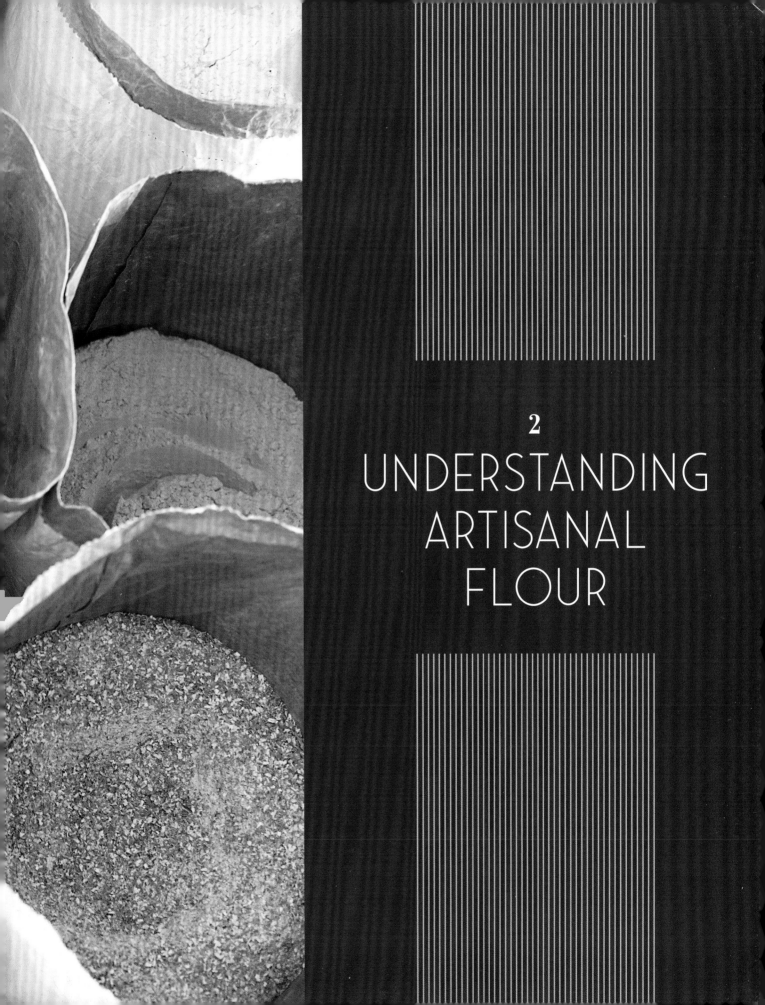

2

UNDERSTANDING ARTISANAL FLOUR

FOUR GENERATIONS OF FLOUR ART AND SCIENCE IN BOUSSAY, FRANCE

BERTRAND GIRARDEAU, MINOTERIE SUIRE, BOUSSAY, FRANCE

Suire is located in a historic old mill building on the banks of the Sèvre Nantaise, a wide tributary of the Loire. The mill, originally powered by water, is a large, multi-storied barn-like structure, stuccoed in pink, with silos and grain elevators attached. I would soon learn that there was room here to store up to 700 tons of grain. The Girardeau family home, a massive stone structure that has housed several generations, faces the mill. Just as I arrived, so did a truckload of 30,000 kilos of wheat.

The Suire staff was expecting it, and they already knew a great deal of technical information about the wheat on this particular truck. The farmer had worked closely with the Suire agronomists before his fields were even planted, discussing the expected demand for the coming year and the wheat varieties that would be needed to make the blends that customers wanted. The Suire staff knew what variety of wheat was on this truck, and the growing conditions that had affected its development. They had already tested samples sent by the farmer immediately after the wheat was harvested, but there was a comprehensive series of tests to be completed before the wheat would be accepted by the mill.

When the truck pulled up to the side of the mill, a syringe-like arm dipped into the cargo bed, pulled up a few kilos of grain, and funneled it directly into a container in the lab. Some of it was poured into a Foss Analytics Infratec grain analyzer, which measured the grain's protein, starch, fiber, oil, and moisture in under a minute. The remaining sample was tested for vomitoxin, herbicides, and pesticides.

The wheat met the mill's first-round requirements, so a few more kilos of grain from the same truck were put through a small test mill and milled into flour. Then, the flour was tested in the lab to determine its baking qualities. First, it was given a falling number test to measure enzyme activity. Wheat contains enzymes that originate in the germ of the grain kernel and progress to the endosperm during the plant's sprouting and maturation. For the baker, these enzymes are extremely important because they break down starches into simple sugars in dough, spurring fermentation. To test the flour, a small amount is mixed with water in a test tube and agitated to activate enzymes in the grain. The more active the enzymes, the less viscous the mixture will become as the enzymes begin to break down thick starches into simpler sugars. Viscosity is measured by the time it takes a piston placed on top of the mixture to fall to the bottom of the test tube. A high falling number indicates a lower level of enzyme activity. A low number means that enzymes have been very active, converting thick starches into thinner sugars. Falling numbers range from above 300 to under 200. Falling number noted, the lab techs moved on to mineral, or ash, content. The bran of a wheat kernel is rich in minerals, which resist burning. Depending on how much bran has been extracted during milling, flour will have a higher or lower ash content. To test for the presence of minerals in the flour, a small sample is placed in an oven and incinerated. The minerals remaining behind (the ash) are weighed. The weight represents the ash content. A flour with 5 percent ash content has .5 grams of minerals per 100 grams flour.

At this point, some of the sample flour was mixed with a salt solution to form a dough. Extensibility, elasticity, and strength of dough was measured on an alveograph, an instrument that records how long it will take for a precisely scaled disk of the dough to be blown into a bubble to the point that it bursts. In Europe, the al-

veograph is one of the prime indicators of flour qualities, evaluating strength in relation to extensibility and elasticity. These values appear on the flour's Certificate of Analysis (COA). The driver of the truck didn't have time to lose patience as he waited for the okay to unload 30 tons of grain. The testing was completed in under an hour.

Minute differences in test results from truckload to truckload can make big differences in the baking properties of flour. After all of this testing, the truck moved to a long garage, where the floor was covered with metal grates. The driver tilted the truck bed, releasing a dramatic and dusty sea of grain onto the floor. It noisily dinged the grates as it fell into a holding area below. Later, massive, long augers would lift it to a grain elevator, where it would be stored until it could be cleaned, blended with grain from other truckloads, and milled. Blending

profile continues

profile continued from previous page

grain from different fields and farms is part of the process that allows the millers at Suire to deliver a final product with all of the qualities promised by the numbers—protein, ash, strength, extensibility.

After observing the lab work and touring Suire's storage elevators, I finally got a look at the famed stone mill. The mill operates on three levels. On the top level is the tempering room, where the grain passes through humidifying equipment to make it easier to grind and to make sure it has the proper moisture content, as close to 14 percent as possible. The heart of the mill is a large room on the middle level with eleven pairs of 2½-meter-wide, 2-ton mill stones. The action of the stones is truly something to see and feel. The levers that release the grain into the centers of the rotating stones are topped with bronze horse heads, so eleven horse heads bob up and down continually as the grain flows through the machinery. The whole mill vibrates, as there are several tons of stones turning at all times. The stones are made not from granite but from a special flint that Bertrand told me was gentler on the grain. The grain is ground once (multiple grinding stones allow Suire to grind several batches at the same time), and then whatever grain hasn't been adequately ground is sifted and put through the stones again. A very small percentage may be ground a third time. On the level below, large boxes fitted with mesh screens of varying fineness sit on top of vibrators which shake, sifting the flour to get to Type 65 and Type 85 (Type 45 and Type 55 are exclusively roller-milled at Suire).

Suire has two roller mill operations, one for organic flour and one for conventional flour. The organic operation is adjacent to the stone mill, and I visited this mill next. The grain begins its journey on the top level of a multi-level setup, moving from the hopper and through pairs of corrugated rollers that break it into large particles. The particles are then sifted, separating the endosperm from the germ and bran. Additional trips through rollers continue to break down the kernels and separate smaller pieces of bran that still cling to the endosperm. Then, the endosperm is put through a series of smooth rollers to reduce the endosperm pieces (now called *middlings*) to flour. All pairs of rollers in a roller mill have one slow roller and one fast one. The rolls turn in opposite directions, toward each other, pulling the stock between them. The cut, depth, and spiral of the corrugation, together with the rotation differential, determine the aggressiveness of the milling at any particular step. The process is called *gradual reduction*. The grain may be rolled and sifted up to 12 times before it is transferred to a holding container, where it sits until it can be blended with other flours. Bertrand let me put my hand under the stream of flour coming out of a final set of rollers. I didn't have a thermometer, but I would guess it was about 85 degrees, the temperature of tepid water, and no warmer than the flour I had touched at the stone mill.

Suire grinds flours at a variety of extraction rates at each mill. It produces two different types of whole wheat flour. Flour from the stone mill that contains 100 percent of the bran is called *integral*. Flour from the roller mill, from which the bran has been completely sifted and then completely re-introduced, is called *complete*. And then there are Type 45, Type 55, Type 65, Type 80, Type 110, and Type 150 flours, with varying amounts of bran sifted. In addition, they mill and blend over 200 custom flours for a long list of bakeries. To custom blend flour, there is a batch blending machine, which can blend 2 tons of flour from either the roller mill or the stone mill or a combination of the two. Freshly ground and blended flour is naturally aged, meaning it is exposed to air for about ten days to oxidize its gluten-forming proteins, strengthening their links and improving baking performance.

Testing is far from over at Suire after flour is milled. In fact, some of the most important tests are performed not in the lab but in the on-site test bakery. Bertrand's commitment to this part of the process is total: Suire has four full-time bakers who do nothing but test flour and recipes as well as train professional bakers from around the country and the world.

Suire's head baker, Fabrice Guéry, invited me to bake alongside him as he evaluated flour following BIPEA's strict standards. In the mixing room, there were five miniature fork mixers and five miniature spiral mixers. Each mixer is hooked up to a mixograph machine that measures the strength, extensibility, and the elasticity of the dough. Five different flour samples are placed in the mixing bowls. Each sample is given a BIPEA scorecard. Each batch of flour is used to make the same test recipe.

The day I was there, Fabrice was testing Type 65 flour using the BIPEA-approved Baguette de Tradition recipe. Each dough was prepared in exactly the same way—same mixing speed, same mixing time, same fermentation, same baking time and temperature. Each batch is color-coded with a small sticker at every step. At the end of the day, the cooling baskets held 50 baguettes, marked with stickers. Fabrice and his bakers began meticulously evaluating the breads. They measured each baguette's height and width, the expansiveness of the scoring, and crust thickness. They assigned a value to each one's color, volume, and alvéolage. Finally, they evaluated its flavor characteristics. The results provided the information that Suire's millers would need to formulate reliable and consistent flour from the grain that was continually arriving at the mill.

The oldest flour mill
in Altamura, Italy

Important Dates in the History of Milling

*10,000 BCE: Humans first crush wheat berries between stones, making the wheat's nutrients available to humans.

*5,500 BCE: The saddle quern, consisting of a flat stone bed and a rounded stone operated manually against it, is used to grind grain.

*500 BCE: Rotary querns in Catalonia, Spain, were comprised of two circular stones, one of which is rotated above the other with a projecting handle.

*200 BCE: Introduction of the rotary mill, powered by teams of animals or slaves, to drive larger wheels to crush wheat.

*1000 AD: Mills powered by water and wind allow for faster milling of larger quantities of grain.

*1782: Oliver Evans, a pioneering mechanical engineer from Delaware, invents a fully automated grain mill. Powered by water, Evans's mill is a continuous system, with five machines that form a production line, moving grain on conveyors and bucket elevators through the mill automatically without hand labor.

*1800: In Hungary, where hard wheat varieties grow well, rollers are first used to break open the grain, which is then sifted and reground in a conventional stone mill. This hybrid process, called Hungarian high milling, is still much quicker than traditional stone milling, although it requires a large labor force for sifting.

*1870-1880: Wisconsin miller John Stevens takes Evans's idea of automation and combines it with an efficient system of rollers and sifters, eliminating the use of stones in the process. Stevens secures patents for his invention in 1880. To this day,

the highest grade of commercial wheat flour, consisting of the center portion of the endosperm, is referred to as *patent flour,* in reference to Stevens's patents.

*1900: U.S. milling transforms from a constellation of small local stone mills to big central facilities using rollers to process tons of grain at high speed. The shift to roller milling coincides with a shift in the geography of U.S. wheat growing. In 1839, the geographic center of wheat growing was north and west of Washington, D.C., where soft red wheat varieties thrive. In the 1870s, the center shifts to the Plains, as wheat farming expands exponentially in Kansas and North Dakota, where hard red wheat grows cheaply and well.

*1944: Introduction of pneumatics in mill manufacturing. Transport of grain and grist via an Airstream revolutionizes mill designs worldwide. Grain or flour no longer needs to be arduously transported in sacks or lifted in bucket elevators into the upper floors, where they were then emptied.

*1970s-1980s: Stone milling is revived as part of the health food movement. Milling enthusiasts begin restoring antique mills and putting them back into use.

Understanding Artisanal Flour

When I first traveled to France in the early 1980s, I learned about flour from bakers I admired, asking them to explain what Type 55, Type 65, and Type 85 meant. Whenever I had the chance, I'd place my hand in an open bag of flour, squeeze a fistful and examine the color and texture, then examine breads to understand the flour from the bag to the finished loaf. I became familiar over time with the

Alessandro Riggi examining some Senatore Capelli wheat

difference in feel between coarse, stone-ground flour with large flecks of bran and smooth, cream-colored roller-milled flour. I'd often take samples back home to show my miller. Many smaller artisan bakers in France were using stone-ground Type 55, a creamy white flour ground from winter wheat with 10 to 11 percent protein, to make baguettes, so I asked my miller if he could approximate this type, which was unavailable commercially in the U.S., for Bread Alone.

Back then, it was unusual but not unheard of for a baker to study milling and work closely with a miller to develop a unique flour blend. I remember talking to the late Bernard Ganachaud, a Meilleur Ouvrier de France and at that time one of the most influential and celebrated bakers in Paris. We'd have long conversations about the mill he chose and why he chose it, while standing in front of his Llopis wood-fired oven while his bakers loaded and

unloaded breads in his original bakery on the Rue Ménilmontant. Bernard attributed the success of his famous *flûte gana* in part to his top-secret flour blend. He wouldn't reveal much to me, but he did say that it was roller-milled, because he preferred a finer texture for his flour.

Basile Kamir, the young firebrand baker who took me under his wing, was another artisan who cared very much about milling. He was a little bit more forthcoming with details. He preferred stone-milled flour, ground from wheat grown in Burgundy. His flour was milled at Moulin Decollogne, outside of Paris, and he visited the mill often to consult with the miller and check on the grain.

During this period, French millers were in the process of adopting an industry-wide set of standards, under the direction of BIPEA, a non-profit organization that provides guidelines for a variety of fields, including animal feed, soil, and cosmetics. The BIPEA was accredited in 1970 to help millers precisely analyze flour and its baking characteristics to ensure consistency and quality. These millers, many of them second- and third-generation, already possessed inherited knowledge and experience to mill grain into the flour that bakers expected. During the next 30 years, the fledgling BIPEA system would make the process more professional and codified, guiding the testing of flour's physico-chemical properties and its baking characteristics.

As European artisan baking has evolved, bakers have become more knowledgeable about the details of milling. At the same time, mills specializing in artisan flour have evolved, too. Just as bakers have embraced innovations like temperature-controlled liquid sourdough tanks, retarder-proofers, and thermal oil deck ovens to ensure consistency while increasing production, so too have millers taken a technology-focused approach to quality milling. Employing agronomists who work with university

seed banks, partnering with farmers to help choose what varieties of wheat to grow and provide support in how to grow them, testing grain to thoroughly understand its baking properties and flavor, blending flour so it is consistent from season to season, putting it through its paces during extensive baking testing: French milling, like baking, is an increasingly complex fusion of science and art.

Understanding Flour Across Borders

Although milling practices are similar in France, U.S., Germany, and Italy, each country has a distinct milling language, labeling standards, and style. Wheat varieties are different from country to country, so the raw materials of milling are slightly different. Guidelines for milling vary greatly from place to place in accordance with national law, types

The roller mill at Riggi

of equipment, production expectations, and in response to the local wheat.

Molino Grassi in Italy makes a stone-ground Tipo 0 flour that has a similar protein content as stone-ground Type 65 flour from French mill Minoterie Suire. But because Molino Grassi blends 20 percent *grano duro* semolina wheat from Puglia with *grano tenero* soft wheat and hard wheat from Parma, bread made with the Italian flour will have a slightly golden crumb and lower protein level, while bread made with the French flour will be a creamy off-white with brown undertones.

Thirty years ago, imported flours were seldom available in the U.S., and European-style flours weren't yet being milled here. Today, European milling practices are more common in the U.S. and European flours are increasingly available. Understanding how flour is classified and sold is valuable in helping to choose the flour you want to bake with. If you are going to take the time to go to the Molino Grassi online store to order flour for ciabatta, you'll need to know the difference between the 00 flour that has a W value of 270, which is too strong for such a soft, flat bread, and their 00 flour with a W value of 220, which is just right. The same is true when you order from an artisan mill like Central Milling, where product specs will tell you that Organic Artisan Bakers Craft flour has 11.5 percent protein and 0.60 percent ash content, while Keith's Best has 12.5 percent protein and 0.55 percent ash. The first flour will give you a more extensible dough with a nuanced crumb structure, great for baguettes. The second flour would work better in a large boule or a pan bread that requires strength and lift.

For me, choosing flour is a subtle art based on a scientific foundation. It requires knowledge and practice to understand the baking characteristics of different flours. It also takes practice to get the best baking results.

Authentic Flours for Authentic Breads

The flour industry has undergone incredible changes in the last 30 years and the evolution continues. It's increasingly easy to find specialty flours, either milled to European standards at American mills or imported from European mills. I expect that availability will continue to improve.

Out of respect for the bakers I interviewed for this book, and with the idea of helping readers produce the most authentic breads, I've suggested specific flour types in each recipe that reflect the original bakers' choices. Some are available at supermarkets, natural foods stores, and specialty foods stores around the country. Others are available online, either directly from mills or via Amazon

Me at Molino Grassi

Top: Alveograph in action. Bottom right: Preparing a beaker for the falling number test.

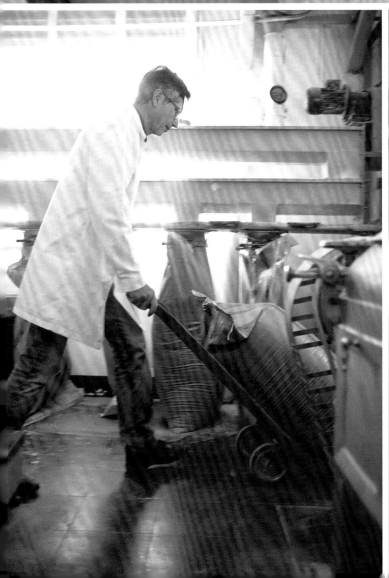

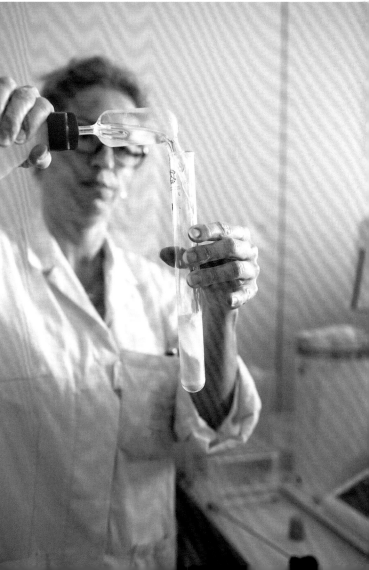

and other retailers. As interest in authentic artisan baking grows, availability is less of an issue for home bakers. Overnight, you can have 10 kilos of Type 65 or Tipo 00 flour delivered to your doorstep. Your local artisan bakery might also be a source. See Resources (page 347) for locating particular flours called for in the recipes.

I encourage you to make the small effort to source high-quality artisanal flour, looking beyond basic bread and all-purpose flour. Your breads will be better for it.

How U.S. Flours Are Classified

Traditionally, flours in the U.S. are identified by names—all-purpose, pastry, bread, and names like Harvest King—that offer a broad yet undefined set of characteristics. I have always found buying flour in the States difficult, because knowing the brand name of a flour does not give any indication of the baking qualities of that product. This is changing somewhat as an expanding number of U.S. millers catering to artisan bakers are beginning to mill small batches of heritage grain and/or adopt French and Italian numbering systems for some of their products. Heartland Mill in Marienthal, Kansas, for example, sells all-purpose and bread flour blends milled from hard winter wheat grown on a select number of organic farms, but has recently begun to offer "single source" Type 65 Turkey wheat flour, containing a single type of heritage wheat from a single field on a single farm. But in general, the following classifications are the norm here.

Flour is divided into types according to protein content and types of wheat, to help bakers identify a particular flour's best use.

CAKE FLOUR (made with soft wheat) has less protein than other flours (typically 6 to 8 percent), and is suitable for delicate and tender items like pound cake.

ALL-PURPOSE FLOUR is made of a blend of soft and hard wheat and typically contains 10 to 12 percent protein. It is called for in a variety of baked goods requiring both structure and tenderness.

PASTRY FLOUR, with a protein content somewhere in between cake and all-purpose flour, is used for crumbly shortbread cookies, tart dough, and American-style Danish pastry.

BREAD FLOUR typically refers to flour milled from a blend of hard red spring and winter wheat with a protein content of 11.5 to 13 percent. Despite its name, this higher-protein flour can be used in a wide range of recipes beyond bread, including doughnuts and yeast-raised pastries, that require a well-defined crumb.

HIGH-GLUTEN FLOUR, usually milled from hard red spring wheat, has a protein content of at least 14 percent, making it the strongest flour on the market. High-gluten flour is used in products that require chewiness, like bagels and certain kinds of pizza. It can also help fortify breads made with low-gluten grains such as rye and buckwheat.

Complicating matters, different brands have different names for their flour types. Take a look at the choices at King Arthur and you will see Sir Lancelot (high-gluten flour with 14 percent protein), Sir Galahad (with 11.7 percent protein, which the company describes as "all-purpose or low-protein bread flour"), and Special Patent (12.7 percent protein, recommended for hearth breads and machine production). Additionally, protein content of a particular type of flour varies by brand. King Arthur's all-purpose flour has 11.7 percent protein, while Gold Medal's all-purpose flour has 9.8 percent protein. So it is crucial to look at the labeling before you buy, to determine that you are buying the right flour for a particular bread.

STONE MILLING VS. ROLLER MILLING

The idea of returning to stone milling has powerful appeal. In my first book, I advocated for it. My generation of U.S. artisan bakers generally defaulted to stone-ground flour from a small miller if we could find it. The alternative was a trial-and-error process of choosing from available brand-name flours geared towards commercial baking.

Over the years, however, I've come to understand that the question of best milling practices is not simply answered by turning to a stone mill. In the U.S., there are very few stone mills to choose from. The mills that do exist produce flour in relatively small quantities. The largest stone mill grinds about 500 pounds of flour per hour, while a roller mill may put out more than twice as much in the same amount of time.

One of the debates surrounding milling is whether roller mills overheat the grain, compromising its nutritional value by destroying healthy enzymes and oils. At about 130 degrees, this damage will begin to occur. According to some of the most experienced millers I've spoken to, it all depends on how efficiently grain is ground and how the milling is managed. Stone grinding must be done with great skill. If turned too quickly and with too much pressure, stones can easily heat up from friction. It is true that roller milling can generate heat. But good millers are careful to control the process. Bertrand Girardeau says that his flour, whether stone-ground or roller-milled, never gets warmer than 5 degrees above the ambient temperature. Mark Nightengale of Heartland Mill in Marienthal, Kansas, says his roller-milled grain only gets as hot as 115 degrees, even when it is 100 degrees outside. These seasoned expert millers argue that the short contact time between the grain and rollers may result in less loss of unsaturated lipids and greater enzyme activity and nutrient retention than if the grain had been ground for a longer time between stones.

The best artisan flours, whether roller or stone milled, come from mills where grain varieties are carefully chosen and then handled with handcrafted bread in mind. Every fine miller has his or her own set of best practices. Advocates of stone milling like Craig Adams at Great River Organic Milling in Arcadia, Wisconsin, believe that stone-grinding results in more nutritious and flavorful flour: "Grain flowing into the stones becomes very thin, flat flakes which integrate all parts of the wheat immediately into the flour, and give the flour more flavor."

Nicky Giusto of Central Milling in Utah argues that his restored 1920s vintage roller mills, hand-operated and water-powered, produce flour with a rustic quality that you can't get with newer machinery. Bertrand Girardeau, owner of Minoterie Suire in France, refuses to fetishize stone milling, even though he has one of the most beautiful and sophisticated stone mills in the world. Alongside his stone mill, he runs a roller mill that is more appropriate for some grains and some products, and allows him to meet the increasing demand for his organic flour. Other leading mills, including Moulins Bourgeois and Moulin de Brasseuil, both outside of Paris, and Moulin Marion near Macon, use both rollers and stones. Mark Nightengale is an American proponent of this hybrid approach, and he is using a vintage Allis-Chalmers roller mill for sifted flour and a stone mill for whole grain flour.

European mills serving artisan bakeries have set the standard for sourcing grain, milling it to precise specifications, and blending it for consistent results. U.S. mills that take European mills as their models, working closely with farmers and producing flour in the European style, are the best bet for domestic flours that will produce superior artisan breads.

Flour in France

The same straightforward system of flour classification is used throughout France. Flour is assigned a number that corresponds to its ash content in milligrams per 10 grams flour. Because minerals are concentrated in the bran of the wheat kernel, ash content corresponds with color. Darker flours have a higher ash content than lighter flours, which have had more bran extracted during milling.

Type 55 is the standard hard-wheat white flour for baking, including puff pastries (*pâte feuilletée*). Type 45 is often called pastry flour, and is a finer extraction flour (this corresponds to what older French texts call *farine de gruau*). Some recipes use Type 45 for croissants although many French bakers use Type 55 or a combination of Types 45 and 55. Types 65, 80, and 110 are stronger bread flours of increasing darkness, and Type 150 is a whole wheat flour.

FRENCH FLOUR TYPE	ASH CONTENT
Type 45	Less than 0.50 %
Type 55	0.50 to 0.60%
Type 65	0.62 to 0.75%
Type 80	0.75 to 0.90%
Type 110	1.00 to 1.20%
Type 150	More than 1.40%

Stone mills at Suire

German Flour

A similar system of classification is used in Germany as in France, where numbers are assigned to flour types depending on ash content. The numbers are different, but still coordinating with ash content:

FRENCH FLOUR TYPE	GERMAN FLOUR TYPE	ASH CONTENT	USES
Type 45	Type 405	Less than 0.50%	Typically used in baguettes, croissants, and soft white breads
Type 55	Type 550	0.50% to 0.60%	Slightly stronger than Type 405, used similarly in wheat bread
Type 65		0.62% to 0.75%	
Type 80	Type 812	0.75% to 0.90%	Used in darker wheat and mixed grain breads
Type 110	Type 1050	1.00% to 1.20%	High protein content and strong flavor, ideal for mixed grain and other hearty breads
	Type 1600	1.50%+	An even darker color and has the highest mineral content among wheat flours except for whole wheat; suitable for dark mixed bread and for hearty, rustic wheat bread
Type 150	Type 1700	1.50%+	Whole wheat flour

Type 550 is comparable to American all-purpose flour. Type 405 is the equivalent of American pastry flour. Types 812 and 1050 are bread flours of increasing strength. Type 1600 is almost 100 percent whole wheat flour.

Rye in several forms is so extensively used in Germany that German millers have developed a separate classification for rye flours.

GERMAN RYE FLOUR	ASH CONTENT	CHARACTERISTICS
Type 815	0.815%	Finely ground white, the lightest and finest rye flour; suitable for light rye bread, more common in southern Germany than in the north
Type 997	0.997% to 1.09%	Light rye flour with some bran, suitable for mixed grain breads
Type 1150	1.15%	Medium to dark rye flour, good for mixed-grain and sourdough breads
Type 1370	1.37%	Medium to dark rye flour, very flavorful and especially good for 100% rye breads
Type 1740	1.18%	Medium-ground whole rye flour, used for hearty rye and mixed grain breads but also for gingerbread and fruit bread
Type 1800	1.37%	Coarsely ground whole rye, strongly flavored and used in traditional German seeded whole rye breads

The Complicated Case of Italian Flour

In the U.S., flour is classified primarily by its protein content. In Italy, the story is more subtle and more complicated.

First of all, most Italian mills do double duty, selling flour to pasta makers as well as bakers. Flours milled from hard wheat are labelled *grano duro*. Flours milled from softer wheat are labeled *grano tenero*, meaning "tender grain." Mills blend these two wheat varieties based on the type of flour required.

Italian mills market their baking flours according to two systems of classification. The first is based on grind, ranging from fine to coarse. Numbers range from Tipo 00 to Tipo 2 and are obtained by measuring the quantity of flour in kilograms after milling 100 kg of wheat. The higher the number, the coarser the flour. Tipo 00 is ground as fine as talcum powder, Tipo 0 is less finely ground, and so on. These numbers also indicate the ash content and extraction rate of flour. Tipo 00 has maximum ash of 0.5 percent. The most highly processed of Italian flours, it has an extraction rate of just 50 percent. Tipo 0 can have an ash content of 0.51 to 0.65 percent, and an extraction rate of 72 percent. Tipo 1 has an ash content of 0.66 to 0.80 percent. And Tipo 2, with an ash content of 0.81 to 95 percent and an extraction rate of 95 percent, is almost whole wheat.

The most common misconceptions in the U.S. about Tipo 00 flour are that the classification has something to do with the flour's protein content and that it is *the* indication that a flour is good for pizza. Neither of these is true. In fact, Italian millers grind grain of varying protein levels into this extra-fine flour, for a variety of baked goods, from the most tender shortbread cookies to the chewiest artisan breads. Molino Grassi in Parma, for example, sells five types of white flour with the des-

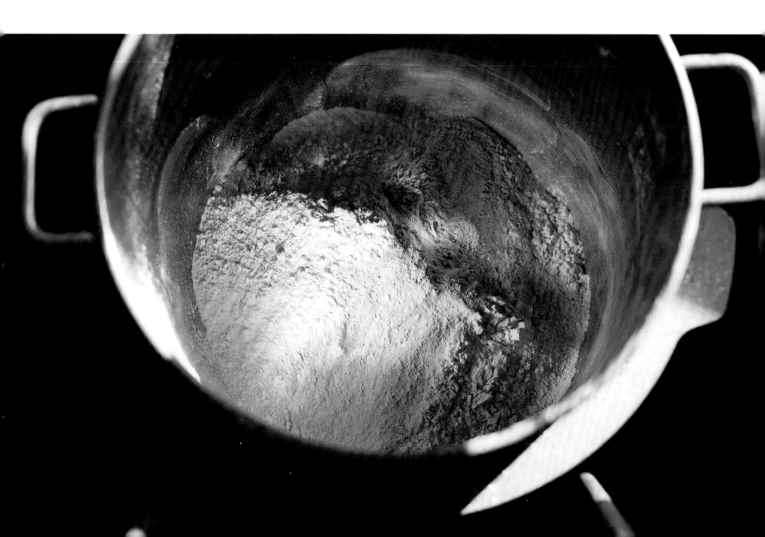

ignation "00," with protein contents ranging from 10.5 to 14 percent.

In this country, 00 flour has been sold to consumers as pizza flour, but Italian pizzaioli don't just look for the 00 designation when buying flour. Molino Iaquone also caters to pizza makers, with a line of six 00 pizza flours, ranging in protein content from 11 to 16 percent. Italian bakers choose a flour depending on the kind of pizza they make: A thin, Neapolitan-style pie with a quick rising time calls for a low-protein 00 flour. A thick, chewy pan pizza with a long rising time requires a 00 with a lot of protein.

Because protein content is not necessarily an indicator of gluten quality, Italian bakers also rely on an alvéograph assessment before choosing a flour. The essential number for Italian bakers, along with "Tipo," is a flour's "W" value, which indicates the relationship between a dough's rising power (strength) and its extensibility and elasticity. Generally, Italian mills recommend the following W value flours for the corresponding uses.

W VALUE	CHARACTERISTICS
<120	Poor-quality flours, unusable for bread making
120 to 160	Weak flours, appropriate for the production of biscotti
160 to 250	Medium or average strength flours, used for soft doughs (*paste molli*) in the production of *Pugliese*, ciabatta, *Francese*, *pane piuma*, etc.; for firm doughs (*paste dure*) in the production of *pane ferrarese*, and also for the refreshment of natural yeast (*lievito naturale*)
250 to 310	Flours of strength obtained from high-quality national wheat and strong wheat of national or foreign origin, used in the production of *maggiolino*, baguette, *rosetta*, *soffiato*, and *biove*
310 to 320	Flours extracted from strong wheat, used primarily for doughs with a long fermentation; indirect method doughs employing a biga or *lieviti* (natural yeasts) with long rises; or for sweet raised doughs such as *pandoro*, panettone, *Veneziane*, etc.

Molino Iaquone advertises a flour's W value right beneath the Tipo on its website. Their Sacco Verde flour has a W value of 210 to 220, making it a good choice for *pane Pugliese* or ciabatta. Sacco Rosso's W value is 320 to 340, and indicates that it will work well in long-fermented sourdough breads as well as sweet raised doughs like panettone.

Claudio Grossi's
hillside wheat fields

MILLER/BAKER PIONEER

HEINZ WEICHARDT, WEICHARDT-BROT, BERLIN, GERMANY

Berlin baker Heinz Weichardt has been milling his own flour daily for 40 years. In 1971, Heinz, a trained pastry chef, was working in the kitchen of a Rudolf Steiner–influenced rehab hospital near Lake Constance when he and his wife, Mucke, encountered the Steiner's philosophy of biodynamic farming, the first modern system of organic agriculture. Introduced to the world in 1924 by Steiner, biodynamics is a program that considers the farm as a self-sustaining system that should produce its own fertilizer and animal feed. The Demeter Biodynamic program, created in 1928, was the first certification system for organic farm products and exists to this day to ensure that Demeter-approved farms meet organic standards as well as post-harvest handling and processing guidelines.

Heinz and Mucke began baking bread at home in the evenings with Demeter-certified flour and other Demeter-certified ingredients including butter and honey, and Mucke would sell the loaves outside the Waldorf kindergarten where their daughter Yvonne was a student. The bread became so popular among parents that some of them raised money to stake the Weichardts in a real bakery. The Weichardts were pioneers of organic baking in pre-unified Berlin, opening the first whole-grain Demeter-certified organic bakery in the city, in the Zehlendorf neighborhood, in the mid-1970s. In 1981 they opened a larger shop in Wilmersdorf, which features three large Sextener natural stone mills where their flour is freshly ground daily from Demeter-certified grain sourced from farms the Weichardts have been working with since they opened.

Heinz is a tall, bespectacled man with a sweep of slicked back snow-white hair and a matching manicured white mustache. The Wilmersdorf shop is charmingly simple and old-fashioned. Honey-colored wooden shelves behind the counter are lined with whole grain loaves and accessorized with sheaves of wheat in ceramic crocks and antique baking molds. Pendant lamps made from willow baskets illuminate glass cases filled with a mix of rustic and somewhat decadent German pastries. Counter people in bright green aprons continually check on customers, refilling water glasses and offering samples. The oven room in the back of the shop has floor to ceiling white tiled walls, a black and white tiled floor, and large tubs of

starter fermenting on the floor, with a large vintage stainless-steel deck oven in the far end of the bakery. Wooden racks suspended from the ceiling and on the walls hold a variety of willow bread forms, peels, and oven tools.

The Weichardt starter is initiated with *backferment,* a dried starter culture made with biodynamically grown wheat and honey. Backferment was developed in the 1920s by German baker Hugo Erbe, an early student of Rudolf Steiner's theories. In the 1960s, shortly before Heinz began baking bread, the German firm Sekowa began to produce backferment commercially. The yeast existing in the honey is activated when the starter is mixed with flour and water in the bakery. Once active, this starter, like a conventional sourdough, can be maintained indefinitely, although bakers who work with it generally prefer to mix a new starter daily. Backferment generates more lactic than acetic acids, producing breads with a particularly mild flavor.

Heinz doesn't simply purchase Demeter-certified flour. It has always been critical for him to be an active participant in the biodynamic loop. He frequently drives out to the fields in a restored green convertible Volkswa-

gen *Käfer* ("beetle" in German), so he is there when his farmers plant their fields and when they harvest their grain. He is the only baker I've ever visited who grinds 100 percent of his own flour. He is as fully committed to the art of milling as any of the master millers I know. The milling room, adjacent to the shop and ovens, is visible through large plate glass windows on the street. Three towering wooden framed mills with 100-kilo composite grinding stones take up most of the space in the 10- by 20-foot room. An overhead pipe, connected to a grain storage room behind the milling room, feeds grain into the hoppers above the slowly moving stones. Heinz chooses to grind his wheat, rye, and spelt flour on the coarse side. When I dipped my hand into a bag next to the mill I was surprised at how gritty it felt. Although the mills make a thunderous sound when operating, the neighbors don't mind. Typical of the Weichardts' good manners, they installed soundproofing along with the equipment when they moved into the space.

Weichardt breads have a mild sweetness, which Heinz attributes to the backferment. The freshly milled flour has a creamy, grassy aroma that gives the bread a lively flavor. Most of the rye breads contain a small percentage of wheat flour, which gives them a higher rise and lighter texture than traditional German 100 percent rye breads.

With four shops now, and about 30 employees, Weichardt-Brot is still a small business, but one with an outsize reputation for delicious bread. Heinz and Mucke's daughter Yvonne took over the everyday operations in 2008, allowing them to spend more time at their hobby farm in Schleswig-Holstein, where they raise heritage breed animals and grow small plots of wheat and rye with seed from their farmers.

MILLING YOUR OWN FLOUR

Home milling enthusiasts praise freshly milled flour for its lively flavor and believe it to be nutritionally superior to commercially milled grain. Like Heinz Weichardt, they say that milling their own grain makes them feel closer to the earth from which it grew. With the purchase of a quality home mill, you can decide for yourself which kind of flour suits your life and bakes better bread for you.

There are definitely challenges to baking with home-milled flour. Sometimes it will be more absorbent, sometimes less. Depending on the hardness of the grain and its humidity you might have to adjust the stones. Some home millers like to mix their own flour with commercial flour in order to make their doughs more predictable. To me, this is missing the point. If you want to experience the advantages of freshly milled flour, then make the leap and use it exclusively, knowing that it is going to take some practice. Working with 100 percent home-milled flour will give you the chance to judge your dough and adjust your recipe and technique every time you mill, becoming a better and more sensitive baker in the process.

- **BUY THE RIGHT MILL**: A hand-cranked mill will take you back to the old days, but you may tire of powering it if you bake frequently. For frequent bakers, electric is the way to go. Choose a stone burr mill (which is like Heinz Weichardt's mill in miniature) with a variety of settings from coarse to fine. A flour sifter attachment is useful. The KoMo Classic Grain Mill (see Resources, page 347), handmade in Austria, is my choice.

- **SELECT QUALITY GRAIN**: A wide variety of whole grains is available at natural foods stores, supermarkets, and direct from mills. If you buy your wheat or rye berries from a bin at your local grocery store, you won't know much about them. To mill the kind of flour that will produce the bread you want to bake, you'll need some information: Is it red or white, spring or winter, 12 or 18 percent protein? I recommend buying grain from a mill, like Central Milling (see Resources, page 347), where products come with detailed specs.

- **CHOOSE THE APPROPRIATE GRIND**: This is a process of trial and error. To begin, take some of your favorite commercially milled flour and feel it, rubbing it between your fingers. Mill some grain, tightening the stones until you get something similar. When you think you have

achieved the right consistency, grind enough to use in a familiar recipe, make some bread, and compare it to past loaves. And then adjust and keep baking.

- **USE A SIFTING SCREEN**: Unless you want to bake exclusively with 100 percent whole grain flour, you will want to sift some of the larger bran and germ particles from your milled flour to get the extraction that you need. Sifting out the bran and germ at various percentages will give you flour ranging from very white to whole meal. Leftover bran can be toasted and used in baked goods and on top of breakfast cereal.

- **MILL AS NEEDED**: The biggest difference between home-milled flour and professionally milled flour is fresh flavor. Only grind as much flour as you will use within a day or two to take advantage of this characteristic. Flour may lose nutrients as it oxidizes, another reason to grind only as much as you need on a particular day.

- **HYDRATE AS NECESSARY**: In general, freshly milled flour can absorb more water than aged flour. Use a recipe you are already familiar with to judge how absorbent your flour is compared to commercially milled flour that you use regularly. Evaluate your dough as you mix it, and increase hydration as necessary.

- **WATCH OUT FOR INCREASED FERMENTATION**: The enzymatic activity in dough mixed with freshly milled flour often is significantly higher than in dough mixed with aged flour. Watch doughs carefully. To control fermentation, consider retarding dough, using cold water, and/or keeping the temperature in your kitchen low.

- **ADJUST YOUR EXPECTATIONS**: Freshly milled flour may not produce breads with the same volume as breads made with commercially aged flour. Understand as you embark on baking with home-milled flour that your bread is going to be different. The idea isn't to duplicate bread made with commercially aged flour, but to make bread with home-milled flavor, texture, and volume.

A simple and elegant Komo home mill

3

ESSENTIAL
BAKING
PRACTICES

PROFILE:

COMPAGNON DU DEVOIR

FABRICE GUÉRY, MINOTERIE SUIRE, BOUSSAY, FRANCE

When I first met Fabrice Guéry, the director of innovation and research at Minoterie Suire, there was something distinctive about his demeanor, an understated focus. He was quietly confident and exceptionally patient. I wondered how he had acquired such wide-ranging knowledge about traditional French breads, and admired his ability to evaluate flour by touch and make minute adjustments to a recipe to achieve the result he had in mind. He was perfectly suited to his job, which included teaching experienced bakers like me to look at the craft with fresh eyes.

He told me that he was a member of the Compagnons du Devoir et du Tour de France, a French organization of craftsmen and artisans with roots in the guilds of the Middle Ages. To become a Compagnon, Fabrice, already a trained baker, had to take a practical baking exam and submit to a probing and personal interview assessing his character and potential. He then undertook a five-year apprenticeship, spending a year at a time under the tutelage of a different master baker in a different location in France. He learned to bake fougasse and other Provencal specialties in Marseilles and kugel-hopf and pretzels in Alsace.

This program is much more than a way for young bakers to learn about new breads. They each make a moral commitment to transmit not just their baking know-how but their way of life as good workers and good people. Compagnons are initiated into a community, living in a house with other apprentices. Being a Compagnon means coming together with people of differ-

ent generations and different backgrounds and helping each other flourish in their chosen craft.

After the first year, young apprentices present projects demonstrating what they have learned so far, and become Aspirants in a private ceremony that includes only Compagnons and other Aspirants. Aspirants are given sashes and ceremonial walking sticks, signifying the journey to come. The next few years consist of more work and traveling. During their final years as Aspirants, the young bakers choose

where to live and work and begin to teach the practical and moral components of the trade to beginners.

For 20 years, Fabrice has chosen Minoterie Suire as his home base, where he transmits his Compagnon skills and code of conduct. He works with hundreds of bakers, giving him a chance to share his passion and humanity as well as his knowledge about flour and bread. In the mill's state-of-the-art test bakery, he refines his skills and teaches these refinements to bakers from around the world. It's not what he does, but how he does it. Take bassinage, for example. When Fabrice adds water to dough midway through mixing, he does it drop by drop, constantly evaluating and calculating, looking for subtle changes in the dough so that it is perfectly hydrated. Although he is extremely precise, he recognizes how variable the craft is, depending as it does on the minute differences between one flour blend and the next. Watching him shape dough is a master class in itself. His movements are quick, gentle, and effortless. He handles bread dough delicately so he doesn't damage its internal structure, creating perfectly shaped breads. Working with him at Suire one day, I casually overturned a tub of fermented dough onto the counter, lightly banging it to loosen the dough and free it. Fabrice then took another container and, without criticizing my style, made it clear that his way was better, when he gently loosened the dough from the container's sides with a spatula and let it slip onto the counter in a perfect square.

I asked Fabrice to help me bake the breads to be photographed for this book, because I knew he would make the platonic version of each one. Graciously, he accepted my invitation. As is his custom when visiting a bakery, he arrived with a small container of his own sourdough. Like a jazz saxophonist who knows he will get the unique sound he is searching for with a particular reed, Fabrice wanted to use the starter that would bring out the subtle and subdued qualities of flavor, structure, and texture in the breads. One afternoon in the Berlin bakery where we were working, I watched him as he took some dough from its rising container midway through bulk fermentation, folding it to help it build strength. Folding completed, Fabrice gently patted the dough, as if to give it encouragement, before placing it back in the container. The gesture, one of great respect and the transferring of good energy, is representative of Fabrice's Compagnon philosophy and explains why he is a joy to work with and learn from.

Thinking Like an Experienced Baker

The recipes in this book assume a knowledge and familiarity with the basic practices of bread making. They follow a straightforward and recognizable sequence:

· A starter is built and fermented over several hours to reach maturation.

· Dough development is most often achieved by machine or, for those so inclined, by hand.

· The final dough rises in a very lightly oiled container at a specific temperature for a specific time.

· Folding is often suggested to build strength in soft doughs.

· Scaling, dividing, and shaping into bâtards, baguettes, or rounds is done with a Zen-like focus and a gentle touch.

· Final loaves are proofed in a banneton or couche and then baked on a preheated baking stone, Dutch oven, or home brick oven.

And yet, each bread in this book has its own distinct look and personality, lent to it by the baker who created it.

I have watched with fascination at dozens of bakeries across Europe as my baker friends and colleagues have made differently shaped breads, both refined and rugged: Airy dimpled focaccias shiny from olive oil and fragrant with fresh herbs, dense ryes packed with whole soaked grains and pungent with rye sour, elegantly shaped baguettes with crispy tips and a bubbly crumb that beg to be eaten warm, large volcanic-looking rounds with explosive ridges and thick crusts, dark fruit- and nut-packed loaves with caramelized crusts encouraged by the natural sugars in dried fruit. Almost unbelievably, each one starts with a very similar formula.

Simple practices employing simple equipment, executed carefully and well, will make the most dramatic differences in your baking. The following is a list of the various and nuanced techniques that the bakers I have visited use in unique combinations to customize and personalize their recipes. Employ them as indicated to bake exemplary breads.

Ingredient Selection

All recipes in this book use natural, simply processed, and untreated ingredients. My preference is always for certified organic whole grains and seeds, and organic stone-ground or roller-milled flours made without additives or preservatives. Many recipes call for flours you might not be familiar with. These flours will give your breads unique color, depth of flavor, and notable texture and are worth the extra effort in sourcing. For example, Maurizio Spinello uses Tumminia flour from Sicily to make his Pane Nero di Castelvetrano (page 252). The specialty flour market is growing and changing rapidly. New "old" grains and unusual varieties are being grown and milled domestically and abroad. Traditional artisan flours from France and Italy are entering the U.S. market. Locally grown and specialty flours that just a few years ago were unattainable are easily sourced.

I exclusively use dry instant yeast (*not* rapid rise), in very small quantities, because it is reliable and doesn't need to be dissolved in warm water before use.

Nearly every baker I visited uses untreated mined or specialty sea salt for the pure flavor. Chemically treated salt can interfere with fermentation.

See page 347 for ingredient resources.

Metric Measuring

Every baker I visited while writing this book, without exception, uses the metric system to scale ingredients. The metric system is more accurate and inherently easier than volume measurement. It is more precise when weighing out small quantities of ingredients than the system of pounds and ounces that most Americans are familiar with. When working with Fabrice Guéry in the Minoterie Suire test kitchen, where he tests thousands of batches of bread under strict conditions every year, I watched him scale ingredients for test batches only slightly larger than the recipes in this book, measuring *to the gram:* not 4 grams of salt, but 5; not 999 grams of flour but 1,000. The first skill of a great baker is scaling with precision. An inexpensive metric digital scale, scaling down to one gram, is all you need to go metric. Some recipes call for less than 1 gram of yeast. In these cases, weigh out 1 gram on your digital scale and then return a portion (half for 0.5g, three-quarters for 0.25g) to the container and use the remaining portion in your recipe.

Baker's Percent

As I visited with bakers in different countries, with different baking backgrounds and different training, the one constant, no matter what language was spoken, was our shared understanding of *baker's percent.* Each ingredient is expressed as a percentage of the total flour weight (if more than one flour is involved in the formula), and the total flour weight is always expressed as 100 percent. This allows professional bakers to easily see the precise relationships between ingredients, and to scale up or down according to need. It also allows them to precisely adjust a recipe as necessary, cutting back on the percentage of sourdough starter in the summer when the weather is warmer, for example, or varying the water percentage depending on the strength of the flour. When Florian Domberger shared his recipe for Seele (page 259), we were in the middle of baking breads for our photo shoot. He simply jotted quantities of starter, flour, water,

Baker's magic

and salt based on 1,000 grams of flour. I stuck the piece of paper in my pocket and was able to write up a complete recipe at the end of the day.

I've included baker's percent alongside metric measurements in these recipes to help readers think like professionals. With baker's percent, a recipe is no longer just a list of ingredients. Now you are looking at every ingredient in relation to the flour. When you bake with this larger understanding of the way your ingredients are working together, you start thinking like a baker. Eventually, you will be able to communicate with other bakers, using this universal language.

For the sake of simplicity, I've calculated separate baker's percent for starters and pre-ferments. This way, you can see the baker's percents at both the level of the starter and at the level of the final dough.

A simple example of baker's percent alongside metric weight of ingredients, from Richard Ruan's baguette recipe. Here, the 375 grams of water comes from dividing 375 by 500 and then multiplying the result, .75, by 100:

INGREDIENTS	BAKER'S %	METRIC WEIGHT
FINAL DOUGH		
Type 65 or equivalent flour (11 to 11.5% protein)	100	500 g
Water	75	375 g
Salt	2	10 g
Dry instant yeast	.2	1 g

Building a Better Starter

Pre-Ferments

While sourdough is the foundation of many artisan breads, yeast-based pre-ferments, including sponges, poolishes, and bigas, are also essential. A pre-ferment is simply a small quantity of flour and/or whole grains mixed with water and yeast and allowed to ferment for several hours before being employed to build and raise a final dough. A pre-fermented dough adds moisture, structure, and depth of flavor to your bread. It also contributes to the caramelization of the crust and gives breads a longer shelf life, often many days longer. It is not uncommon for a yeast pre-ferment to make up a high proportion of a final dough. The Baguette au Germe de Blé Grillé (page 132), inspired by Bernard Ganachaud's *flûte gana*, has a baker's percentage of 80 percent of the final flour weight.

Soakers

Seed Soakers

One of my favorite sensory experiences at Bäckerei Hinkel in Dusseldorf was the sight and smell of the soaking seeds filling large plastic tubs. There was a little bit of fermentation, due to the presence of so much sourdough in the room, giving the soakers a bit of effervescence. Soaking grains and seeds in water before adding them to dough ensures that they don't rob the final dough of moisture. It prevents the seeds from stealing water from the crumb of the finished product, increasing its shelf life. Soaking also improves the texture of the seeds, diffusing their flavor into the final products and increasing volume. Soakers are often used in combination with sponges and sours. Sometimes yeast is added to a soaker, so it acts as a pre-ferment.

Old Bread Soakers

Northern European bakers use this traditional technique, grinding stale bread and soaking it in water or adding it to a sourdough starter, to economize as well as lend flavor and moisture to dough. This technique is very common in Germany and is actually regulated by law, which mandates how much old bread can be added to dough. One of my favorite examples is Jochen Gaues's Kohl-Speck Brot (page 283), which is made with lightly toasted rye bread crumbs that are then soaked in water. Toasting the crumbs before soaking adds an extra layer of caramelized flavor to an already complex bread.

Flour Soakers

Specialty flours like quinoa, rice, and millet as well as cornmeal have no gluten and when added directly to bread dough can weaken its structure. Hydrated flour won't weaken the dough as much as unsoaked flour would. A flour soaker also increases the amount of water that can be added to a final dough. Pane Giallo (page 286), an Italian bread that includes polenta, or cooked cornmeal, gets its bubbly, earthy, and moist crumb this way.

Liquid Sourdough Handling

Certain recipes in this book, such as Pain au Levain Moderne (page 220), call for stirring your liquid sourdough starter at regular and timed intervals as it ferments. This mimics the action of temperature- and timed-controlled sourdough tanks that are increasingly common in small and midsize artisan bakeries. Giving your fermenting starter a stir every 2 hours ensures even and active fermentation by making sure that the starter's temperature is even throughout and the wild yeast and bacteria are distributed evenly, so they can feed on all available flour granules. The action also oxygenates the mixture, further encouraging fermentation. With a minimal amount of work, this technique gives dramatic results. At Bread Alone, we used to mix our liquid sourdough in buckets by hand, stirring intermittently. When we switched to stainless-steel timed tanks manufactured by the German company IsernHäger, we saw a dramatic improvement in the quality of the fermentation, the stability of the sourdough, and the flavor of the starter and finished products.

Hot Water Sourdough Starters

Sometimes in rye baking, very hot water is used in the final build of a sourdough starter. The warm starter accelerates the wild yeast activity while minimizing the proliferation of lactic and acetic acids, producing a starter with robust leavening power and a milder flavor than conventional rye sourdoughs. The first time I watched Pierre Nury prepare his rye sourdough to make a Tourte de Seigle (page 266), I was shocked when he stirred very hot water into the sourdough. It was counterintuitive. Wouldn't such hot water cause the starter to ferment wildly, causing the dough to be extra sour? He explained that the very short fermentation time does indeed allow yeast to proliferate but doesn't give acids time to grow, resulting in one of the mildest rye breads I've tasted.

Developing Your Dough

Strategic Kneading

There are several focused kneading techniques for dough development, depending on the style of the bread. Almost every recipe in this book assumes the use of a heavy-duty home mixer like one from the KitchenAid Professional series or a small professional spiral mixer like the Häussler Alpha (see page 347 for sources), which kneads as thoroughly as my larger professional mixers. The recipes describe in detail the best settings and timing for mixing a particular dough for optimal development. Some rye breads, like the Tourte de Seigle (page 266), are mixed briefly on a relatively low speed, so as not to damage the fragile strands of gluten that are developing. Highly hydrated wheat doughs like the Pizza Bianca di Forno Campo de' Fiori (page 120) require a long mixing time on a high speed before they will cohere and develop the characteristic silky and elastic structure. Mixing time can vary according to the type of mixer being used, but the goal is to achieve the desired gluten structure at the end of the mixing time.

Autolyse

This technique was popularized by Raymond Calvel and adopted by a generation of French bakers for making smooth, elastic, easy-to-work-with doughs and breads with a bubbly crumb. Before other ingredients are added to the bowl, flour and water are mixed together to form a rough, often shaggy, dough. Covered and left to stand at room temperature for a minimum of 15 minutes or up to 1 hour, gluten development is initiated and starches are broken down into sugars. When the starter, salt, and other ingredients are kneaded in, the dough will already have developed some elasticity and will be easier to work with. In addition, the amount of time necessary to develop a dough is reduced. Mahmoud M'Seddi of the 2M bakery in Paris, who won the 2018 Grand Prix de la Baguette, attributes the richly flavored crust and light interior of his bread in part to a 1½-hour autolyse.

Bassinage

Bassinage is primarily employed for maximizing hydration without overworking the dough. This technique is employed in Rodolph Landemaine's Baguette de Tradition (page 190). In the final stage of mixing, the mixer is returned to low speed. A small drizzle of water is added to the dough while the mixer is running. When it is fully incorporated, another small drizzle of water is added until absorbed. This process continues until the baker feels the dough is holding its full capacity of water. My understanding of bassinage expanded when I watched Fabrice Guéry employ the technique. When his dough had developed to 80 percent of its full strength, he slowly drizzled in just 10 grams of water at a time, waiting until it was fully incorporated and then judging the dough's development before adding another small amount of water. The process took 8 to 9 minutes, because he had the mixer set at the lowest speed. He had increased the hydration to almost 90 percent in the most gentle way possible. He knew his dough, so he knew when to stop at just the right level of hydration, while the dough was very soft but still holding its shape. You may pass this point a few times before you get a sense of when to stop. Keep practicing and you will learn to recognize it.

Controlling Dough Temperature

In a professional baking environment, bakers go to great lengths to maintain a dough temperature of 75 to 77 degrees. Consistent dough temperature is key to achieving consistent high-quality results.

The pre-ferment or starter, flour, and ambient environment each have their own temperatures. While it is difficult for the baker to adjust any of those numbers, it is easy to adjust water temperature to arrive at what is called Desired Dough Temperature (or DDT), generally 77 degrees for the final dough. All it takes are some simple calculations to get an average. Let's say that the starter is 78 degrees, the flour is 75 degrees, the ambient temperature of the room is 80 degrees, and the mixer heats up dough on average by 11 degrees. Those four numbers are added together to get 244. That number is subtracted from the DDT (77) multiplied by the number of temperatures (4), which is 308. Giving you 308−244 = 64. So the water added to the flour and the starter will have to be 64 degrees to ensure that the final dough has a temperature of 77 degrees.

If you want consistent results at home, you can approximate this method by estimating the friction factor of your mixer by using an instant read thermometer to take the temperature of several batches of bread dough, both before and after kneading.

Checking the pH of Pre-Ferments and Sourdough Starters

pH is a scale, from 0 to 14, used to express the relative acidity of a solution. More acidic solutions have a lower pH, and less acidic solutions have a higher pH. pH is an important indication of the ripeness of a sourdough starter or a yeasted pre-ferment and its ability to raise bread. Using a digital pH meter (see Resources, page 347) is a simple way to monitor the maturation of your starters. We do it multiple times a day at Bread Alone. A ripe sourdough will have a lower pH, 3.9 to 4.2, while a yeasted pre-ferment will have a higher pH, between 5.2 to 5.5. It's helpful, while developing your skills, to measure the pH level of your starters at the same time that you taste them, to develop a familiarity with various pH levels. If the pH isn't low enough in your sourdough, wait another hour and check again.

Folding

Highly hydrated doughs especially benefit from being folded at regular intervals during the first fermentation. Folding strengthens gluten without overworking the dough. It also encourages a pleasingly irregular crumb structure. Pierre-Julien Bouniol of Boulangerie Utopiste in Avignon folds his Pain de Campagne (page 226) dough at least twice during fermentation. Folding, along with long, gentle mixing and a very short final proofing time, gives his loaves their characteristic dense, chewy, moist texture. It is important to avoid folding the dough too much or it will be too strong and very difficult to work with during shaping.

Retarding

Chilling doughs, a technique that some bakers call *retarding*, slows down fermentation activity while developing flavor and altering the texture of the dough and crust. Dough is most often retarded for

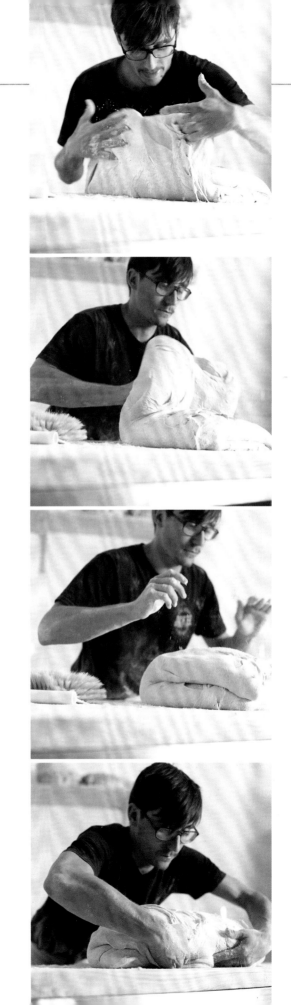

FOLDING

up to 24 hours, either in bulk or already shaped, in order to improve flavor and for the sake of convenience. Rodolphe Landemaine retards his Baguette de Tradition (page 190) overnight, which gives them a mildly sour flavor. I know bakers who keep their doughs in retarder/proofers (a special machine designed for this purpose; home bakers simply use the refrigerator) for up to 48 hours, but there is a danger that your dough will begin to break down and/or the yeast will burn out during such a long period of time.

Dividing

Using a dough scraper or bench knife to cut the dough to divide it will ensure a clean cut and preserve the gluten structure of the dough by avoiding excessive tearing, This is especially important when you are working with highly hydrated doughs, which require both a delicate touch and gentle handling to preserve the fragile gluten structure.

Pre-Shaping

Pre-shaping helps to prepare the dough for final shaping and cuts down on overhandling that might damage dough structure during final shaping. Dough is generally shaped into loose rounds before being shaped into boules or bâtards. For longer baguettes, dough is pre-shaped into ovals or rectangles. It's important to handle the dough at this point as minimally as possible in order to preserve its cell structure for the finished product.

Resting

Resting the loaves after pre-shaping gives the dough a chance to relax, so it requires less handling during final shaping. Because the fermentation activity continues during this step, the resulting breads will have a more open crumb structure than unrested breads. Resting is usually no more than 20 to 30 minutes. In a bakery setting, dividing, pre-shaping, and shaping is a cyclical process. Bakers will divide a couple hundred pieces at a time. As soon as the loaves are all divided and pre-shaped, the bakers will cycle back to the first pre-shaped loaves, shape them, and continue until all breads are shaped.

Shaping Tips

Boules (Rounds), Baguettes, and Bâtards

Unless otherwise indicated, the breads in this book are shaped into boules or rounds, baguettes, or bâtards before being shaped into their final form.

To shape a round, collect the dough into a rough ball. Cup your hands over the ball and then move them in tight circles as you pull the ball toward you with the heels of your hands, pulling any rough bits underneath the ball and creating a taut skin around it.

To shape a baguette, pat the dough into a rough rectangle. With the longer side facing you, fold the top of the dough down about one third of the way toward the center. With the fleshy part of your thumbs, gently press along the seam. Fold the bottom of the dough about one-third of the way toward the center and seal the seam. Fold this skinny rectangle in half, bringing the top edge down to meet the bottom. Press again with your thumbs firmly along the seam to seal. Roll the log back and forth a few times slightly adding more pressure to the tips.

To shape a bâtard, start with a log shape and place your hands together, palms down over the middle of the log. Using light, even pressure, roll the log back and forth as you spread your hands apart. Repeat two or three times until the bâtard is the desired length, tapering the ends by increasing downward pressure at the tips.

To shape a pan loaf or rectangular free-form

bread, press the dough into a rectangle. Fold each end of the rectangle towards the center of the dough. Press once or twice with your fingertips to seal. Press the dough into a rectangle again. This time, fold the long edges toward the center. Press with your fingertips to seal the seam. Place seam side down in a loaf pan, and seam side up in a banneton.

Using a Couche

This is a common technique across Europe, helpful for proofing a large number of loaves in a small space. A piece of natural flax linen, strategically folded, holds loaves in place as they proof. This fabric is naturally nonstick, and becomes easier to work with over time. A couche can easily be improvised using a piece of parchment paper and some kitchen towels, and instructions for doing so are included in the recipes. But if you are a frequent baker, you should consider investing in a high-quality linen couche, which will wick away a little bit of the dough's surface moisture, encouraging a crisp crust.

Richard Ruan moving his baguettes from the couche to the loader

Bannetons

Baskets made from a variety of materials, rattan, willow, and plastic, in a large variety of shapes, are used to keep soft dough in shape while it is rising. Decorative bannetons also beautify your breads.

Shaping Rye Breads

Because rye is low in gluten, rye doughs are much softer, stickier, and potentially more difficult to shape than wheat doughs. They are only rarely shaped without a banneton or a bread pan. Bakers sometimes use wet hands to scale and shape doughs to place into pans. Alternatively, they generously flour their hands and the bannetons before placing the rye dough into the banneton or other containers

to avoid sticking. Use short quick strokes with the heels of your hands so that the dough doesn't stick to your fingers.

Scoring

Scoring can be highly decorative, but it is primarily functional, a way to control the rise and direct the expansion of the dough in the oven. One way or another, bread dough that is teaming with yeast and sourdough is going to expand in the heat of the oven. Instead of letting it burst where it may, a baker can strategically slash a loaf to give it a place to expand in the first few minutes in the oven. I recommend using a clean and sharp razor blade (supported by a blade holder), also known as a *lame*. A

BAGUETTE

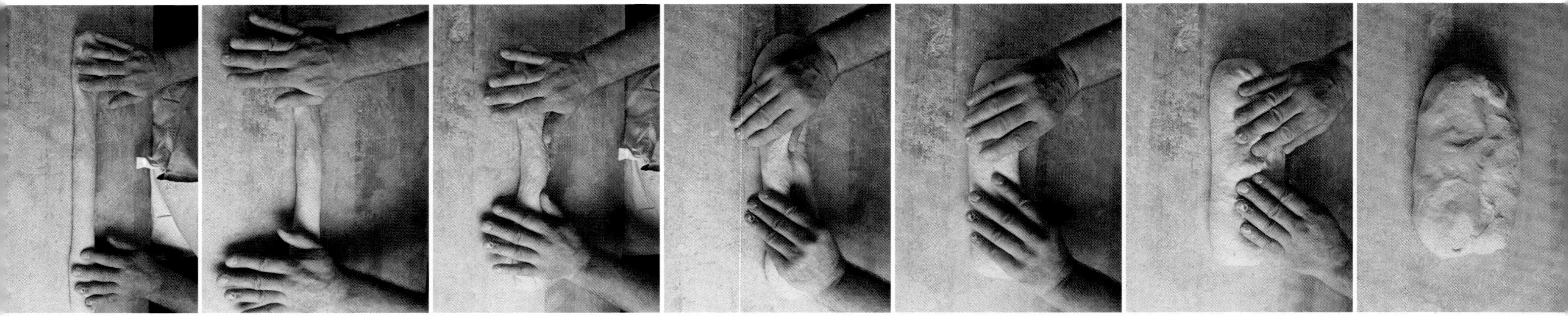

BANNETON

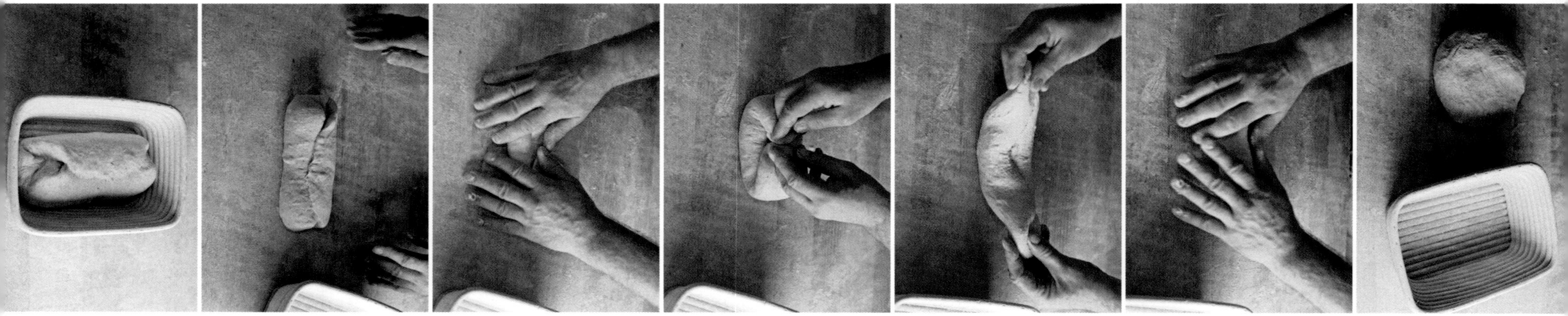

BÂTARD

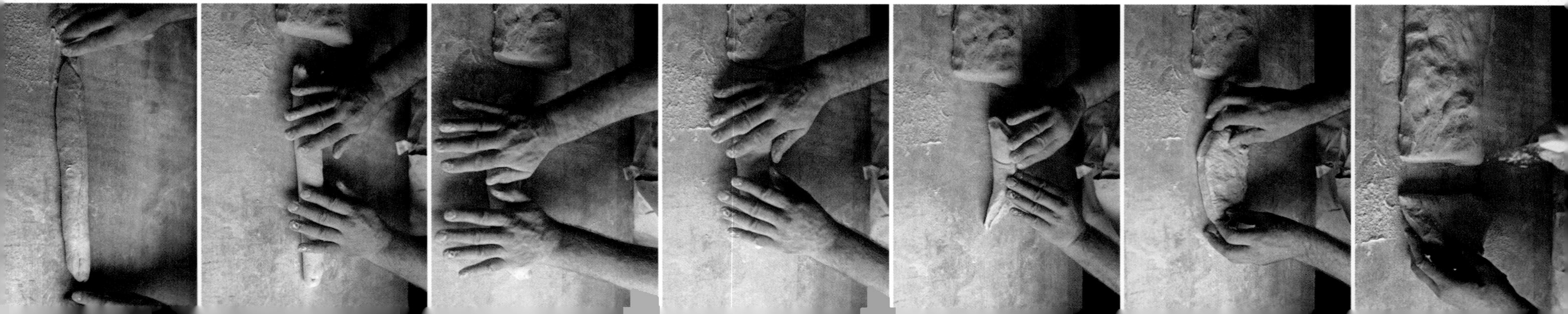

BOULE

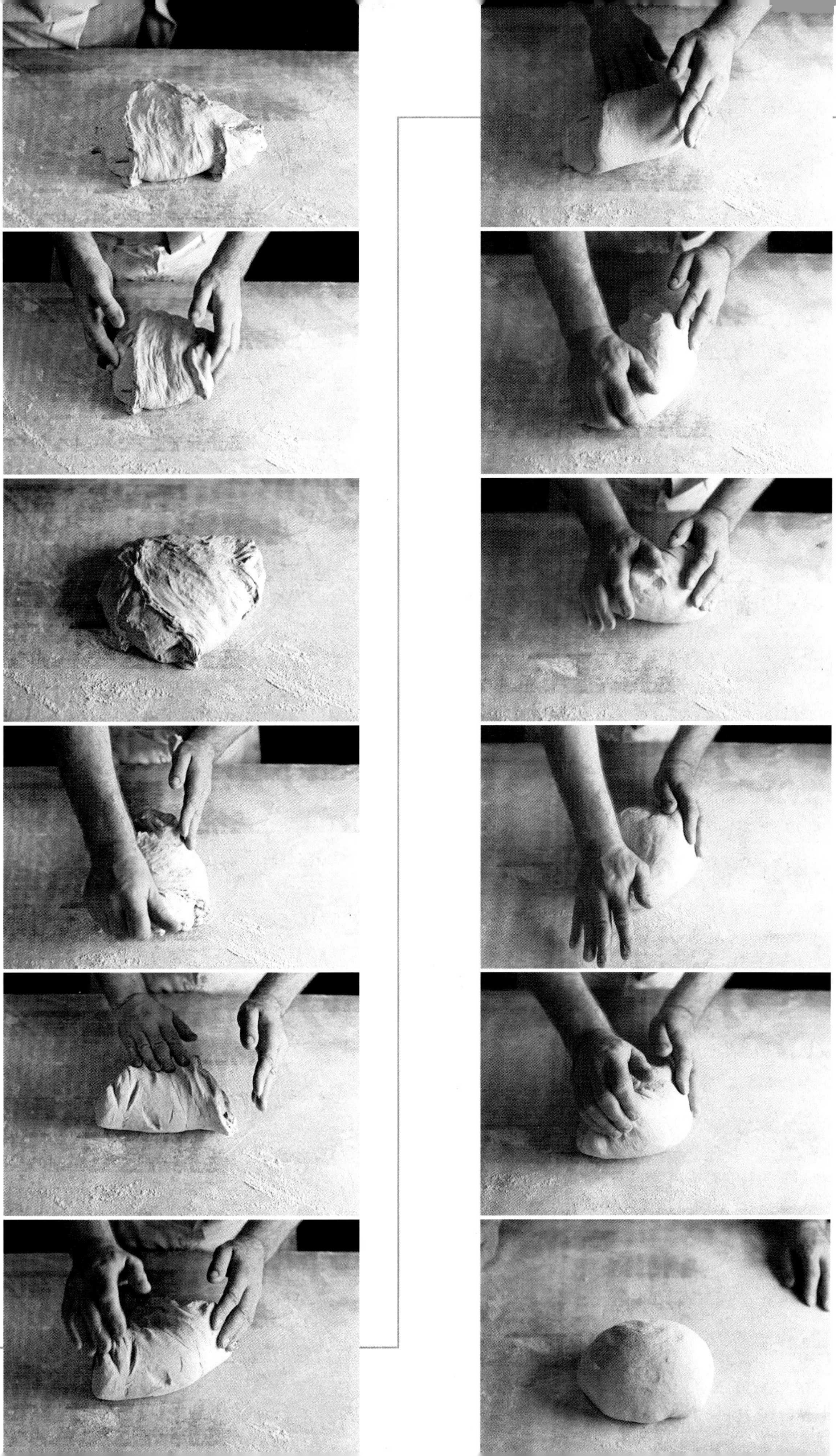

Classic scoring

sharp serrated knife or paring knife are alternatives for scoring the dough. And here is a bonus pro tip: When Didier Rosada was shaping the Pompe à l'Huile (page 160) for our photo shoot, he asked me for my credit card. Since I trust him implicitly, I handed over my American Express. He used it to make clean cuts through each oval to create a classic fougasse shape.

Baking

Approximating a Hearth Oven

A baking stone coupled with a cast-iron skillet for steam or a Dutch oven will help you get good oven spring and crust development, but won't exactly replicate the results from a professional oven. For truly professional results, there's a new generation of steam-injected stone hearth ovens for the home from manufacturers including Rofco, Miele, and Häussler (see Resources, page 347). Breads baked in these ovens attain great volume and develop delicious crusts. Even heat distribution and abundant steam give results comparable to a professional deck oven. Home wood-fired ovens are also now more popular and available. Maine Wood Heat distributes Le Panyol wood-fired home ovens. We recently bought one to use as a mobile bread and pizza oven at Bread Alone.

Steam

Steaming the dough during the first minutes of baking keeps the crust temporarily soft so that it can expand to its full potential while the yeast is still alive. Steaming will give your loaves a glossy crust as they bake by encouraging the gelatinization of starches on the dough's surface during baking. Steaming also improves the crispiness of the crust by delaying its formation. A thinner crust will create a crustier bread. There are a variety of ways to do this. I prefer to preheat a cast-iron skillet on the lower rack of the oven and then place a cup of ice cubes in the skillet when I load the bread on the baking stone, which produces steam neatly and without the risk of shattering the oven's lightbulb. Baking in a preheated cast-iron Dutch oven is an alternative to baking on a baking stone. It can be tricky to transfer large doughs from a banneton or couche to a hot, heavy pot, so you must take care. But with practice, you can easily master the technique. The results are outstanding, and eliminate the need to add extra steam.

Cooling

Professional bakers use ventilated metal screen or bins to hold bread while it cools, to allow good air circulation and prevent condensation, preserving the crispiness of the crust. You can use wire racks for cooling at home to allow air to circulate all around breads.

Par-Baking and Freezing Breads

Many bakeries do this to have their full variety available at the same time. To do this at home, shorten the baking time by 5 to 8 minutes, then cool the loaves for 20 minutes and put them immediately in the freezer unwrapped. Let them freeze for 2 hours, and then wrap them and return to the freezer. To finish, put them in a 350-degree oven for 15 to 20 minutes to defrost and finish baking at the same time. These breads taste perfectly fresh and delicious.

Reflections on Becoming a Better Baker

One of the most impressive bakers I met on this journey, Arnd Erbel, told me that he thinks of bread baking as a single recipe, and that every time he bakes he adjusts the recipe to suit the particular circumstances of that day's production. Arnd bakes more than a dozen types of bread, but because he thinks of each one as a variation, he can apply the lessons he has learned about one bread to any other.

His words reminded me of something Apollonia Poilâne had said, that it is enough to continually try to make one bread well. Some of the most beloved bakers follow this tradition of focusing on a single bread, including Nunzio Ninivaggi in Altamura, who also uses one type of dough to bake his celebrated Altamura breads, and Marco Bocchini, who makes Genzano bread and pizza according to his father's recipe and following IGP (Indicazione Geografica Protetta) guidelines.

I don't believe in a perfect bread, but I do believe in working towards that ideal. My goal is to continually find ways to improve. When I worked at Minoterie Suire with test baker Fabrice Guéry, I became fascinated by the BIPEA scorecard (see page 87) he used to note subtle differences in every batch of dough he mixed and every bread he baked, objectively grading the process and the breads. His detailed notes reminded me of the obsessive records Thomas Jefferson made while working on his garden, jotting down the date that blossoms appeared, what size the vegetables were when harvested, and how many bugs he killed in a particular gardening session, all in the service of doing better next year. I realized how much knowledge you could acquire, very quickly, when you analyzed the process following such a precise system.

I recommend, as a learning tool, making the same bread over and over, keeping a record of the details of the process and noting the characteristics of the dough at every step. This will make you a better baker. Choose a recipe that you'd like to master, and commit to baking the bread at least four times in a period of two weeks. Use the same high-quality artisanal flour, and each time take careful notes throughout the process, recording variables such as hydration, mixing time, proofing time, baking time. Evaluate the finished bread, judging its cut opening, volume, crust color, crust crispiness, alvéolage, crumb color, and flavor. You will gain knowledge that only experience and repetition can provide.

Oven dance at
Forno a Legna da Sergio

ARTISAN BREAD SCORECARD

Use the following checklist, inspired by the BIPEA scorecard that bakers at French mills use to evaluate flour, to get to know your bread over the course of several bakes.

	BREAD #1	BREAD #2	BREAD #3	BREAD #4
Water temp				
Kneading time				
Dough temp				
Final dough temp				
Evaluation (describe the dough: is it tacky, dry, elastic, well-developed, slack, etc.)				
Fermentation time				
Evaluation (describe the dough)				
Resting time				
Pre-shaping and evaluation (describe the dough)				
Final proof time				
Baking and steam time				
Baking temp				
Steam (how much water added)				
Baking Characteristics: Cut opening Volume Crust color Crust crispiness Alvéolage Crumb color Flavor				

BABA COOL IN AVIGNON

PIERRE-JULIEN BOUNIOL, BELLA CIAO
BOULANGERIE UTOPISTE, AVIGNON, FRANCE

In 2015, Pierre-Julien Bouniol was a frustrated journalist who dreamed of a simpler way of life. On a whim, he quit his job and applied to the École Internationale de Boulangerie in Noyers-sur-Jabron. The school, founded in 2005 by biologist Thomas Teffri-Chambelland to certify bakers in natural sourdough baking with organic grain, takes a very small number of students every term with the goal of giving them the skills to open their own organic bakeries within a year of graduation. While teaching traditional recipes and techniques, the program is decidedly modern in its insistence on organic ingredients, and in welcoming career changers

and training them to operate small businesses. Until relatively recently, most French bakers began as apprentices in their early teens, often working in family businesses. Pierre-Julien is part of a movement in France of professionals who change careers, focusing on specialty foods and working within the artisan tradition.

Pierre-Julien's knowledge of both baking and business, along with his poetic spirit and suave manner, helped convince a local bank to lend him money for his bakery. In the summer of 2016, he opened Bella Ciao Boulangerie Utopiste. When I met him, he reminded me of myself at his age. He hasn't yet accumulated a lifetime of experience, but he has the passion and desire to create something special, and his excellent and unusual bread is proof that you don't have to have inherited knowledge or years in a bakery to make delicious bread if you focus on simple techniques and perfect your hand work.

The bakery is in a quieter district of Avignon, filled with quirky little shops selling everything from handmade hats to hand-forged knives. As you approach the bright blue cafe, you might see customers parking bikes in the rack out front or someone strumming a guitar at the cafe table in front of the large plate glass window. Inside, the shop is tiny and simple, with a counter made of reclaimed wood and just a couple of types of rustic bread (identified by little chalkboard signs) overflowing from large baskets. Utopiste ("utopian") is the perfect name for Pierre-Julien's place. He and his assistants work as a collective,

and are determined to have lives outside the bakery, taking Sundays and Mondays off, and opening at the late (for a bakery) hour of 11 a.m. the other five days of the week.

The place has a young hipster, or "baba cool," vibe. Pierre-Julien is about 30 years old, and the two bakers who work with him are even younger. One sports a man-bun, another a trendy goatee. Reggae music plays in the tiled workroom, which is visible beyond the cash register. Yet the clientele are all ages, from young moms with babies in backpacks to elegantly dressed retirees in cardigans, tweed jackets, and berets. They come for the bread, which Pierre-Julien dreamed up after absorbing the fundamentals of traditional sourdough baking and using his knowledge to develop a style of his own. His idea, fostered by the progressive education he received, was to make breads with robust, uncomplicated texture and a rich, dense crumb by manipulating the dough as little as possible.

His technique is simple. He mixes his dough on the slow speed for 20 minutes in a very old Artofex mixer. Bakers who choose this machine are willing to devote the extra time it requires because of the result. The slow, deliberate, very delicate kneading action produces a dough with gentle elasticity, giving the finished bread a dense, chewy, and less developed quality similar to bread slowly kneaded by hand. After kneading, Pierre-Julien cuts the dough into 10-kilo pieces. He lets the pieces ferment in plastic tubs for an hour and a half, then he folds the dough, lets it rest another hour and a half, and folds it again. After a final fermentation, the dough is turned onto a worktable, cut into rough rectangles with a bench knife, and put right in the oven with no shaping and little final proofing. It oddly reminded me of being in Altamura, where the breads go immediately into the oven. Like the Altamura breads, Pierre-Julien's loaves are unstructured with a dense, moist crumb. It doesn't matter that the loaves are not identical, or even if they are different sizes, since the bread is sold by weight.

4

STRAIGHT
DOUGHS

To prepare a straight dough, you simply combine the ingredients in one step. These simple doughs are raised with commercial yeast, so there is no pre-ferment or sourdough culture to make before mixing. Sourdough enthusiasts may consider straight doughs to have less flavor, character, and aroma than breads made with a natural starter or pre-ferment. But as some of the best bakers in Europe prove, well-made straight doughs can be as satisfying as more complex doughs, and they hold an important place in the artisan repertoire.

Bakers like Richard Ruan have good reasons for choosing commercial yeast. When developing his baguette recipe, Richard was striving for a bread with a clean, sweet, warm flavor and a light texture, without any underlying sour notes. A pre-ferment or sourdough starter would have given the bread unwelcome acidity. But he didn't want bland or uninteresting loaves. To ensure the opposite, Richard employs several techniques. He uses just a tiny amount of yeast in his dough, as low as 1 gram per kilo and then ferments it for an unusually long time in the refrigerator. This long fermentation allows the bread to develop its sui generis wheaty flavor.

Adding flavorful ingredients is another way of enhancing a straight dough. Provencal bakers sprinkle their fougasse dough with olives or cheese. German bakers add dried fruit and nuts. Pierre-Julien Bouniol makes irresistible chocolate rolls using a straight dough: Cocoa powder and chopped bittersweet chocolate add flavor and richness. Fermented overnight in the refrigerator, batches can be shaped and baked on demand throughout the workday so his customers can enjoy warm treats whenever they stop in.

The following recipes are among the easiest and most satisfying in this book. That doesn't necessarily mean they are quick. While Pierre-Julien's Pitchou Chocolat can be made start to finish in 4 hours, Richard's baguettes require at least 16 hours. Of course, most of this time you won't be actively working on your bread. While it rests and develops, you'll have the time to listen to all nine of Beethoven's symphonies.

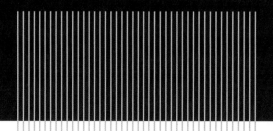

THE MINIMALIST BAKER

RICHARD RUAN, LA BOULANGERIE DES CARMES, ANGERS, FRANCE

I felt more than a bit intimidated on my way to meet Richard Ruan at La Boulangerie des Carmes in Angers, at the edge of the Loire Valley in western France. Richard is well known as a baker's baker. He was recommended to me by no less than the legendary Hubert Chiron, author of *Les Pain Français*, considered the bread bible by a generation of French artisan bakers.

Very few bakers in France have more breadth of experience than Richard. He grew up in a baking family, working alongside his father and grandfather. Not content to stay in one place, he impulsively traveled to the U.S. and helped establish an authentic boulangerie, La Chatelaine, in Columbus, Ohio. He returned to France and continued to develop his knowledge and skills at some of the country's most rigorously traditional shops.

He was present at the moment mills began to hire skilled bakers to test flour outside of a lab and in realistic bakery conditions. Realizing that the quality of bread in France would continue to decline unless a new generation of bakers were trained in artisan techniques, these mills also hired bakers to teach their customers the best baking practices. In 1993, the same time the government passed a law detailing the characteristics and acceptable methods for producing a true *baguette de tradition,* he was hired by Bellot Minoterie in western France, a mill that exclusively grinds local wheat from Poitou-Charentes and develops flour blends and mixing techniques. He traveled to over 700 bakeries that were customers of the mill to train their bakers in how to best use this flour and how to refine and improve their baking. Not only is he an expert on bread, but he is also vastly knowledgeable about wheat varieties, wheat blending, and specialty flours. After years of preparation he put his skills to the test by competing in France's most prestigious craft competition, the Meilleur Ouvrier de France, which he was awarded in 2000.

Before we met, he had told me that he had spent his entire career dreaming about the ideal bakery he would open if he could. La Boulangerie des Carmes is the embodiment of these dreams. When I arrived in Angers, I expected to see a large, militaristic workplace in the French tradition, with an army of assistants, and Richard as the general. Instead, I found a 300-square-foot room, smaller than my office at Bread Alone. Breads were displayed on a 4-foot-long zinc-topped counter and on simple wooden shelves lined with baskets. When the counter and baskets are full of bread, a new customer might be afraid to help himself to a loaf, out of fear that a chain reaction would destroy the display.

He took in my shocked expression as I surveyed his domain and explained why this tiny space was his *boulangerie ideal.* Although he was making a good salary as an expert teacher, he told me, he realized he wanted to open his own business. After countless visits to hundreds of bakeries, he realized, "I'm a minimalist. If I had my own place, it would contain nothing but the essentials. A mixer, worktable,

profile continues

Pain des Carmes
400 gr - 3,12€/Kg   1.25 €

Sac Echangeable
à vie
0,50 €

Boule au levain
r - 3.60€/Kg   1.80 €

Boule des carmes
400 gr - 3,12€/Kg   1.25 €

oven." He made a deal with his wife, who was wary of the impact this business would have on their savings: He'd hire a minimal staff, make a minimal investment, and simply produce fresh bread all day long. "I didn't want to have a place where I had to work just to pay for expensive machines." Instead, he has a vintage Artofex mixer and a small oven. He hired one assistant, and together they produce just a few varieties of bread. It doesn't bother him that demand outstrips supply. "I want there to be a line out the door all the time." Stepping into the shop feels like a step back in time. The staff wears old world baking smocks. The low-tech philosophy extends to the front of the shop, where there isn't a cash register, just a drawer. Richard likes his clerks to perform calculations in their heads before making change, which to him feels more human. His stripped-down aesthetic is evident even in the car he drives—an economical three-seat French-made electric Mia that resembles a bread wagon.

Richard's streamlined recipes are similarly minimalist. He maintains a single traditional firm levain for his spelt breads and his levain bread. He doesn't even fuss with sourdough for his baguettes. To ensure that his loaves have great flavor, he adds just a pinch of leavener, and ferments his dough an unusually long time in the refrigerator. After he mixes the dough, he stores bins of different types—seeded, buckwheat, fruit and nut—in a cold room. He never knows what the demand will be. Sometimes the dough sits for a day, sometimes it sits for two. Whenever he runs out of loaves, the dough is shaped and then goes right into the oven. He is closed on Sundays and Mondays, and Saturday's dough keeps until he comes back to work on Tuesday morning.

He uses a relatively low-gluten flour, which gives his breads a tender crumb with a gentle chew. The long-fermented dough has enough time to develop the strength it needs to keep its shape. And because Richard shapes all of his breads by hand, he doesn't have to worry that the dough is too soft to go through a baguette moulder.

While simple and handmade, Richard's loaves are as elegant as you might expect from a Meilleur Ouvrier de France. Just before baking, he adds a decorative flourish to each baguette: Sometimes it is a simple slash. Sometimes he cuts a little strip of dough away from the side of each loaf and wraps it around the loaf like a piece of bakery twine.

BAGUETTE DE RICHARD RUAN

INGREDIENTS	BAKER'S %	METRIC WEIGHT
FINAL DOUGH		
Type 65 or equivalent flour (11 to 11.5% protein)	100	600 g
Water	75	450 g
Salt	2	12 g
Dry instant yeast	0.2	1 g

1. **MAKE THE FINAL DOUGH**: Using a rubber spatula, combine the flour and 400 g of the water in the bowl of an electric mixer fitted with a dough hook. Mix with a rubber spatula just until a rough dough forms.

2. **AUTOLYSE**: Cover and let rest 45 minutes.

3. Add the salt and yeast to the bowl. With the dough hook, mix on the lowest setting for 2 minutes. Increase the speed to low (2 on a KitchenAid mixer) and, with the mixer on, slowly drizzle the remaining 50 g water into the bowl, about 1 minute. Continue to mix until the dough is very soft, elastic, and shiny, another 10 minutes. Turn the mixer to medium-low (4 on a KitchenAid mixer) and mix another 2 minutes.

4. **RETARD**: Use a dough scraper to transfer the dough to a lightly oiled, clear 3-quart container with a lid. Turn the dough over so all sides are oiled. Cover and let stand at room temperature for 60 minutes. Turn the dough out onto a lightly floured counter. Pat into a 6- by 8-inch rectangle and fold like a business letter. Slide both hands under the dough and flip it over. Slip it back into the container, cover, and refrigerate for 12 to 24 hours.

5. **REST**: Remove the dough from the refrigerator and let stand for 45 minutes to warm up. On a floured countertop, divide the dough into three equal pieces and pre-shape into rounds. Cover and let rest for 30 minutes.

recipe continues

START TO FINISH:
17 to 29
hours

AUTOLYSE
45 minutes

KNEAD
15 minutes

REST
30 minutes

RETARD
12 to 24 hours

WARM UP
45 minutes

REST
30 minutes

FINAL PROOF
45 minutes

BAKE
25 to 30 minutes

MAKES
three 354-gram baguettes

recipe continued from previous page

6. **FINAL PROOF**: Cover a baker's peel or rimless baking sheet with parchment. Shape each piece of dough, adding additional flour to the work surface as needed, into a baguette with pointed tips (see page 78) about 14 inches long. Dust the parchment-covered peel or baking sheet with flour and place the baguettes on the parchment, seam side down, 2 inches apart. Lift the parchment paper between the loaves, making a pleat and drawing the loaves close together. Tightly roll up two kitchen towels and slip them under the parchment paper along the sides of the outer loaves to support each baguette. Lightly dust with flour and drape with plastic wrap. Let rise until pillowy, about 45 minutes.

7. **BAKE**: About 1 hour before baking, place a baking stone on the middle rack of the oven and a cast-iron skillet on the lower rack. Preheat the oven to 425 degrees for 1 hour. Uncover the breads, remove the rolled-up towels, and stretch the parchment paper out so that it is flat and the loaves are separated. With a *lame,* a single-edged razor blade, or a serrated knife, make one long slash, about ¼ inch deep, down the length of each loaf. Slide the loaves, still on the parchment, onto the baking stone. Place 1 cup of ice cubes in the skillet to produce steam. Bake until the loaves are golden brown and well risen, 25 to 30 minutes. Slide the loaves, still on the parchment, onto a wire rack. Cool completely. Store in a brown paper bag at room temperature for up to 2 days.

Baguette
de Richard
Ruan,
page 97

Baguette
Sarrasin,
page 100

Baguette
with Grains,
page 102

BAGUETTE SARRASIN

INGREDIENTS	BAKER'S %	METRIC WEIGHT
FINAL DOUGH		
Type 65 or equivalent flour (11 to 11.5% protein)	90	540 g
Buckwheat flour	10	60 g
Water	75	450 g
Salt	2	12 g
Dry instant yeast	0.2	1 g

START TO FINISH:

16 to 29

hours

AUTOLYSE
45 minutes

KNEAD
15 minutes

REST
30 minutes

RETARD
12 to 24 hours

WARM UP
1½ to 2 hours

REST
15 minutes

FINAL PROOF
30 to 45 minutes

BAKE
25 to 30 minutes

MAKES
three 354-gram baguettes

1. **MAKE THE FINAL DOUGH:** Combine the wheat flour, buckwheat flour, and 400 g of the water in the bowl of an electric mixer fitted with a dough hook. Mix with a rubber spatula just until a rough dough forms.

2. **AUTOLYSE:** Cover and let rest 45 minutes.

3. Add the salt and yeast to the bowl. With the dough hook, mix on the lowest setting for 2 minutes. Increase the speed to low (2 on a KitchenAid mixer) and, with the mixer on, slowly drizzle the remaining 50 g water into the bowl, about 1 minute. Continue to mix until the dough is very soft, elastic, and slightly gritty from the buckwheat, another 10 minutes. Turn the mixer to medium-low (4 on a KitchenAid mixer) and mix another 2 minutes.

4. **RETARD:** Use a dough scraper to transfer the dough to a lightly oiled, clear 3-quart container with a lid. Turn the dough over so all sides are oiled. Cover and let stand at room temperature for 60 minutes. Turn the dough out onto a lightly floured counter. Pat into a 6- by 8-inch rectangle and fold like a business letter. Slide both hands under the dough and flip it over so the folds are underneath. Slip it back into the container, cover, and refrigerate for 12 to 24 hours. The dough will be pillowy and relaxed.

5. **REST:** Remove from the refrigerator and let stand for 1½ to 2 hours to warm up. On a lightly floured countertop, gently press the dough into a 9- by 14-inch rectangle. Dust with flour. With a bench scraper, cut the rectangle into three 14-inch strips. Cover and let rest for 15 minutes.

6. **FINAL PROOF**: Cover a baker's peel or rimless baking sheet with parchment. Dust the parchment-covered peel or baking sheet with flour and place the dough strips on the parchment, 2 inches apart. Let rise until pillowy, 30 to 45 minutes.

7. **BAKE**: About 1 hour before baking, place a baking stone on the middle rack of the oven and a cast-iron skillet on the lower rack. Preheat the oven to 425 degrees for 1 hour. Uncover the breads. Slide the loaves, still on the parchment, onto the baking stone. Place 1 cup of ice cubes in the skillet to produce steam. Bake until the loaves are golden brown and well risen, 25 to 30 minutes. Slide the loaves, still on the parchment, onto a wire rack. Cool completely. Store in a brown paper bag at room temperature for up to 2 days.

AUTOLYSE
1 hour

KNEAD
7 minutes

REST
30 minutes

RETARD
12 to 24 hours

WARM UP
1½ to 2 hours

REST
30 minutes

FINAL PROOF
45 minutes

BAKE
25 to 30 minutes

MAKES
three 342-gram baguettes

BAGUETTE WITH GRAINS

INGREDIENTS	BAKER'S %	METRIC WEIGHT
FINAL DOUGH		
Type 65 or equivalent (11 to 11.5% protein) flour	100	520 g
Water	78	405 g
Flax seeds	7	35 g
Whole millet	7	35 g
Sunflower seeds	7	35 g
Salt	2	12 g
Dry instant yeast	0.2	1 g

1. **AUTOLYSE**: In the bowl of an electric mixer fitted with a dough hook, combine the flour, water, flax, millet, and sunflower seeds. Mix with a rubber spatula just until a rough dough forms. Cover and let stand for 1 hour.

2. **MAKE THE FINAL DOUGH**: Add the salt and yeast to the bowl. With the dough hook, mix on the lowest setting for 2 minutes. Increase the speed to low (2 on a KitchenAid mixer) and continue to mix on low until the dough is very soft and elastic, but bumpy from the seeds, another 5 minutes.

3. **RETARD**: Use a dough scraper to transfer the dough to a lightly oiled, clear 3-quart container with a lid. Turn the dough over so all sides are oiled. Cover and let stand at room temperature for 60 minutes. Turn the dough out onto a lightly floured counter. Pat into a 6- by 8-inch rectangle and fold like a business letter. Slide both hands under the dough and flip it over so the folds are underneath. Slip it back into the container, cover, and refrigerate for 12 to 24 hours.

4. **REST**: Remove from the refrigerator and let stand for 1½ to 2 hours to warm up. On a lightly floured countertop, divide the dough into three equal pieces and pre-shape into rounds (see page 78). Cover and let rest for 30 minutes.

5. **FINAL PROOF**: Cover a baker's peel or rimless baking sheet with parchment. Shape each piece of dough, adding additional flour to the work surface as needed, into a baguette with pointed tips (see

page 78) about 14 inches long. Dust the parchment-covered peel or baking sheet with flour and place the baguettes on the parchment, seam side down, 2 inches apart. Lift the parchment paper between the loaves, making a pleat and drawing the loaves close together. Alternatively, use baker's linen instead of parchment. Tightly roll up two kitchen towels and slip them under the parchment paper along the sides of the outer loaves to support each baguette. Lightly dust with flour and drape with plastic wrap. Let rise until pillowy, about 45 minutes.

6. **BAKE**: About 1 hour before baking, place a baking stone on the middle rack of the oven and a cast-iron skillet on the lower rack. Preheat the oven to 425 degrees for 1 hour. Uncover the breads, remove the rolled-up towels, and stretch the parchment paper out so that it is flat and the loaves are separated. With a *lame,* a single-edged razor blade, or a serrated knife, cut a ¼-inch-thick strip of dough, about 2½ inches long, from the side of the dough, leaving it attached to the baguette at the tip. Drape the dough piece over the top of the loaf and tuck it underneath. Repeat three times, for a total of four decorative strips. Slide the loaves, still on the parchment, onto the baking stone. Place 1 cup of ice cubes in the skillet to produce steam. Bake until the loaves are golden brown and well risen, 25 to 30 minutes. Slide the loaves, still on the parchment, onto a wire rack. Cool completely. Store in a brown paper bag at room temperature for up to 2 days.

Note for Professional Bakers

In a production environment, when working with a hydraulic dough divider, it is best to scale the exact quantity of dough needed for one press right after mixing, then place the tubs in the cooler for the first fermentation. Once the first fermentation is completed, the dough can be directly transferred to the hydraulic dough divider to be divided, making the scaling process very efficient. It is best to lightly oil the tubs for an easy transfer.

BUCKWHEAT METEIL

For this book, I wanted to create a simple recipe, a learning bread, that has all of the characteristics of a great artisan bread: A rugged crust, a rich and moist crumb, a mix of flours to create a unique flavor. I wanted to leave out the sourdough for people who aren't yet ready to take that step. For inspiration, I turned to the idea of *pain méteil*. It's not uncommon in French bakeries to see a *pain méteil*, which generally includes a mix of flours, most often wheat and rye. This *pain méteil* has a mix of whole wheat, whole rye, and buckwheat. The buckwheat contributes an earthy flavor. The long, cool fermentation in the refrigerator offers flexibility in terms of when you want to bake. Baking in a Dutch oven creates a thick, flavorful crust without the need for a baking stone and steam. This streamlines the process for people who might not have that equipment on hand. And if your shaping skills are rudimentary, using a Dutch oven will give you a perfectly shaped loaf with ease.

INGREDIENTS	BAKER'S %	METRIC WEIGHT
FINAL DOUGH		
Type 65 or equivalent flour (11 to 11.5% protein)	60	375 g
Whole wheat flour	10	63 g
Whole rye flour	10	63 g
Buckwheat flour	20	125 g
Water	80	500 g
Salt	2	13 g
Dry instant yeast	0.3	2 g
Currants (optional)	30	187 g

1. **MAKE THE FINAL DOUGH:** In the bowl of an electric mixer fitted with a dough hook, combine the Type 65 flour, whole wheat flour, whole rye flour, buckwheat flour, 450 g of the water, the salt, and yeast. Stir with a rubber spatula until a rough dough forms. With the dough hook, mix on the lowest setting (2 on a KitchenAid mixer) until the

recipe continues

START TO FINISH:

17 to 21

hours

KNEAD
13 minutes

REST
45 minutes

RETARD
12 hours

WARM UP
1½ to 2 hours

FINAL PROOF
1 hour

BAKE
50 to 55 minutes

MAKES
one 1,141-gram loaf
(1,328 g with currants)

recipe continued from previous page

dough comes together, 30 seconds. Turn the mixer to medium (6 on a KitchenAid mixer) and mix until the dough is soft and elastic, with a velvety texture and slightly sticky to the touch, 8 minutes. Pull the dough off the hook. With the mixer on low, slowly drizzle the remaining 50 g water into the bowl. Continue to mix until the dough is very soft, elastic, and shiny, another 4 minutes. Add the currants, if using, and mix until incorporated.

2. **RETARD**: Use a dough scraper to transfer the dough to a lightly oiled, clear 4-quart container with a lid. Turn the dough over so all sides are oiled. Cover and let stand 75 minutes. Refrigerate for 12 hours.

3. **WARM UP**: Remove the dough from the refrigerator and let it warm up on the countertop for 1½ to 2 hours.

4. **FINAL PROOF**: Shape the dough into a loose boule (see page 78). Place in a lightly floured banneton, seam side up. Alternatively, line a large bowl with a clean cotton dish cloth, dust with flour, and place the boule, seam side down in the bowl. Cover and let stand about 1 hour.

5. About 30 minutes before baking, place a 6-quart round Dutch oven with lid on the lower rack of the oven. Preheat the oven to 425 degrees.

6. **BAKE**: With heavy-duty oven mitts, transfer the hot Dutch oven to a cool stovetop burner or other heatproof surface. Remove the lid. Lightly flour your hands. Turn the dough out of the banneton and into your hands. Gently drop it into the preheated pot. With a *lame*, a single-edged razor blade, or a serrated knife, make two slashes, about ½ inch deep, to form an X. Cover, return to the oven, and bake for 30 minutes. Uncover and bake until golden brown and well risen, another 20 to 25 minutes. Invert the loaf onto a wire rack, re-invert, and let cool completely. Store in a brown paper bag at room temperature for 2 to 4 days.

Note for Professional Bakers

This bread can also be baked in a regular deck oven. After the final proof, transfer the dough to the oven loader or oven peel and baked directly on the stone of the oven. After scoring, bake with steam until the proper color and crust crispiness is achieved.

FOUGASSETTES
AU ROQUEFORT

Traveling in Provence, you'll see many variations on the classic fougasse, some with olives, some with rosemary, some with lardon. Twenty-five years ago, I developed a recipe for olive fougasse for my first book. On a recent trip to Aix au Provence, I saw this variation, with Roquefort cheese. I ate my Fougassette au Roquefort warm from the oven while I sat on a wooden bench outside a blue-trimmed bakery in the distinctly Provencal sunshine. It left a strong sensory impression on me. We occasionally make them now at Bread Alone for special occasions, and for me they always bring back the memory of the first time I tried them.

This is an extremely easy dough to make and it absorbs the flavor of the herbs as it sits overnight in the refrigerator. The shaping is unique and distinctive. You bake the fougasettes soon after shaping, which makes the recipe almost instantly gratifying.

START TO FINISH:
10 to 15
hours

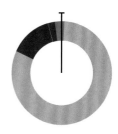

INGREDIENTS	BAKER'S %	METRIC WEIGHT
FINAL DOUGH		
Type 65 or equivalent flour (11 to 11.5% protein)	90	450 g
Whole rye flour	10	50 g
Water	65	325 g
Fresh thyme, finely chopped	0.2	1 g
Fresh rosemary, finely chopped	0.2	1 g
Extra-virgin olive oil	5	25 g
Salt	2	10 g
Dry instant yeast	0.6	3 g
Roquefort cheese, crumbled	20	100 g

KNEAD
8 minutes

RETARD
8 to 12 hours

WARM UP
1½ to 2 hours

REST
20 minutes

BAKE
18 minutes

MAKES
four 240-gram breads

1. **MAKE THE FINAL DOUGH**: Combine the wheat flour, rye flour, water, thyme, rosemary, olive oil, salt, and yeast in the bowl of an electric mixer fitted with a dough hook. Mix with a rubber spatula just until a rough dough forms. With the dough hook, mix on the lowest

recipe continues

recipe continued from previous page

setting for 4 minutes. Turn the mixer to low (2 on a KitchenAid mixer) and mix for another 4 minutes.

2. **RETARD**: Use a dough scraper to transfer the dough to a lightly oiled, clear 4-quart container with a lid. Turn the dough over so all sides are oiled. Cover and let stand 60 minutes. Refrigerate overnight, 8 to 12 hours.

3. **REST**: Remove the dough from the refrigerator and let stand 1½ to 2 hours to warm up. On a lightly floured countertop, divide the dough into four equal pieces. Gently round. Cover and let rest 20 minutes.

4. About 1 hour before baking, place a baking stone on the middle rack of the oven and a cast-iron skillet on the lower rack. Preheat the oven to 425 degrees.

5. **SHAPE**: Cover a baker's peel or rimless baking sheet with parchment. Lightly dust the parchment with flour. Gently press each dough round into a 4-inch-long, 3-inch-wide oval. Transfer the ovals to the parchment-lined peel. Sprinkle with the cheese. With a paring knife or small serrated knife, make a 3-inch-long cut down the middle of each oval. Make two 2-inch-long parallel cuts on either side of this cut.

6. **BAKE**: Slide the loaves, still on the parchment, onto the baking stone. Place 1 cup of ice cubes in the skillet to produce steam. Bake until the loaves are golden brown and the cheese is bubbling, about 18 minutes. Slide the loaves, still on the parchment, onto a wire rack and let stand 10 minutes. Peel from the parchment and let cool on rack completely. Fougassettes de Roquefort are best eaten on the day they are baked.

Note for Professional Bakers

Because of its flat shape, this bread has the tendency to dry out quickly, so it is best to bake it at higher temperature for a shorter period of time to retain as much moisture as possible.

OVERNIGHT GRAIN AND FRUIT LOAF

START TO FINISH:

13½ to 18

hours

SOAKER
2 hours

KNEAD
5 minutes

RETARD
8 to 12 hours

WARM UP
1½ to 2 hours

FINAL PROOF
1 hour

BAKE
45 to 50 minutes

MAKES
one 1-kilo loaf

In many bakeries in France and Germany these days, bakers are frequently using the very simple technique of a long, cool bulk dough fermentation with their whole grain and seeded doughs. The result is bread with a superior crumb structure and complex flavor. I have noticed tubs of pre-scaled dough retarding in walk-in refrigerators for 8 hours or more before shaping. Letting the dough sit overnight allows bakers to increase the hydration, resulting in a bubbly crumb and a more caramelized crust. Another plus: Seeds become more tender both from soaking and also from absorbing additional water in the refrigerator.

It's a bit of an effort in a bakery situation, because large batches of dough take up so much refrigerator space and have to be divided into smaller portions so that the dough can cool down to its center. But for the home baker it is an easy technique, since a single bowl of dough will cool down very nicely in the refrigerator overnight. Once you develop the habit of mixing the dough ahead of time, fermenting it in the refrigerator for anywhere from 8 to 24 hours gives added flexibility and fresh bread when you need it.

I prefer to bake this bread in a large Dutch oven. The cast-iron pan gives the soft, loose dough a consistent and beautiful shape. Hot from preheating, the pan also captures the steam and gives the bread a rugged, rustic crust.

INGREDIENTS	BAKER'S %	METRIC WEIGHT
SOAKER		
Mixed wheat flakes, rolled oats, rye flakes, millet, buckwheat groats, flax seeds, barley, quinoa, teff	100	52 g
Dried apricots, chopped	100	52 g
Currants	100	52 g
Warm water	240	125 g
FINAL DOUGH		
Type 65 or equivalent flour (11 to 11.5% protein)	50	204 g
Whole wheat flour	50	204 g
Water	74	303 g
Salt	2	8 g
Dry instant yeast	1.2	5 g
Soaker	69	281 g

1. **MAKE THE SOAKER**: Combine the wheat flakes, oats, rye, millet, groats, flax, barley, quinoa, teff, apricots, currants, and warm water in a medium bowl. Stir to moisten. Cover and let stand at room temperature for 2 hours.

2. **MAKE THE FINAL DOUGH**: In the bowl of an electric mixer fitted with a dough hook, combine the white flour, whole wheat flour, water, salt, yeast, and soaker. Stir with a rubber spatula until a rough dough forms. Knead on low speed (2 on a KitchenAid mixer) for 3 minutes. Turn the mixer to medium-low (4 on a KitchenAid mixer) and knead an additional 2 minutes.

3. **RETARD**: Use a dough scraper to transfer the dough to a lightly oiled, clear 4-quart container with a lid. Turn the dough over so all sides are oiled. Cover and let stand 90 minutes. Refrigerate overnight, 8 to 12 hours.

4. **WARM UP**: Remove the dough from the refrigerator and let stand for 1½ to 2 hours to warm up.

5. **FINAL PROOF**: Turn the dough onto a lightly floured countertop, Gently round and place in a lightly floured banneton. Cover and let stand until pillowy, about 1 hour.

recipe continues

recipe continued from previous page

6. About 30 minutes before baking, place a 6-quart round Dutch oven with lid on the lower rack of the oven. Preheat the oven to 425 degrees.

7. **BAKE**: With heavy-duty oven mitts, transfer the hot Dutch oven to a cool stovetop burner or other heatproof surface. Lightly flour your hands. Turn the dough out of the banneton and into your hands. Gently drop it into the preheated pot. With a *lame,* a single-edged razor blade, or a serrated knife, make four 3-inch-long slashes, about ½ inch deep, to form a square on the top of the dough. Cover, return to the oven, and bake for 10 minutes. Uncover and bake until golden brown and well risen, another 35 to 40 minutes. Invert the loaf onto a wire rack, re-invert, and let cool completely. Store in a brown paper bag at room temperature for 2 to 4 days.

Note for Professional Bakers

Instead of scaling the seeds separately, you can scale all the seeds for the seed blend at once. To enhance their flavor, the seeds can be lightly toasted before soaking. The seeds could also be allowed to soak overnight.

PANEPEPATO

At Antico Forno Roscioli in Rome, I spent several hours in a compact, crowded, and very hot oven room that was hidden at the end of a maze of hallways behind the bakery counter. On my way out the door, I spotted some dense fruitcake-like patties next to the cash register and impulsively bought two of them to take home with me. Co-owner Pierluigi Roscioli told me that they were a personal favorite of his and a house specialty, not to be missed. I put them in my suitcase, completely forgot about them, and traveled another ten days. I finally rediscovered them when I unpacked at home and took them to Bread Alone the next day. Like fruitcake, they improved over time. Unlike fruitcake, which can be too rich and fruity for me, they were dense, chewy, and moist in just the right combination. When I sliced them and handed out samples, everyone instantly fell in love and we carefully rationed them to keep peace in the office. These are extremely easy to make, require no fermentation time, and keep for days. They are now a personal favorite.

START TO FINISH:

35 minutes

MAKE FINAL DOUGH
15 minutes

BAKE
20 minutes

MAKES
6 ultra-dense little fruit-nut disks,
about 170 grams each

INGREDIENTS	BAKER'S %	METRIC WEIGHT
Whole toasted, skinned hazelnuts	90	147 g
Whole blanched almonds	93	152 g
Toasted pine nuts	23	38 g
Golden raisins	36	59 g
Dried figs, stemmed and chopped	25	41 g
Bittersweet chocolate, chopped	74	121 g
Candied orange peel, chopped	46	75 g
Grated orange zest	3	5 g
Nutmeg	0.3	.5 g
Salt	1	1.5 g
Ground black pepper	0.3	.5 g
Strong brewed coffee	43	70 g
Honey	80	130 g
Tipo OO or equivalent flour (10 to 11% protein)	100	163 g
Confectioners' sugar	10	16 g

recipe continues

recipe continued from previous page

1. MAKE THE FINAL DOUGH: Preheat the oven to 350 degrees. Line a rimmed baking sheet with parchment paper. In a large bowl, combine the hazelnuts, almonds, pine nuts, raisins, figs, chocolate, orange peel, orange zest, nutmeg, salt, pepper, and 25 g of the coffee. In a small microwave-safe bowl, combine the honey and remaining 45 g coffee and heat until the honey is just liquefied. Stir into the nut mixture to coat. Sprinkle 115 g of the flour over the mixture and stir to incorporate, adding more as necessary, 10 g at a time, until the dough holds together.

2. BAKE: Divide the dough into six equal pieces, about 170 g each. With damp hands, form the dough into six patties, 4 inches across and 1 inch thick. Place the rounds on the prepared baking sheet and bake until firm, about 20 minutes. Transfer to a wire rack and let cool completely. Heavily dust with confectioners' sugar before serving. Panepepato will keep in an airtight container at room temperature for up to 2 weeks.

Note for Professional Bakers

It is preferable to mix this dough in a planetary vertical mixer with a paddle attachment to get a better and more efficient incorporation of ingredients.

PITCHOU CHOCOLAT

Every baker has his or her sweet treat, and these chocolate rolls are Pierre-Julien Bouniol's. Surprisingly, the texture isn't soft and delicate. It's chewy, like focaccia. Pierre-Julien makes these in small batches and bakes them throughout the day. His customers schedule their visits to the bakery when they know they can get pitchou still warm from the oven. While Pierre-Julien forms them into traditional small rounds, I prefer the more rustic look of cutting the dough into loose squares. The recipe is straightforward and can be completed in a little more than 3 hours. Alternatively, the dough holds well in the refrigerator overnight.

INGREDIENTS	BAKER'S %	METRIC WEIGHT
FINAL DOUGH		
Type 65 or equivalent flour (11 to 11.5% protein)	100	758 g
Unsweetened cocoa powder	8	61 g
Egg (1 and 1 egg yolk)	10	76 g
Milk, room temperature	22	167 g
Water	38	288 g
Sugar	3	23 g
Dry instant yeast	1	8 g
Salt	2	15 g
Butter, softened	7	53 g
70% cacao best-quality bittersweet chocolate, chopped	20	152 g

START TO FINISH:
3½
hours

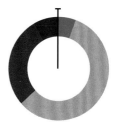

KNEAD
12 minutes

FIRST FERMENTATION
2 hours

REST
1 hour

BAKE
16 minutes

MAKES
sixteen 100-gram squares

1. **MAKE THE FINAL DOUGH**: Combine the flour, cocoa powder, egg, milk, water, sugar, yeast, salt, and butter in the bowl of an electric mixer fitted with a dough hook. Stir with a rubber spatula just until a rough dough forms. With the dough hook, mix on medium-low (4 on a KitchenAid mixer) speed for 10 minutes. Add the chopped chocolate and knead until incorporated, another 2 minutes.

recipe continues

recipe continued from previous page

2. **FIRST FERMENTATION**: Transfer the dough to a lightly oiled, clear 4-quart container with a lid. Turn the dough over so all sides are oiled. Cover and let stand at room temperature for about 2 hours.

3. About 1 hour before baking, place a baking stone on the middle rack of the oven. Place a cast-iron skillet on the lower rack of the oven. Preheat the oven to 350 degrees.

4. **FINAL PROOF**: On a lightly floured countertop, press out the dough into a 12-inch square. Lightly dust with flour. With a bench scraper, cut into 16 squares. Line a baker's peel or rimless baking sheet with parchment. Place the dough squares on the parchment, lightly dust with flour, and drape with plastic wrap. Let stand 1 hour.

5. **BAKE**: Uncover the dough and flip each piece over. Immediately slide the squares, still on the parchment, onto the baking stone. Place 1 cup of ice cubes in the skillet to produce steam. Bake until well risen, 16 minutes. Slide the squares, still on the parchment, onto a wire rack to cool completely. Pitchou Chocolat are best eaten on the day they are baked.

Note for Professional Bakers

The Pitchou Chocolat dough can be mixed and allowed to ferment overnight in the refrigerator or in a retarder. The next day, the dough can be divided (using a 36-part dough divider with no rounding, proofed) and baked when needed in order to be enjoyed as fresh as possible by customers.

PIZZA BIANCA DI FORNO CAMPO DE' FIORI

START TO FINISH:

21 to 28

hours

KNEAD
22 minutes

FIRST FERMENTATION
1 hour

RETARD
18 to 24 hours

WARM UP
1 hour

REST
30 minutes

BAKE
15 to 20 minutes per pizza

MAKES
two 490-gram flatbread pizzas

Because the price of bread is traditionally low in Italy, bakers are always trying to find ways to sell flour and water for more money. Pizza bianca is probably three times the price per kilo as bread. Maybe this is one of the reasons it has become a classic Roman street food. One of my favorite pizza places is Forno Campo de' Fiori, where I enjoy a slice while strolling through the piazza on market days, taking in the colorful sight of fruit and vegetable stalls. Bernardino Bartocci and his cousin Fabio kindly let me spend a few days baking pizza with their team. Every morning and evening, they mix a bubbly, super-soft, nearly pourable dough and ferment it in 2-kilo pieces in large tubs, very slowly at room temperature for 6 hours or more. They then divide the dough into 2-kilo pieces and shape the pieces into large ovals. The ovals are refrigerated for 2 to 10 hours, to relax. After the dough has warmed to room temperature, it is gently pulled and pressed, dimpled, and pulled and pressed again, until it is stretched to 8 feet in length. Topped with a little olive oil and sea salt, crushed tomatoes, or seasonal specialties like shaved artichokes or zucchini blossoms, it is loaded into the oven on an extra-long peel and baked. The hot baked pizzas may be sprinkled with herbs. Every 15 minutes a fresh pizza is pulled from the oven. Customers order the pizza by length, and it is sliced, weighed, wrapped in paper, handed over, and most likely eaten while walking out the door.

Making this style of pizza at home is easy—instead of stretching the dough to 8 feet, you only have to get it to cover the baking stone. It does require many minutes of kneading, a long fermentation, and your confidence that a dough this soft will become extremely elastic and transform in the oven into delicious, bubbly pizza. Ice water keeps the dough cool and ensures slow fermentation.

INGREDIENTS	BAKER'S %	METRIC WEIGHT
FINAL DOUGH		
Tipo OO flour with W value of 250 to 260	100	500 g
Ice water	85	425 g
Salt	2.2	11 g
Dry instant yeast	0.2	1 g
Olive oil	5	25 g
Flaky sea salt	1	5 g
Fresh rosemary or thyme, chopped	3	15 g

1. **MAKE THE FINAL DOUGH**: Combine the flour, 375 g of the ice water, the salt, and yeast in the bowl of an electric mixer fitted with a dough hook. Stir with a rubber spatula just until a rough dough forms. With the dough hook, mix on low (2 on a KitchenAid mixer) for 4 minutes. Turn the mixer to medium-high (8 on a KitchenAid mixer) and continue to mix, very slowly drizzling in the remaining 50 g water over the course of another 12 minutes. The dough will be very loose, almost liquid. Continue mixing for 3 to 4 minutes, until the dough comes together. Turn the mixer to the highest speed and mix until the dough pulls away from the sides of the bowl, another 2 to 4 minutes.

2. **FIRST FERMENTATION**: Transfer the dough to a lightly oiled, clear 4-quart container with a lid. Cover and let stand at room temperature for 2 hours.

3. **RETARD**: Refrigerate the dough for 18 to 24 hours.

4. **WARM UP**: Remove the dough from the refrigerator and let sit on the counter to warm up, about 1 hour.

5. About 1 hour before baking, place a baking stone on the middle rack of the oven. Preheat the oven to 500 degrees. Pour the dough onto a lightly floured countertop and gently press into a rectangle measuring 12 by 20 inches. Use a bench scraper or sharp chef's knife to cut the dough into two rectangles measuring 6 by 20 inches. Lightly drape with plastic wrap. Let rest 30 minutes.

6. **BAKE**: Line two baker's peels or rimless baking sheets with parchment. Dust with flour. Transfer the rectangles to the peels

recipe continues

recipe continued from previous page

or baking sheets and dimple the dough all over with your fingertips. Lift two corners of a rectangle from the peel, stretching it as you lift, and place it back down on the peel several times to stretch the dough to 12 by 18 inches. Gently dimple the dough again. Brush with olive oil and sprinkle with sea salt to taste and rosemary. Repeat with the remaining dough rectangle. Slide one pizza, still on the parchment, onto the baking stone. Bake until the pizza is bubbled and golden brown, 15 to 20 minutes. Slide the pizza, still on the parchment, onto a cutting board. Repeat with the remaining pizza. Slice and serve immediately.

Note for Professional Bakers

To increase dough extensibility and facilitate the stretching of the dough, an autolyse could be used during the mixing process. Alternatively, to decrease the elastic resistance of the dough, you could add 0.1 to 0.2 percent deactivated yeast to the formula.

5

YEASTED
PRE-FERMENTS

I think about bread as a fermented food, like beer, wine, and sauerkraut. Fermentation is what gives all of these foods their flavor and character. Bakers generally agree that the longer a dough is allowed to ferment, the better. To reduce production time while coaxing the most flavor from flour, bakers turn to pre-ferments.

By taking a portion of your dough ingredients, mixing them, and letting this small batch of dough ferment, you can significantly reduce the production time of the bread itself without sacrificing the flavor that comes from long fermentation. Adding a ripened pre-ferment to your dough will give it the benefits of a slow rise in several hours rather than a half or whole day.

There are other benefits to using a pre-ferment. The gluten that develops in a pre-ferment gives the final dough a head start in becoming strong and extensible, resulting in a higher-rising bread. During the long fermentation of certain stiff dough pre-ferments like Italian biga, bacteria and enzymes break down the flour's starches into simple sugars, causing the crust to caramelize beautifully. And because of the acids produced during pre-fermentation, breads baked with a pre-ferment have a longer shelf life than straight doughs.

While pre-ferments are infinitely variable and can be adapted to suit a baker's schedule and needs, every baking culture has its favored styles. American bakers of a certain age will be familiar with the term *sponge*, which is a relatively wet pre-ferment typically fermented for a relatively short time, just a few hours. *Poolish* is the French term for a wet style of pre-ferment. This is the starter that the Boulangerie Utopie bakers use to raise their jet-black Baguette au Charbon Vegetal (page 128). The difference between a poolish and a sponge is fermentation time. European bakers tend to let their starter stand for 8 to 12 hours or longer. *Pâte fermentée* is a stiff dough pre-ferment that is made with the same proportions of flour and water as the bread dough itself, plus a pinch of salt. It ferments more slowly than a sponge or poolish. Didier Rosada's version of Pain Brié (page 149), a bread that was created for fishermen to carry out to sea for many days, has a large percentage of pâte fermentée for a long shelf life. *Biga* is an Italian-style pre-ferment, stiff like pâte fermentée. During fermentation, it becomes very strong and elastic, giving the Olive Filoncini (page 146) of Rocco Princi their pleasantly chewy texture.

BAGUETTE AU CHARBON VEGETAL

START TO FINISH:

13 to 14

hours

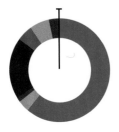

POOLISH
8 hours

AUTOLYSE
30 minutes

KNEAD
10 minutes

FIRST FERMENTATION
2¼ to 2½ hours

REST
40 minutes

FINAL PROOF
40 to 50 minutes

BAKE
25 minutes

MAKES
three 327-gram loaves

In Paris, everyone has an opinion about where to buy the best bread. I was sitting on a bench in the Luxembourg Gardens one morning, tearing into three baguettes I had just purchased from three different bakers, when two women, on either side of me, asked me what I was doing with so much bread. When I explained that I was always looking for the best bread in Paris, they gave me their own recommendations. The older woman was devoted to the classic miche at Max Poilâne, a bread that I was well acquainted with. The younger insisted, "You've got to get the Baguette au Charbon Vegetal at Boulangerie Utopie." She described a jet-black bread with a dark, earthy flavor akin to the hint of volcanic ash in Morbier cheese. I literally sprung from the bench, ran to the Metro, and rode to the Place de Republique.

Boulangerie Utopie partners Sébastien Bruno and Erwan Blanche divvy up the baking, one in charge of bread and the other in charge of pastries. As a result, and unlike at most Paris bakeries, both bread and pastry here are top-notch. There were dozens of people patiently waiting in line outside the shop on the Rue Jean-Pierre Timbaud, everyone chatting about their favorite Utopie item.

Charbon vegetal actif, or active charcoal, can be found in natural foods stores. Relatively unknown in the U.S., it has long been embraced in France for its benefits as a digestive aid and beauty product. It certainly produces a striking bread, a baguette so dark that it looks like someone left it in the oven two hours too long. The charcoal flavor itself is subtly astringent, just sharp enough to make the bread interesting as well as beautiful. Take care when first mixing the dough by hand, so that the charcoal doesn't fly out of the mixer bowl and coat your kitchen with black dust.

INGREDIENTS	BAKER'S %	METRIC WEIGHT
POOLISH		
Type 65 or equivalent flour (11 to 11.5% protein)	100	105 g
Warm water	100	104 g
Dry instant yeast	0.2	0.25 g
FINAL DOUGH		
Poolish	49	210 g
Type 65 or equivalent flour (11 to 11.5% protein)	100	426 g
Charbon vegetal actif (activated charcoal powder)	4	18 g
Water	60	256 g
Lightly toasted sesame seeds	6.1	26 g
Salt	2.5	11 g
Dry instant yeast	0.1	1 g
TOPPING		
Lightly toasted sesame seeds		33 g

1. **MAKE THE POOLISH:** In a small bowl, stir together the flour, warm water, and yeast until well incorporated. Cover and let ferment at room temperature (68 to 77 degrees) until doubled in volume, about 8 hours.

2. **AUTOLYSE:** Combine the poolish, flour, charbon vegetal actif, and water in the bowl of an electric mixer fitted with a dough hook. Mix with a spatula just until a rough dough forms. Cover and let rest 30 minutes.

3. **MAKE THE FINAL DOUGH:** Add the sesame seeds, salt, and yeast to the bowl. With the dough hook, mix on low speed (2 on a KitchenAid mixer) for 10 minutes. The dough should have a silky and elastic texture.

4. **FIRST FERMENTATION:** Transfer the dough to a lightly oiled, clear 4-quart container with a lid. Turn the dough over so all sides are oiled. Cover and let stand 60 minutes. Turn the dough out onto a lightly floured counter. Pat into a 6-by 8-inch rectangle and fold

recipe continues

recipe continued from previous page

like a business letter. Slide both hands under the dough and flip it over so the folds are underneath. Slip it back into the container, cover, and let stand another 45 minutes. Repeat the folding and turning, return to the container, and let stand until the dough is pillowy, another 45 minutes to 1 hour.

5. **REST**: On a lightly floured countertop, divide the dough into three equal pieces, pat into rectangles, and gently fold into cigar-like logs, 4 inches long and 3 inches wide. Dust with flour and cover with plastic. Let rest for 40 minutes.

6. **FINAL PROOF**: Cover a baker's peel or rimless baking sheet with parchment. Shape each piece of dough into a baguette (see page 78) about 12 inches long. If the dough resists, cover and let it rest 15 minutes before shaping again to the full length. Dust the parchment-covered peel or baking sheet with flour and place the baguettes on the parchment, seam side down, 3 inches apart. Lift the parchment paper between the loaves, making a pleat and drawing the loaves close together. Alternatively, use baker's linen instead of parchment. Tightly roll up two kitchen towels and slip them under the parchment paper on the sides of the outer loaves to support each baguette. Dust with flour and drape with plastic wrap. Let rise until pillowy, 40 to 50 minutes.

7. **BAKE**: About 1 hour before baking, place a baking stone on the middle rack of the oven and a cast-iron skillet on the lower rack. Preheat the oven to 425 degrees for 1 hour. Uncover the breads, remove the rolled-up towels, and stretch the parchment paper out so that it is flat and the loaves are separated. With a pastry brush, lightly brush the tops of the loaves with water and then sprinkle with the sesame seeds. With a *lame,* a single-edged razor blade, or a serrated knife, make three slashes, 2½ inches long and slightly angled, down the center of each loaf. Slide the loaves, still on the parchment, onto the baking stone. Place 1 cup of ice cubes in the skillet to produce steam. Bake until the loaves are well risen and the crust is well developed, about 25 minutes. Slide the loaves, still on the parchment, onto a wire rack and let cool completely. Store in a brown paper bag at room temperature for up to 2 days.

Notes for Professional Bakers

It is always a good idea to mix this dough last during production as the charbon vegetal actif will leave black dough residue in the mixer that might color the next batch. Also, it is important to carefully time the bake of this bread as the color of the crust is naturally dark and can't be used as a control point to define the end of the bake.

BAGUETTE AU GERME DE BLÉ GRILLÉ

START TO FINISH:

13

hours

POOLISH
8 hours

AUTOLYSE
30 minutes

KNEAD
13 minutes

FIRST FERMENTATION
2¼ to 2½ hours

REST
20 minutes

FINAL PROOF
1 hour

BAKE
25 minutes

MAKES
three 314-gram loaves

Bernard Ganachaud made his mark in the 1970s when he introduced his *flûte gana,* a trendsetting product that featured a very loose crumb structure (new at the time) and a nutty, earthy, complex flavor. To my knowledge, this was the first time an artisan baker was able to trademark a recipe and product.

To produce a bread he liked that wasn't bound to the schedule of sourdough maintenance, he thoughtfully employed a traditional French pre-ferment called *poolish.* Just a tiny bit of commercial yeast jump-starts a very gentle fermentation. Bread baked with this starter is very fresh, light, and nutty, with a bubbly crumb and no hint of acidity. Folding the dough mid-fermentation develops its strength. If you do it properly, you end up with a nicer, more rounded shape because the dough has a better structure. Bernard guarded his recipe while sharing his knowledge. So this is my version, with some toasted wheat germ added. It is my tribute to him.

I was lucky to meet Bernard in the early 1980s, on my second trip to Paris. Debonair and gentlemanly, with a manicured white mustache and immaculate chef's jacket (always with the blue and red collar signifying the Meilleurs Ouvriers de France), he warmly welcomed me into his bakery. I have great memories of the many hours I spent there. He took great pride in tutoring me on the workings of his bakery. He also helped me expand my French baking vocabulary. To this day, when I meet French bakers they comment with amazement on my proper use of baking terms. A few years later, I was thrilled to host him when he visited Bread Alone and show my mentor how much progress I had made. It was a loss to the baking community when he passed away in 2015. His daughters Marianne and Valerie continue his work, with two shops in Paris and the supervision of multiple licensees all over the world who bake the *flûte gana.*

To toast wheat germ, spread it evenly across a baking sheet and place in a 350-degree oven until lightly browned, about 5 minutes, watching carefully so it doesn't over-brown.

INGREDIENTS	BAKER'S %	METRIC WEIGHT
POOLISH		
Type 65 or equivalent flour (11 to 11.5% protein)	100	150 g
Water	100	150 g
Salt	0.6	1 g
Dry instant yeast	0.6	1 g
FINAL DOUGH		
Poolish	80.5	302 g
Type 65 or equivalent flour (11 to 11.5% protein)	100	375 g
Wheat germ, toasted	12	45 g
Water	56	210 g
Salt	2.6	10 g
Dry instant yeast	0.3	1 g

1. **MAKE THE POOLISH**: In a small bowl, stir together the flour, water, salt, and yeast until well incorporated. Cover and let ferment at room temperature (68 to 77 degrees) until doubled in volume, about 8 hours.

2. **AUTOLYSE**: Combine the poolish, flour, toasted wheat germ, and water in the bowl of an electric mixer fitted with a dough hook. Mix with a spatula just until a rough dough forms. Cover and let rest 30 minutes.

3. **MAKE THE FINAL DOUGH**: Add the salt and yeast to the bowl. With the dough hook, mix on low (2 on a KitchenAid mixer) for 3 minutes. Turn the mixer to medium-low (4 on a KitchenAid mixer) and mix for 10 minutes.

4. **FIRST FERMENTATION**: Transfer the dough to a lightly oiled, clear 4-quart container with a lid. Turn the dough over so all sides are oiled. Cover and let stand 60 minutes. Turn the dough out onto a lightly floured counter. Pat into a 6- by 8-inch rectangle and fold like a business letter. Slide both hands under the dough and flip it over so the folds are underneath. Slip it back into the container, cover, and let stand another 45 minutes. Repeat the folding and turning,

recipe continues

recipe continued from previous page

return to the container, and let stand until the dough is pillowy, 45 minutes to 1 hour longer.

5. **REST**: On a lightly floured countertop, divide the dough into three equal pieces, pat into rectangles, and gently fold into cigar-like logs, 4 inches long and 3 inches wide. Dust with flour and cover with plastic. Let rest for 20 minutes.

6. **FINAL PROOF**: Cover a baker's peel or rimless baking sheet with parchment. Dust with flour. Shape each piece of dough into a baguette (see page 78) about 14 inches long. Place the baguettes on the parchment-lined peel, seam sides down, 3 inches apart. Lift the parchment paper between the loaves, making a pleat and drawing the loaves close together. Alternatively, use baker's linen instead of parchment. Tightly roll up two kitchen towels and slip them under the parchment paper on the sides of the outer loaves to support the baguettes. Lightly dust with flour and drape with plastic wrap. Let rise until pillowy, about 1 hour.

7. **BAKE**: About 1 hour before baking, place a baking stone on the middle rack of the oven and a cast-iron skillet on the lower rack. Preheat the oven to 425 degrees for 1 hour. Uncover the breads, remove the rolled-up towels, and stretch the parchment paper out so that it is flat and the loaves are separated. With a *lame*, a single-edged razor blade, or a serrated knife, make one slash about ½ inch deep down the length of each loaf. Slide the loaves, still on the parchment, onto the baking stone. Place 1 cup of ice cubes in the skillet to produce steam. Bake until the loaves are golden brown and well risen, about 25 minutes. Slide the loaves, still on the parchment, onto a wire rack and cool completely. Baguettes with Germe de Blé Grillé are best eaten on the day they are baked.

Notes for Professional Bakers

For large production, scale the necessary poolish to be used per batch of dough just after mixing it. It is much easier to handle a freshly made poolish then a fermented poolish. Using one bucket of poolish per batch of dough will also speed up the mixing process.

LE PAIN AUX 13 DESSERTS

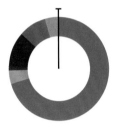

START TO FINISH:

11½

hours

POOLISH
8 hours

AUTOLYSE
30 minutes

KNEAD
8 minutes

FIRST FERMENTATION
75 minutes

FINAL PROOF
1 hour

BAKE
30 minutes

MAKES
one 1-kilo loaf

When the *Dictionnaire Universal du Pain* was published, I was invited to a ceremony to celebrate the achievement at the Compagnons du Devoir headquarters in Paris. Jean-Philippe de Tonnac, the author, invited bakers from all over the world to speak about their craft, and how and why they bake. This is where I first met Dominique Saibron. I had been to his bakery on the Avenue du General Leclerc many times over the years and was thrilled to finally speak to him about his life and work. I made special trips to his bakery, to buy this bread in particular, more times than I can count. It is a unique, beautifully shaped bread, flat and with a crosshatch scoring pattern.

The bread is named after a beautiful Provencal Christmas tradition: The 13 desserts of Provence are a collection of fruits, nuts, cookies, and pastries forming the end of the Christmas Eve feast, or *Gros Souper*, eaten before attending midnight mass. The 13 desserts represent Christ and the 12 apostles at the Last Supper. For his bread, Dominique uses 13 kinds of nuts and dried fruits. With its large size and unique look, it makes a stunning centerpiece for an impressive display of cheeses. It has a perfect balance of crunch and sweetness. I like to eat it thinly toasted with rich French butter or a nutty, aged cheese.

INGREDIENTS	BAKER'S %	METRIC WEIGHT
POOLISH		
Type 55 or equivalent flour (11 to 11.5% protein)	100	100 g
Water	100	100 g
Dry instant yeast	0.1	0.25 g
FINAL DOUGH		
Poolish	80	200 g
Type 55 or equivalent flour (11 to 11.5% protein)	100	252 g
Water	68	171 g
Sugar	15	38 g
Unsalted butter, cut into pieces and softened	15	38 g
Salt	2.8	7 g
Dry instant yeast	0.8	2 g
Candied cherries, chopped	20	50 g
Candied lemon peel, chopped	8	20 g
Candied orange peel, chopped	8	20 g
Dried apricots, chopped	8	20 g
Golden raisins, chopped	8	20 g
Prunes, chopped	8	20 g
Dark raisins	8	20 g
Currants	8	20 g
Dried figs, stemmed and chopped	8	20 g
Toasted and skinned hazelnuts, coarsely chopped	8	20 g
Pistachios, coarsely chopped	8	20 g
Blanched almonds, toasted and coarsely chopped	8	20 g
Walnuts, toasted and coarsely chopped	8	20 g

recipe continues

recipe continued from previous page

1. **MAKE THE POOLISH**: In a small bowl, stir together the flour, water, and yeast until well incorporated. Cover and let ferment at room temperature (68 to 77 degrees) until doubled in volume, about 8 hours.

2. **AUTOLYSE**: Combine the poolish, flour, and water in the bowl of an electric mixer fitted with a dough hook. Mix with a spatula just until a rough dough forms. Cover and let rest 30 minutes.

3. **MAKE THE FINAL DOUGH**: Add the sugar, butter, salt, and yeast to the bowl. With the dough hook, mix on low (2 on a KitchenAid mixer) for 3 minutes, stopping to give the dough a few turns with a spatula if necessary for it to come together. Add the fruit and nuts and continue to knead on low until well incorporated, 4 to 5 minutes.

4. **FIRST FERMENTATION**: Transfer the dough to a lightly oiled, clear 4-quart container with a lid. With wet hands, turn the dough over so all sides are oiled. Cover and let stand 75 minutes.

5. **FINAL PROOF**: Cover a baker's peel or rimless baking sheet with parchment. Dust with flour. Turn the dough out onto the peel. Press into a 14-inch disk. If you have trouble pressing it on the first try, press into an 11-inch disk, then cover and let rest 10 minutes before pressing to 14 inches. Dust with flour and cover with a clean kitchen towel. Let rest for 1 hour.

6. **BAKE**: About 1 hour before baking, place a baking stone on the middle rack of the oven and a cast-iron skillet on the lower rack. Preheat the oven to 400 degrees for 1 hour. Uncover the loaf. Use a flour sifter or mesh strainer to dust with flour. With a serrated knife, slash in a checkerboard pattern, making $\frac{1}{4}$-inch-deep cuts, $1\frac{1}{2}$ inches apart, first in one direction and then crosswise in the other direction at a 45-degree angle. Slide the loaf, still on the parchment, onto the baking stone. Place 1 cup of ice cubes in the skillet to produce steam. Bake until the loaf is golden brown, about 30 minutes. Slide the loaf, still on the parchment, onto a wire rack and cool completely. Store in a brown paper bag at room temperature for up to 4 days.

Note for Professional Bakers

Because of the high percentage of dried fruits and nuts in this dough, it is important to build sufficient strength into it. This is achieved through a good gluten development during mixing and, if this is not sufficient, through some folds during the first fermentation of the dough.

PAIN AU CHATAIGNE

Dominique Saibron is a pastry chef who discovered the world of bread baking and never looked back. He quit his fancy restaurant job and opened his first boulangerie in 1987, on the Place Brancusi in one of the most charming neighborhoods of Paris. It's one of my go-to bakeries when I'm in town, not far from where I stay near the Luxembourg Gardens. Dominique is known for the beauty of his simple and authentic breads. He has won the Grand Prix Baguette competition twice.

He only bakes this chestnut loaf from October to March, when freshly milled chestnut flour is available. In the U.S., chestnut flour is expensive but easy to find online. The dough gets some earthy, smoky character from the flour, and some sweetness from candied chestnuts and a little bit of honey. I had never seen this particular scoring technique before, which creates a pointy crown for the bread. This seasonal and festive loaf would be a charming addition to a Thanksgiving feast.

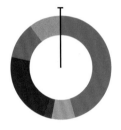

POOLISH
3 hours

AUTOLYSE
30 minutes

KNEAD
9 minutes

FIRST FERMENTATION
1½ hours

FINAL PROOF
45 minutes

BAKE
40 minutes

MAKES
two 607-gram loaves

INGREDIENTS	BAKER'S %	METRIC WEIGHT
POOLISH		
Chestnut flour	100	167 g
Water	100	167 g
Dry instant yeast	0.6	1 g
FINAL DOUGH		
Poolish	67	335 g
Type 65 or equivalent flour (11 to 11.5% protein)	100	500 g
Water	51	255 g
Honey	6	30 g
Salt	2.6	13 g
Dry instant yeast	1.4	7 g
Candied chestnuts, chopped	15	75 g

recipe continues

recipe continued from previous page

1. **MAKE THE POOLISH:** Combine the chestnut flour, water, and yeast in a medium bowl. It will resemble a thick pancake batter. Cover and let stand at room temperature for 3 hours.

2. **AUTOLYSE:** Combine the poolish, flour, and water in the bowl of an electric mixer fitted with a dough hook. Mix with a spatula just until a rough dough forms. (Chestnut flours can vary in absorbency; if the mixture is too dry, add water, 10 g at a time, to reach the desired consistency.) Cover and let rest 30 minutes.

3. **MAKE THE FINAL DOUGH:** Add the honey, salt, and yeast to the bowl. With an electric mixer fitted with a dough hook, knead on medium-low (4 on a KitchenAid mixer) for 5 minutes. Turn the mixer to medium (6 on a KitchenAid mixer) and knead another 4 minutes. Add the candied chestnuts and mix until well distributed.

4. **FIRST FERMENTATION:** Transfer the dough to a lightly oiled, clear 4-quart container with a lid. Turn the dough over so all sides are oiled. Cover and let stand until doubled in volume, about 1½ hours.

5. **FINAL PROOF:** Turn the dough onto a lightly floured countertop, divide into two equal pieces, and shape into two rounds. Place in two lightly floured bannetons, seam side up. Dust with flour and lightly drape with plastic wrap. Let stand until slightly puffy, about 45 minutes.

6. **BAKE:** About 1 hour before baking, place a baking stone on the middle rack of the oven and a cast-iron skillet on the lower rack. Preheat the oven to 425 degrees for 1 hour. Line a baker's peel or rimless baking sheet with parchment paper. Gently overturn the loaf onto the peel. With a sharp, pointed scissors, make a series of ¼-inch-deep snips, at a 45-degree angle and 1 inch apart, in a circle about 2 inches from the center of the loaf. Slide the loaf, still on the parchment, onto the baking stone. Place 1 cup of ice cubes in the skillet to produce steam. Bake until the loaf is golden brown and well risen, about 40 minutes. Slide the loaf, still on the parchment, onto a wire rack to cool completely. Store in a brown paper bag at room temperature for up to 4 days.

Notes for Professional Bakers

To ease production, the chestnut poolish could be fermented overnight. This way, the baker would be able to mix the dough right away in the morning without waiting 3 hours for the poolish to ripen. For a longer-fermented poolish, reduce the quantity of yeast to 0.1 percent. Add the difference—0.5 percent—to the final dough.

LEINSAMENBROT

Many German bakeries have at least one stainless-steel vat of sourdough—like sourdough on tap—that is held at the proper temperature and automatically stirred to keep the starter well blended and active. The bakeries also have an area where seeds are soaked, and another zone where old bread is ground and soaked. All of this contributes to making complex breads in a streamlined way.

This recipe will give you an idea of what a traditional, 100 percent whole grain German bread tastes like without the complex components I just described. There is no sourdough starter to worry about. The seed soaker and pre-ferment are combined into one step. The combination of wheat flakes, rye flakes, and flax seeds give the bread great flavor, especially because they've been allowed to ferment with the yeast. After you have some success with this bread, you may feel ready to take on a sourdough bread with multiple soakers, like the Schwarzbrot (page 292) or the Roggenmischteig (page 296).

START TO FINISH:

8

hours

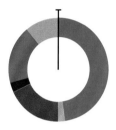

INGREDIENTS	BAKER'S %	METRIC WEIGHT
YEASTED SOAKER		
Flax seeds	100	40 g
Whole wheat flakes		22 g
Rye flakes	62	25 g
Dry instant yeast	5	2 g
Water, 100 degrees	300	120 g
FINAL DOUGH		
Whole wheat flour	82	425 g
Medium rye flour	18	95 g
Soaker	41	212 g
Dry instant yeast	0.4	2 g
Salt	2.5	13 g
Water	59	307 g
Dark molasses	7.3	38 g
TOPPING		
Whole wheat flakes		22 g

SOAKER
4 hours

KNEAD
10 minutes

FIRST FERMENTATION
1½ hours

REST
15 minutes

FINAL PROOF
1 to 1½ hours

BAKE
45 to 55 minutes

MAKES
two 557-gram pan loaves

recipe continues

recipe continued from previous page

1. **MAKE THE YEASTED SOAKER**: In a medium bowl, stir together flax seeds, whole wheat flakes, rye flakes, yeast, and warm water until well incorporated. Cover and let soak at room temperature (68 to 70 degrees) for about 4 hours.

2. **MAKE THE FINAL DOUGH**: Combine the whole wheat flour, rye flour, soaker, yeast, salt, water, and molasses in the bowl of an electric mixer. Stir with a rubber spatula until a rough dough forms. With the dough hook, mix the dough on low speed (2 on a KitchenAid mixer) for 2 minutes. Scrape the dough towards the center of the bowl with a spatula. Turn the mixer to medium-low speed (4 on a KitchenAid mixer) and mix for 8 minutes, stopping as necessary to scrape the sides and bottom of the bowl with a spatula.

3. **FIRST FERMENTATION**: Transfer the dough to a lightly oiled, clear 4-quart container with a lid. Cover and let rise until it has almost doubled, about 1½ hours.

4. **REST**: Turn the dough onto a lightly floured countertop, divide into two equal pieces, and pre-shape into rectangles (see page 79). Dust with flour and cover with plastic. Let rest 15 minutes.

5. **FINAL PROOF**: Shape the doughs into pan loaves. Nestle into two 9 by 5-inch loaf pans. Gently brush the tops of the loaves with water and sprinkle with the wheat flakes. Let rise, uncovered, until the loaves have expanded to 1½ times their original size, 1 to 1½ hours.

6. **BAKE**: Preheat the oven to 375 degrees. Place the loaves on the middle rack of the oven. Bake until the loaves pull away from the sides of the pans and the crusts are deep brown, 45 to 50 minutes. Invert onto a wire rack and then turn right side up. Cool completely before slicing. Store in a brown paper bag at room temperature for 3 to 4 days.

Note for Professional Bakers

Extra care should be taken during the mixing of the final dough. Because of the high proportion of coarse ingredients and rye and whole wheat flour, a gentle mixing is advised. In a spiral mixer, it is best to achieve most of the mixing in first speed as the action of the hook into the dough is gentler.

BIGA
25 hours

KNEAD
9 minutes

FIRST FERMENTATION
1 ½ hours

REST
10 minutes

FINAL PROOF
30 minutes

BAKE
20 to 25 minutes

MAKES
fourteen 50-gram sticks

OLIVE FILONCINI

In Milan, baker Rocco Princi worked with Giorgio Armani's store architect to design stunningly sleek and modern bakeries. The breads at Princi themselves are impeccably stylish but with a rustic and classic appeal. These olive sticks are stacked in a graphic display, like little wood piles, on the bakery countertop. I've sampled olive sticks at other bakeries, but these are exemplary. Petite, yet packed with delicious green olives, they are elegant and substantial. The recipe follows the traditional Italian biga fermentation cycle. As a result, the breads have a dense, chewy, moist texture. To get evenly, elegantly shaped little loaves, roll the dough into a rectangle and use a pizza wheel to cut it into identical strips.

INGREDIENTS	BAKER'S %	METRIC WEIGHT
BIGA		
Tipo OO flour with W value of 250 to 260	100	83 g
Water	54	45 g
Dry instant yeast	1.2	1 g
FINAL DOUGH		
Biga	52	129 g
Tipo OO flour with W value of 250 to 260	100	250 g
Water	65	162 g
Salt	2.5	6 g
Dry instant yeast	0.4	1 g
Large pitted Sicilian green olives, halved	62	155 g

1. **MAKE THE BIGA**: In a small bowl, stir together the flour, water, and yeast until well incorporated. Knead into a firm dough, about 5 minutes. Cover and let stand 1 hour at room temperature, and then refrigerate for 24 hours. It will have doubled in volume.

2. **MAKE THE FINAL DOUGH**: In the bowl of an electric mixer fitted with a dough hook, combine the biga, flour, water, salt, and yeast. Stir with a rubber spatula until a rough dough forms. With the

recipe continues

recipe continued from previous page

dough hook, knead the dough on low speed (2 on a KitchenAid mixer) for 5 minutes. Pull the dough off the hook, add the olives, and knead on low speed until they are well incorporated, stopping and turning the dough over with a spatula as needed, about 4 minutes.

3. **FIRST FERMENTATION**: Transfer the dough to a lightly oiled, clear 4-quart container. Turn the dough over so all sides are oiled. Cover with plastic wrap and let rise until it has almost doubled, about 1½ hours.

4. About 1 hour before baking, place a baking stone on the middle rack of the oven and a cast-iron skillet on the lower rack. Preheat the oven to 425 degrees.

5. **REST**: On a lightly floured countertop, roll the dough into an 8- by 14-inch rectangle. Dust with flour and cover with plastic. Let rest 10 minutes.

6. Cover a baker's peel or rimless baking sheet with parchment. With a pizza wheel, cut the dough into fourteen 8-inch-long strips. Dust the parchment-covered peel or baking sheet with flour and place the filoncini 2 inches apart on the prepared peel. Gently pick up each one and twist gently three times. Cover and let rest 30 minutes.

7. **BAKE**: Place 1 cup of ice cubes in the skillet to produce steam. Slide the filoncini, still on the parchment, onto the baking stone. Place 1 cup of ice cubes in the skillet to produce steam. Bake until golden brown, 20 to 25 minutes. Slide the filoncini, still on the parchment, onto a wire rack and cool completely. Olive filoncini are best eaten on the day they are baked.

Notes for Professional Bakers

For large quantities of sticks, after the first fermentation the dough can be rolled out through a sheeter and cut into strips. For even larger quantities, a stress-free dough divider could be used to laminate and cut strips of dough that can then be guillotined to the desired length.

PAIN BRIÉ

I've always been intrigued by the history of D-Day and the intricacies of the invasion. The last time I visited Normandy, I bought some pain brié and cider at a bakery in Saint-Laurent-sur-Mer, near Omaha Beach, and took it to the war memorial overlooking the ocean. Above the bluff, where the D-Day battle once raged, and not far from the cemeteries, serene and majestic fields of wheat now grow. I was told by the baker that his flour came from the wheat in the nearby fields.

Didier Rosada, who knows as much about bread history as he does about baking, shared his pain brié recipe with me. He told me that pain brié is a traditional Norman bread. Its name comes from the pounding of the dough, as *brie* is derived from the Old Norman verb *brier,* "to pound." The bread, with a large percentage of pre-ferment and a low percentage of water, has a long shelf life and was created for fishermen to carry out to sea for many days. The preparation includes a long kneading period and involves aggressively punching down the dough to produce a yeasted bread with a tight crumb. Here, an electric mixer does the same job. The loaves are scored before the final proof, to guarantee the distinct definition of the cuts.

INGREDIENTS	BAKER'S %	METRIC WEIGHT
PÂTE FERMENTÉE		
Type 65 or equivalent flour (11 to 11.5% protein)	100	442 g
Water	65	288 g
Salt	2	9 g
Dry instant yeast	0.6	3 g
FINAL DOUGH		
Pâte fermentée	297	742 g
Type 65 or equivalent flour (11 to 11.5% protein)	100	250 g
Water	60	150 g
Salt	2	5 g
Dry instant yeast	0.8	2 g
Unsalted butter, softened	10	25 g

recipe continues

START TO FINISH:
15 to 16
hours

PATE FERMENTEE
12 hours

KNEAD
6 minutes

FIRST FERMENTATION
1 to 1½ hours

REST
30 minutes

FINAL PROOF
1 hour

BAKE
30 minutes

MAKES
two 585-gram loaves

recipe continued from previous page

1. **MAKE THE PÂTE FERMENTÉE**: In a large bowl, stir together the flour, water, salt, and yeast until well incorporated. Cover and let stand at room temperature (68 to 77 degrees) for 2 hours. Refrigerate until doubled in volume, another 10 hours.

2. **MAKE THE FINAL DOUGH**: Combine the pâte fermentée, flour, water, salt, yeast, and butter in the bowl of an electric mixer fitted with a dough hook. Stir with a rubber spatula until a rough dough forms. Mix on low speed (2 on a KitchenAid mixer) for 4 minutes, turn the speed to medium (6 on a KitchenAid mixer) and mix for another 2 minutes.

3. **FIRST FERMENTATION**: Transfer the dough to a lightly oiled, clear 4-quart container with a lid. Turn the dough over so all sides are oiled. Cover and let rise until doubled in volume, 1 to 1½ hours.

4. **REST**: On a lightly floured countertop, divide the dough into two equal pieces and pre-shape into rounds (see page 78). Dust with flour and cover with plastic. Let rest for 30 minutes.

5. **FINAL PROOF**: Shape each round into a short bâtard (see page 78) about 10 inches long. If the dough begins to resist shaping, let it rest for a few minutes before continuing, until you can get to 10 to 12 inches. Place on a parchment-lined peel or rimless baking sheet. With a *lame*, single-edged razor blade, or serrated knife, make six parallel slashes about ½ inch deep, end-to-end, down each bâtard. Dust with flour and cover with plastic. Let rest until pillowy, about 1 hour.

6. **BAKE**: About 1 hour before baking, place a baking stone on the middle rack of the oven and a cast-iron skillet on the lower rack. Preheat the oven to 425 degrees for 1 hour. Uncover the breads. Slide the loaves, still on the parchment, onto the baking stone. Place 1 cup of ice cubes in the skillet to produce steam. Bake until the loaves are golden, about 30 minutes. Slide the loaves, still on the parchment, onto a wire rack. Cool completely. Store in a brown paper bag at room temperature for 3 to 4 days.

Notes for Professional Bakers

The easiest way to mimic the slow pounding action on the dough is to knead this stiff dough strictly in first speed. This also preserves the life of the motor of the mixer. The dough is so stiff that mixing in second speed would put too much stress on the machine. In order to achieve well-defined cuts, scoring is usually done right after the shaping of the loaves.

PRESERVING BIODIVERSITY IN PARMA

CLAUDIO GROSSI

Parma is one of my favorite places in Italy. A small, elegant city of 200,000 in Emilia-Romagna, it has the sophistication of Milan without the crowds and congestion. Its narrow, marble-paved streets are lined with well-maintained antique buildings in pinks, yellows, and rose tones. Tiny piazzas with burbling fountains are surrounded by old chapels, umbrella'd cafes in little nooks, gelaterias. A sparkling river, a tributary of the Po, meanders through its center. In addition, it is a Unesco City of Gastronomy, an epicenter of Emilia-Romagna cuisine that is celebrated for its Parmigiano cheese and prosciutto. I didn't realize until I visited that it is also a major agricultural center. Fields of soft *grano tenero* wheat surround the city. Several large mills are based in the region.

As is the case with nearly all of the farmers I've met during my career, I was introduced to Claudio Grossi by a miller, Silvio Grassi of the fifth-generation Parma mill Molino Grassi, the largest organic mill in Italy. Molino Grassi offers a full range of flour types for making pasta, pizza, and bread. It has staked its organic milling business on Italian wheat, with a focus on *grani antichi,* the many varieties of heritage wheat, along with emmer, einkorn, khorasan, and spelt grown by nearby farmers. I planned my visit to the mill to coincide with the harvest, in early July. It had been particularly good weather for wheat, Silvio remarked, with sufficient rain in the spring and long periods of bright sun in the summer, which helped strengthen the wheat's root structure and encourage the stalks to grow tall. He was particularly excited about Claudio's crop of heritage wheat, which he had arranged to purchase in its entirety. Claudio had named his wheat Grano del Miracolo, referring both to its miraculous health and baking properties, and the story of its accidental rediscovery.

First thing the next morning we were headed out of town in Silvio's monster Range Rover to Claudio's farm. The level landscape of the city immediately gave way to rugged hills covered in a checkerboard pattern of wheat, barley, and corn fields, punctuated by a farmhouse here, a post office or cafe there. We turned off the main road and onto a narrow track, winding through wheat-covered hills and olive groves. Following the road into a valley, we arrived at an unembellished farmhouse, a rust-colored two-story brick building. A row of sunflowers framed the yard. An open toolshed housed a few tractors and farm implements. A typical Italian vegetable garden, with neat rows of basil, tomatoes, peppers, and greens was the only landscaping on the ¼-acre yard. Claudio, slender and fine-featured, was waiting for us outside. Sinewy but not brawny, with sensitive eyes and expressive hands, he looked more like a piano tuner or violin maker than a fieldworker.

The wheat encroached upon the driveway. I brushed against it as I opened my car door. In a couple of steps, we were walking directly into Claudio's fields as he explained what we were seeing. He pointed out that the wheat

varied in color, the shape of the heads, and the height of the stalks, which ranged from 4 to 7 feet tall, even taller than the Senatore Cappelli wheat I had experienced in Sicily. Claudio said that having wheats of different heights prevented the tallest wheat from bending to the ground (*lodging* in farm parlance) and potentially sprouting. Compared to fields planted with a single variety, Claudio's fields were riotously diverse, as I had read that many wheat fields were before the Industrial Revolution. We crossed the road and walked down a tractor path through another field that continued up a steep hillside. I lingered to examine the heads of wheat, walking more slowly than Claudio, as we made our ascent. The wheat was so dense and tall that it swallowed me up, so I lost sight of Claudio. I had to call out to him

several times, following his voice until I found him again.

As we continued up the hillside, he told me the story of Grano del Miracolo wheat. His grandfather, he said, had begun to farm the land in 1890. He was drafted into the army during World War I. On his return to the farm, he was swept up in the Fascist party's *Battaglia di Grano*, forced by the government to grow newly developed varieties of higher yielding wheat to help Italy become independent from the rest of the world for wheat. Claudio's grandfather wasn't happy about it, but he had no choice. He expressed his resistance by secretly storing several years' worth of seeds from the old wheat in a grain bin in his dry, secure storage barn. After his grandfather retired, Claudio's father continued to plant standard varieties of durum

profile continues

profile continued from previous page

wheat, as did Claudio when he took over from his father in the late 1980s.

Soon afterwards, Claudio unearthed the old wheat seeds and took them to a lab at the University of Padua. They were a mixture of many old wheat varieties, he discovered, including Virgilio, Ardito, and Fiorello, and some varieties so rare that they didn't appear in the University's registry. Intrigued, he planted a test plot with his grandfather's seeds to see what would grow. He wasn't surprised at the variegated field, but he was surprised when he returned to the lab with his grandfather's wheat and had it tested to evaluate its baking and nutritional qualities. The biodiverse wheat was revealed to be a mixture of soft and hard varieties, containing 43 percent more phosphorus and 25 percent more iron than standard wheat. Its low protein content suggested that it would be more digestible than standard wheat. Usually, a low protein level would be hard to develop. But when the wheat was milled into a test batch of flour and run through modern baking tests, the dough displayed an unusual strength and extensibility. Bread baked with this flour attained good volume, had a sweet and earthy flavor, a lingering perfume, and beautiful pale yellow crumb. The bread itself stayed fresh for days.

Claudio continued to plant test plots of this wheat, hand-selecting particularly large or well-shaped heads, drying them in his attic and cleaning them until he had a sufficient quantity of seeds to test plant again. Eventually, he planted all of his fields exclusively with this blend, which he improved on every year. He started selling his grain to a few natural foods stores, and some local bakers. Locally, his reputation grew.

In 2012, he attended a grain fair where he met Silvio, and the two discovered their shared passion for maintaining the region's grain biodiversity. It wasn't long before Silvio offered to buy all of his wheat, every year, relieving Claudio of the small farmer's uncertain ability to make a living. Knowing that his wheat would be purchased regardless of his varying success year to year gave Claudio the freedom to experiment in order to expand his seed stock and evolve his farming techniques. The partnership continues, with Claudio producing 180,000 pounds of Grano del Miracolo a year. Claudio, still practicing low-impact, small-scale organic wheat farming, told me that his crop changes slightly from year to year, depending on growing conditions that may favor one type of wheat over others. Every year he holds back enough seeds for two years' worth of planting, to ensure that even after a bad season he'll have enough to plant in the future. Grano del Miracolo is now available to consumers in the U.S. (see page 347), so you can bake a loaf of bread with this flour to experience a living example of what grew in the hills around Parma 100 years ago.

The opposite of an exercise in nostalgia, baking with this flour is an affirmation of a biodiverse future. During the time that Claudio's grandfather's wheat was in storage, the world of wheat and milling changed dramatically. The biodiversity represented by this unique blend was almost lost. The effort of a single farmer determined to preserve his legacy and the commitment of a miller to mill this special grain into flour is a model for other farmer/miller collaborations.

PANE CON FARINA DI MONOCOCCO

After I spent a day with farmer Claudio Grossi and miller Silvio Grassi, they took me to Panificio Franco Frati, a bakery in a small town just outside of Parma, where the baker, Franco Frati, works with many of the ancient grains milled by Silvio. I first saw his name on one of the fields on the outskirts of town, signifying that the grain was destined for his bread. One of his specialties was this einkorn (*monococco* in Italian) bread. He told me that he really liked the nutty character of the type of einkorn that grew nearby, and in fact he had helped that farmer identify, over several years of selective breeding, grain with the flavor characteristics he was looking for.

He explained that because einkorn has less gluten than wheat flour, he uses Claudio's Grano del Miracolo flour (see Resources, page 347) as the foundation of the dough. He chills his loaves for 16 to 18 hours after shaping them, which helps develop structure and rich flavor.

INGREDIENTS	BAKER'S %	METRIC WEIGHT
BIGA		
Grano del Miracolo flour	100	160 g
Water	60	96 g
Dry instant yeast	0.6	1 g
FINAL DOUGH		
Biga	52	258 g
Whole einkorn flour	40	200 g
Grano del Miracolo flour	60	300 g
Water	70	350 g
Salt	2.5	12.5 g
Dry instant yeast	0.2	1 g
Honey	4	20 g

recipe continues

START TO FINISH:
34 to 36
hours

BIGA
25 hours

KNEAD
8 minutes

FIRST FERMENTATION
3 hours

REST
10 to 15 minutes

RETARD
16 to 18 hours

WARM UP
1 ½ hours

BAKE
25 to 30 minutes

MAKES
two 570-gram loaves

recipe continued from previous page

1. **MAKE THE BIGA**: In a small bowl, stir together the flour, water, and yeast until well incorporated. Knead it into a firm dough, about 5 minutes. Cover and let stand 1 hour at room temperature and then refrigerate for 24 hours.

2. **MAKE THE FINAL DOUGH**: In the bowl of an electric mixer fitted with a dough hook, combine the biga, einkorn flour, Grano del Miracolo flour, water, salt, yeast, and honey. Stir with a rubber spatula until a rough dough forms. With the dough hook, knead the dough on low speed (2 on a KitchenAid mixer) for 2 minutes. Pull the dough off the hook and continue to mix on low until the dough is smooth and elastic, another 6 minutes.

3. **FIRST FERMENTATION**: Transfer the dough to a lightly oiled, clear 4-quart container with a lid. Turn the dough over so all sides are oiled. Cover with plastic wrap and let rise until it has almost doubled, about 3 hours.

4. **REST**: On a lightly floured countertop, divide the dough into two equal pieces and pre-shape into rounds. Dust with flour and cover with plastic. Let rest for 10 to 15 minutes.

5. **RETARD**: Cover a rimless baking sheet with parchment. Shape each round into two 10- by 3½-inch snub-nosed bâtards (see page 78). Dust the parchment-covered peel or baking sheet with flour and place the bâtards on the parchment, seam sides down, 3 inches apart. Lift the parchment paper between the loaves, making a pleat and drawing the loaves close together. Alternatively, use baker's linen instead of parchment. Tightly roll up two kitchen towels and slip them under the parchment paper on the outer sides of each loaf to support the logs. Alternatively, place the bâtards in two lightly floured 10-inch-long bannetons. Cover loosely with a towel or plastic wrap. Refrigerate for 8 to 12 hours.

6. **WARM UP**: Remove the loaves from the refrigerator and let stand on the countertop to warm up for 1½ hours.

7. **BAKE**: About 1 hour before baking, place a baking stone on the middle rack of the oven and a cast-iron skillet on the lower rack. Preheat the oven to 400 degrees for 1 hour. Place 1 cup of ice cubes in the skillet to produce steam. Uncover the breads, remove the rolled-up towels, and stretch the parchment paper out so that it is flat and the loaves are separated. Transfer the loaves, still on the parchment, to the oven. Or, if in bannetons, gently flip loaves right onto the baking stone. Bake until the loaves are well risen and dark brownish-red, 25 to 30 minutes. Slide the loaves, still on the parchment, onto a wire rack. Cool completely. Store in a brown paper bag at room temperature for up to 4 days.

PROFILE:

DAME FARINE

MARIE-CHRISTINE ARACTINGI,
BOULANGERIE DAME FARINE, MARSEILLE, FRANCE

On the short walk in Marseille from my waterfront hotel to Marie-Christine Aractingi's bakery, I basked in Mediterranean warmth and light. Hundreds of sailboats bobbed in the harbor, which is guarded by the imposing Fort Saint Jean, a giant pink granite fortress built by Louis the XIV at the entrance to the Old Port. Fish restaurants dotted the sidewalks overlooking the circular harbor. In the distance, I could see the peaks of various church spires and domes, from the gothic Eglise des Reformes to the neo-Byzantine Notre-Dame de la Garde. As I made my way down the Avenue de la Corse, under a canopy of plane trees, I passed a vegetable shop with produce arranged in perfect pyramids, as is the French custom. A few steps from the bakery was a small butcher shop and then a fromagerie. I could still smell the strong salt air as I approached the bright blue door of Marie-Christine's storefront.

A tiny, bubbly, electrically energetic woman of 31 who wears a striped French sailor shirt under her apron welcomed me into her little jewel box of a bakery. She pointed to the loaves arranged like precious gems on a pretty counter made from an antique kneading table. "Today I made fourteen *demoiselles*," her whimsical name for her delicate white baguettes, "and nine *miche Cleopatre*," rounds made with ancient khorasan. With her small-scale production and pride in her work, she conveys the idea that each loaf has a personality and beauty of its own. Just as she knows every loaf, she knows every customer who walks into the shop, chat-

ting with each one about the day's breads, giving samples, even scolding them when they ask for croissants, which they should know she doesn't make. She has strong convictions about a baker being a baker and not a pastry chef.

Although she was trained by the new generation of artisan bakers in Paris, her roots and her heart are clearly in Provence. She was first exposed to baking at home. When she was 18 and a literature student at the Sorbonne, her roommates asked her to bake a *pompe à l'huile*, a typical Provencal holiday bread. She was overcome with wonder when she returned to the kitchen an hour after mixing the dough and saw how it had risen. *"Whoosh!* What did I do? What did I create? The explosion in the bowl captivated my curiosity." She left the University to pursue her newfound passion.

After years of training, she returned to Marseille and opened Dame Farine (which translates as "the flour lady"), working alone at first, baking all night and selling all day. She cultivated two simple sourdoughs, one wheat and one rye, that she keeps in separate pots in the back room. She told me that they like being close to the sea. I could smell and taste the Mediterranean in these starters. She gets her flour from Moulin Saint Joseph (see Resources, page 347), an organic water-powered mill, in business since 1850, that mills wheat grown in Provence exclusively for local bakers. Her breads feature local honey, fruit, and olives. "It was quite hard. By the end of the day you get very *disagreeable*. People stopped liking me because of my bad mood." Her determination to work against the steady decline of French bread, traveling back in time to recover old recipes and techniques, ultimately made her very popular. She notes with satisfaction that when she started, a lot of old-school bakers looked her tiny frame up and down and wondered if she could do the work, but now no one doubts her command of her business and her bread.

Marie-Christine embodies the French artisan spirit: so opinionated, so refined, so devoted to her life's work and her customers. Her business is small by design. The bakery is open five days a week and she is there every one of those days. In the rare case when she has to be out of town, she closes up the shop. She has a small number of employees and a small menu of breads. Too many of either would get in the way of the focus and attention she places on each loaf. While some bakers roughly roll their dough, she carefully shapes bread with her delicate fingers. When she places a round in a couche, she does so with precision, pinching the seam perfectly closed. Each of her finished breads is beautiful and a little bit different, the way a fine potter's hand-thrown bowls are one of a kind and unique.

POMPE À L'HUILE

Marie-Christine Aractingi of Boulangerie Dame Farine in Marseille makes this sweet bread, perfumed with orange flower water and orange peel and rich with eggs and olive oil, for the holidays. It is unique to the South of France and a local favorite. Knead the dough in two stages—first, give it a very short slow mix, and then a longer mix on medium. The dough has a high percentage of sugar, which has to be incorporated in two stages as well. Different bakers often experiment with the cuts to make unique shaped breads. This shape is a fun one: First, pre-shape the dough into loose rounds, then roll each round into an oblong disk. Make sharp cuts in the dough with a *lame* or sharp paring knife, or use the edge of a credit card. Then stretch the dough while lifting it onto a parchment-lined baking sheet or peel to create the bread's characteristic openings.

START TO FINISH:

21 to 28
hours

SPONGE
8 to 10 hours

KNEAD
20 minutes

RETARD
8 to 12 hours

WARM UP
1½ to 2 hours

REST
20 minutes

FINAL PROOF
2½ hours

BAKE
30 minutes

MAKES
two 726-gram loaves

INGREDIENTS	BAKER'S %	METRIC WEIGHT
SPONGE		
Type 65 or equivalent flour (11 to 11.5% protein)	100	200 g
Water	60	120 g
Dry instant yeast	0.5	0.25 g
FINAL DOUGH		
Sponge	64	320 g
Type 65 or equivalent flour (11 to 11.5% protein)	100	500 g
Extra-virgin olive oil	20	100 g
Water	2	10 g
Salt	2	10 g
Dry instant yeast	2	10 g
Eggs	30	150 g (about 3 large)
Sugar	25	125 g
Butter	20	100 g
Orange flower water	6	30 g
Anise seed	1.6	8 g
Candied orange peel, coarsely chopped	18	90 g

recipe continues

recipe continued from previous page

1. **MAKE THE SPONGE**: In a small bowl, stir together the flour, water, and yeast until well incorporated. The mixture will be stiff. Cover and let ferment at room temperature (68 to 77 degrees) until doubled in volume, 8 to 10 hours.

2. **MAKE THE FINAL DOUGH**: Combine the sponge, flour, oil, water, salt, yeast, eggs, sugar, butter, orange flower water, and anise seed in the bowl of an electric mixer fitted with a dough hook. Stir with a rubber spatula until a dough forms. With the dough hook, mix on medium-low speed (4 on a KitchenAid mixer) for 3 to 4 minutes. Turn the speed to medium (6 on a KitchenAid mixer) and mix for 15 minutes. Add the candied orange peel and mix until just incorporated, another minute or two.

3. **RETARD**: Transfer the dough to a lightly oiled, clear 4-quart container with a lid. Turn the dough over so all sides are oiled, cover, and let stand 1½ hours. Refrigerate 8 to 12 hours.

4. **WARM UP**: Remove the dough from the refrigerator and let warm up for 1½ to 2 hours.

5. **REST**: On a lightly floured countertop, divide the dough into two equal pieces and pre-shape into rounds (see page 78). Dust with flour and cover with plastic. Let rest 20 minutes.

6. **FINAL PROOF**: Line two rimless baking sheets with parchment paper. Press or use a rolling pin to roll each round into a 7- by 9-inch oval. Using a sharp paring knife (or a credit card), starting and finishing 1½ inches from the edge, make a cut lengthwise down the center of each piece of dough. On either side of the long cut, make 3 shorter cuts at a 45-degree angle, stopping 1½ inches from the edge of the dough. Lift onto the prepared baking sheets, gently stretching them so the cuts open up. Dust with flour and cover with plastic. Let rest until pillowy, about 2½ hours.

7. **BAKE**: Preheat the oven to 350 degrees. Arrange racks on the top third and bottom third of the oven. Bake, switching the position of the baking sheets after 15 minutes. Continue to bake until the breads are golden, another 15 minutes. Slide the breads, still on the parchment, onto wire racks. Cool completely. Pompe à l'Huile is best eaten on the day it is baked. If you have a leftover bread, wrap it tightly in plastic and then in foil and freeze for up to 1 month; reheat in a 350-degree oven.

Notes for Professional Bakers

Because of the high percentage of sugar in the dough, it should be added in two steps to ensure good gluten development, the first addition at the beginning of the mixing process and the second addition when the gluten is about 40 percent developed. Instead of a paring knife, a dough cutter could be used to cut the dough after stretching. This will speed up the process in a production environment.

PANE CON PEPERONCINI, OLIVE, E POMODORO

Rocco Princi is a gifted baker with a supreme sense of style. His vision was to sell refined pastries and rugged breads in the same location, and to design that location to be elegant and beautiful but inviting. He now has shops in Milan, London, and Shanghai. It's a sign of his ambition that he recently partnered with Starbucks to bring his pastries and breads to an even wider audience. I hope he is able to expand in a way that allows him to maintain his very special standards.

Of his many creations, the bread with tomatoes and olives is one of my favorites and I wanted to adapt the recipe for the home baker. Long fermentation of both the biga and the dough give it great flavor. In addition, the dough has plenty of time to absorb the flavors of the tomatoes and olives.

INGREDIENTS	BAKER'S %	METRIC WEIGHT
BIGA		
Tipo OO flour with W value of 250 to 260	100	156 g
Water	64	100 g
Dry instant yeast	0.6	1 g
FINAL DOUGH		
Biga	51	257 g
Tipo OO flour with W value of 250 to 260	100	500 g
Water	80	400 g
Salt	2.5	12.5 g
Dry instant yeast	0.4	2 g
Large Sicilian green olives, pitted and halved	15	75 g
Sun-dried tomatoes packed in oil, drained and chopped	15	75 g
Crushed red pepper flakes	0.2	1 g

recipe continues

START TO FINISH:
37 to 42
hours

BIGA
25 hours

KNEAD
7 minutes

RETARD
8 to 12 hours

WARM UP
1½ to 2 hours

FINAL PROOF
1½ hours

BAKE
50 minutes

MAKES
one 1.3-kilo loaf

recipe continued from previous page

1. **MAKE THE BIGA**: In a small bowl, stir to-gether the flour, water, and yeast until well in-corporated. Knead it into a firm dough, about 5 minutes. Cover and let stand 1 hour at room temperature, then refrigerate for 24 hours. It will have increased about 1½ times in volume.

2. **MAKE THE FINAL DOUGH**: In the bowl of an electric mixer fitted with a dough hook, combine the biga, 00 flour, water, salt, and yeast. Stir with a rubber spatula until a rough dough forms. With the dough hook, knead the dough on lowest speed for 2 minutes. Increase the speed to medium-low (4 on a KitchenAid mixer) and knead another 2 minutes. Add the olives, tomatoes, and pepper flakes and continue to knead until they are well incorporated, about 3 minutes.

3. **RETARD**: Transfer the dough to a lightly oiled, clear 4-quart container with a lid. Turn the dough over so all sides are oiled. Cover with plastic wrap and refrigerate overnight, 8 to 12 hours.

4. **WARM UP**: Take the dough out of the refrig-erator and let it warm up for 1½ to 2 hours.

5. **FINAL PROOF**: On a lightly floured countertop, gently round the dough. Place in a lightly floured banneton, seam side up. Cover with plastic wrap or a kitchen towel and let rest until pillowy, about 1½ hours.

6. **BAKE**: About 1 hour before baking, position an oven rack in the bottom third of the oven and set the Dutch oven (with the lid on) on the rack. Preheat the oven to 425 degrees for 1 hour. Cover a baker's peel or rimless baking sheet with parchment. Wearing oven mitts, carefully remove the Dutch oven to a heatproof surface and take off the lid. Tip the dough onto a peel or your hands and put in the Dutch oven. Dust the top of the loaf with flour. Gently dimple the top of the loaf with your fingertips. Put the lid on and bake for 30 minutes. Remove the lid and bake until the loaf is a rich golden brown, about 20 minutes more. Carefully turn the loaf out onto a wire rack. Cool completely. Store in a brown paper bag at room temperature for up to 4 to 5 days.

Note for Professional Bakers

When baking this bread in a deck oven, I strongly recommend you load the dough on parchment paper. This will keep the oven floor free from grease from the olives, tomatoes, and olive oil, which is very difficult to remove.

QUINOA TWIST WITH SEEDS

START TO FINISH:

16 to 17
hours

SPONGE AND SOAKERS
12 hours

KNEAD
7 minutes

FIRST FERMENTATION
1½ to 2 hours

FINAL PROOF
1¼ to 1½ hours

BAKE
40 minutes

MAKES
two 604-gram loaves

In response to the increased interest in whole grains and seeds, many German bakers are experimenting with unusual combinations in their traditional recipes and expanding their repertoires to include nontraditional whole grain breads. Christa Lutum and Antonius Beumer, of Bäckerei Beumer & Lutum in Berlin, are a prime example. They combine flax, sesame, and rolled oats with quinoa, the seeds of an Andean plant that was domesticated by pre-Columbian civilizations at least 5,000 years ago. Quinoa is notable for its rich flavor and for its high-quality protein (unlike comparable grains and legumes, quinoa contains all eight essential amino acids). Soaking the whole seeds and rolled oats ensures that they are fully hydrated before they go into the bread. It also softens them so they're edible, improves their flavor, makes them more digestible, and prevents them from stealing water from the final dough. In addition to soaking the seeds, they also soak the quinoa flour, which gives the bread a moist crumb and unique texture.

There's no need to go out and buy quinoa flour if you have some quinoa in your pantry. Weigh it out and then put it in your blender. Blend into a fine powder and proceed with the recipe.

INGREDIENTS	BAKER'S %	METRIC WEIGHT
SPONGE		
Type 65 or equivalent flour (11 to 11.5% protein)	100	80 g
Water	60	48 g
Dry instant yeast	1.2	1 g
SEED SOAKER		
Sesame seeds	25	27 g
Flax seeds	25	27 g
Quinoa	25	27 g
Rolled oats	25	27 g
Water	100	108 g
QUINOA SOAKER		
Water	100	85 g
Quinoa flour	100	85 g
FINAL DOUGH		
Sponge	30	129 g
Quinoa soaker	40	170 g
Type 65 or equivalent flour (11 to 11.5% protein)	70	298 g
Whole wheat flour	30	128 g
Water	55	234 g
Salt	2.5	11 g
Dry instant yeast	1.1	5 g
Honey	4	17 g
Seed soaker	51	216 g
FINISHING		
Quinoa flour or quinoa flakes for sprinkling		

1. **MAKE THE SPONGE**: In a small bowl, stir together the flour, water, and yeast until well incorporated. Cover and let ferment in the refrigerator until doubled in volume, 12 hours.

2. **MAKE THE SEED SOAKER**: In a medium bowl, combine the seeds, quinoa, oats, and water. Cover and let stand at room temperature for 12 hours.

recipe continues

recipe continued from previous page

3. **MAKE THE QUINOA SOAKER**: Combine the water and quinoa flour in a small bowl. Cover and let stand at room temperature for 12 hours.

4. **MAKE THE FINAL DOUGH**: In the bowl of an electric mixer fitted with a dough hook, combine the sponge, quinoa soaker, white flour, whole wheat flour, water, salt, yeast, and honey. Stir with a rubber spatula until a rough dough forms. With the dough hook, knead the dough on low speed (2 on a KitchenAid mixer) for 2 minutes. Increase the speed to medium-low speed (4 on a KitchenAid mixer) and mix until the dough is smooth and strong to the touch, 5 minutes. Pull the dough off the hook. Add the seed soaker and knead just until evenly distributed. Do not over-knead, or the seeds might break down the dough.

5. **FIRST FERMENTATION**: Transfer the dough to a lightly oiled, clear 4-quart container with a lid. Turn the dough over so all sides are oiled. Cover with plastic wrap and let rise until it has almost doubled, 1½ to 2 hours.

6. **FINAL PROOF**: On a lightly floured countertop, gently press the dough into a 6- by 8-inch rectangle. Use a dough knife to cut the dough into two 3- by 8-inch rectangles. Sprinkle lightly with some quinoa flour. To shape into twists, place your hands next to each other in the middle of a dough piece. Rotate the dough with your left hand while using your right hand to rotate in the other direction, creating one twist. Repeat as your hands move towards the ends of the dough piece, twice more. Repeat with the remaining dough piece. Cover a baker's peel or rimless baking sheet with parchment. Dust the parchment-covered peel or baking sheet with flour and place the twists on the parchment, seam sides down, 3 inches apart. Lift the parchment paper between the loaves, making a pleat and drawing the loaves close together. Alternatively, use baker's linen instead of parchment. Tightly roll up two kitchen towels and slip them under the parchment paper on the outer sides of each loaf to support the loaves. Lightly brush with water and sprinkle with quinoa flakes. Cover loosely with a towel or plastic wrap. Let rest until pillowy, 1¼ to 1½ hours.

7. **BAKE**: About 1 hour before baking, place a baking stone on the middle rack of the oven and a cast-iron skillet on the lower rack. Preheat the oven to 425 degrees for 1 hour. Uncover the breads, remove the rolled-up towels, and stretch the parchment paper out so that it is flat and the loaves are separated. Place 1 cup of ice cubes in the skillet to produce steam. Bake until the loaves are well risen and dark brownish-red, about 40 minutes. Slide the loaves, still on the parchment, onto a wire rack. Cool completely. Store in a brown paper bag at room temperature for 4 to 6 days.

Note for Professional Bakers

When working with a spiral mixer, extra care should be taken to avoid overmixing the dough. Quinoa flour contains a lot of proteins, but they are soluble in water and don't contribute to gluten formation, therefore the gluten structure of this dough remains very fragile. Shorter mixing time in second speed is advised.

Le kilogramme
15,50 F

EPICERIE
Perrette

6
SOURDOUGH

Reading a recent *New York Times* article about Ötzi, Europe's oldest mummy, I skipped past details like his shoe size and the gap between his front teeth and went straight to the contents of his stomach. The Copper Age man's last meal, eaten 3,300 years ago and just 30 minutes before his death, consisted of ibex meat, ferns, and einkorn wheat. The fine grind of the einkorn suggested to investigators that the grain had been processed into flour and then baked into bread. They hypothesized that Ötzi had stowed the bread in his knapsack before heading high into the Italian Alps (he was found at 10,500 feet). I thought about what that whole grain bread must have tasted like. It would be easy to approximate the recipe for Ötzi's bread, not just because flour made from einkorn, an unhybridized relative of wheat, is readily available these days, but also because the bread had to have been raised with a spontaneous sourdough starter not that different from the one I always have on hand.

We don't know too many facts about prehistoric baking, but we do know that a naturally fermented starter teeming with wild yeast and bacteria was used to bake the very first leavened bread thousands of years ago. It's not much of a stretch to speculate that this starter gave the bread flavor, aroma, and texture and helped keep it fresh for days. Pane di Altamura, the Italian bread that has been baked continuously with the same grain and starter and sometimes in the same primitive ovens for over 1,000 years, gives us an idea of how sourdough bread tasted back then. While this celebrated loaf has in recent years made Altamura a serious baker's destination, it originally fed farmers and shepherds. Its

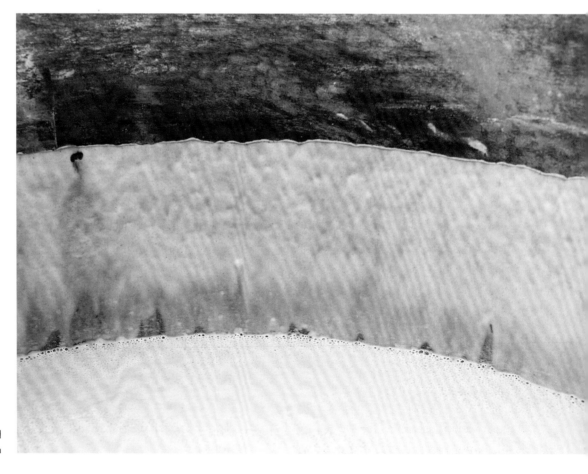

Deflated liquid
sourdough

thick crust, unique flavor, color, and dense crumb, the product of natural yeast fermentation, preserve its freshness for many days in the fields.

Sourdough is the heart and soul of the best traditional artisan baking and remains the foundation of the unique, best-tasting, longest keeping, and most nutritionally complete and digestible breads. In choosing to bake with your own sourdough, you become part of a rich tradition reaching back in time to ancient days and an active sustainer of this time-honored process.

What Is Sourdough?

Fermentation is the term for the breakdown of compound molecules in organic substances by yeast, mold, and bacteria. When yeast and bacteria get to work on milk, they transform it into cheese. Yeast and bacteria turn grape juice into wine. Sourdough is another type of fermentation. For newcomers to the concept, here is the basic idea: Wild yeast, which are ubiquitous microscopic non-filamentous fungi, live in flour and the air. When water hydrates flour, it triggers enzymes in the dough to break down the flour's starches into simple sugars. The yeast feed on these simple sugars, producing carbon dioxide, which causes the mixture to bubble and rise. (Yeast also produce ethanol alcohol, which evaporates in the heat of the oven.) The well-fed and oxygenated yeast multiply rapidly, and with care and under the right conditions, the sourdough culture becomes a powerful leavener. Once a healthy wild yeast colony is established in the starter, it is added in precise amounts to bread dough, causing the dough to ferment and rise on the countertop and in the oven.

Although fermentation is a complex biological and chemical transformation, there is nothing complicated about growing a sourdough starter. When flour is mixed with water and allowed to stand, wild yeast in the flour and in the air *will* feed

on the grain's simple sugars, producing carbon dioxide gas that is entrapped in the dough's viscoelastic structure and causes the mixture to bubble and rise. As Lionel Poilâne famously said, "The baker's savoir-faire is not art. Making bread is nothing more than breeding microscopic animals."

Yeast and Acids in Balance

Sourdough gets its name from the acids that build up in the dough during fermentation. These acids are not produced by yeast, but by different bacteria (mainly a group of lactic acid bacteria called *lactobacilli*) that exist in the environment alongside yeast and feed off sugars in the dough. As they feed and multiply, lactobacilli produce organic acids, chiefly lactic and acetic acids, and other compounds that flavor the bread. As with yeast, there are thousands of known strains of lactobacilli. The various and changing combinations of yeast, lactobacilli, and their byproducts in the culture affect bread's fermentation and its flavor.

Both yeast and lactobacilli are abundant in flour, which, by one estimate, contains 13,000 wild yeast cells and 320 lactobacilli cells per gram. But these microorganisms need specific conditions for multiplication. Hydration, temperature, and the type and grind of flour all contribute to how the microbial culture will grow. Too little yeast in the culture might result in under-developed bread. Too little acid and your bread won't benefit from its flavor. Too much acid will slow down the growth of the wild yeast. So while cultivating a culture of microorganisms is easy, understanding how it is growing, making adjustments in caring for it, and determining when it is ready to use require knowledge of its components and sensitivity to its environment.

While bakers work with what they can see and taste, laboratory scientists study various sourdoughs under the microscope to establish the exact variety of lactobacilli in order to understand what happens on a molecular level during microbial cultivation and, ultimately, to determine when a culture is optimally ready to raise bread. Professor Luc De Vuyst, head of Research in Industrial Microbiology and Food Biotechnology at the Vrije Universiteit Brussel, uses microbiological and physico-chemical parameters to assess the performance of starters sent to him by curious bakers. Microorganisms are counted. When a lactobacilli-to-yeast ratio of 100:1 is achieved in a sourdough, the culture is in optimal condition to raise and flavor bread dough. Genetic and phenotypic analyses are performed. Professor De Vuyst has catalogued the behavior of multiple strains of yeast and lactobacilli in order to determine the strengths and weaknesses of each one. He and his colleagues offer bakers suggestions for refining their techniques, depending on the microbiomes in their bakeries—adjusting times, temperatures, and pH—to get more powerful, tastier, and more reliable results.

Sourdough and Its Environment

One of the most interesting conclusions of scientific studies of sourdough is that environment is the wild card variable. Professor De Vuyst has found that while in the lab, the particular strains of yeast and lactobacilli dominant in a culture can be predicted and controlled. However, once a culture is taken out of this setting and brought to a bakery, there is no certainty that these strains will continue to dominate. I told him about the time I took some of my friend Steve Sullivan's sourdough from his San Francisco bakery, Acme Bread Company, and brought it to Bread Alone, hoping to re-create the flavor of Steve's bread. Using the same flour that Steve uses, I fed it on Steve's schedule. But when I baked with it, the bread tasted more like the loaves I have always made than like Steve's.

Professor De Vuyst confirmed what I suspected. "If you import a foreign microorganism, there is a

chance you will lose it. It depends on how competitive the strain is in the dough matrix." In contrast to my experience with Steve's sourdough, when Vincenzo Benvenuto, owner of Caffetteria del Viale in Altamura, gave me 200 grams of sourdough and a kilo and a half of semolina flour as a parting gift, I was able to keep his starter alive and bake some very authentic-tasting bread when I got home (see "A Sourdough Souvenir" on page 177). Professor De Vuyst did not discount the possibility that imported strains of lactobacilli could become the dominant culture in another bakery. But there is no guarantee. "If your own microbiota is dominant, it will take over. You would have to disinfect the whole bakery—walls, floors, baking apparatus," he replied. I've found it much easier to work with and appreciate what is already here. This isn't a bad thing. In fact, working with your microbiota is part of developing your own signature breads.

Sourdough and Good Health

One of the features of sourdough that has interested me from the beginning of my baking life is its relationship to good health. I've been happily surprised by the number of my bread-sensitive customers who have told me that they are able to enjoy our organic sourdough breads. From my experience and based on the research I have done, I believe that natural sourdoughs create breads that are easier to digest.

Probiotics, including lactobacilli, "predigest" certain food components, making them easier for your stomach to break them down and for nutrients to be absorbed. This is why people who are lactose intolerant can eat fermented dairy products like yogurt: The active bacteria in yogurt breaks down the lactose that otherwise can be difficult to digest. Like yogurt, an active sourdough culture teems with just such "healthy" bacteria. Of course, we don't eat active culture, we eat the bread made with that culture, and by the time we eat sourdough bread, the bacteria have been killed off in the heat of the oven. What's intriguing, however, is the effect that lactobacilli have on the chemistry of the bread dough before it is baked and concomitantly in the physico-chemical and nutritional properties of the final sourdough bread.

Phytic acid, which is found in wheat and other cereal seeds, inhibits the enzymes produced by the microbiome of our digestive system that break down proteins and starches. Scientists hypothesize that for a number of people who struggle to digest proteins and starches, ingesting wheat bread made with commercial yeast can upset the stomach. In addition, phytic acid chemically bonds to minerals, including calcium, magnesium, iron, and zinc, blocking their absorption. This is the case not just for commercial white bread, but for supermarket bread advertised as "whole grain." Commercial whole wheat bread may be just as tough on the gut as white bread, because it contains just as much, if not more, phytic acid. And ironically, that phytic acid may prevent the body from absorbing some of the nutrients that supposedly make whole grain bread healthier.

In contrast to bread made with commercial yeast, sourdough bread can be easier on the stomach. The theory is that during the long, gradual fermentation, wild yeast and lactic acid bacteria in the dough neutralize phytic acid in bread dough as well as begin to "pre-digest" the dough's starches and proteins. This reduction in phytic acid, along with the dismantling of some of the protein and starch molecules, results in a less problematic bread whose remaining proteins and starches are more easily broken down by the body. Another benefit is that the minerals are no longer held hostage and are again available for the body to absorb.

The enzymes and lactic acid bacteria in sourdough are today providing cutting edge relief for

It's alive!

celiac disease sufferers. Starting with the scientific fact that sourdough bread has a lower gluten content than bread made with commercial yeast, Dr. Marco Gobetti, of the Free University of Bozen-Bolzano, is the author of *The Handbook on Sourdough Biotechnology*. He and his team of microbiologists specializing in sourdough technology research have isolated over a thousand strains of lactobacilli to determine which strains are most effective at breaking down gluten in wheat flour. By developing a sourdough culture with these strains, using it to slowly ferment wheat flour, and then semi-drying the fermented wheat flour so it has the same moisture content as regular flour, Gobetti and his team have produced a gluten-free wheat flour. In clinical trials, celiac patients exhibited 100 percent tolerance to baked goods made with this flour.

The Process

Microorganisms need three things to grow and reproduce: food, in the form of carbohydrates and other nutrients in flour; water, which unlocks the starches in the flour, making them accessible as food; and oxygen, supplied by air that is naturally incorporated into the culture during mixing. To initiate the process of cultivating a sourdough, the baker simply has to feed the microbiota naturally occurring in flour by stirring it together with water.

Some bakers add lactobacilli-rich yogurt to the mix. Others throw in a potato peel, pressed grapes, or rehydrated dried fruit to provide extra food for hungry microorganisms. Malt, which is rich in simple sugars, is another nutrient sometimes added to the initial dough. Because of the classic French tradition I come from, my own recipe is simple.

I use organic wheat flour in my starter. To initiate the culture, I combine organic white flour with organic stone-ground whole wheat flour. The whole wheat naturally contains more microorganisms and nutrients for these microorganisms—minerals contained in the bran of the kernel of wheat. I typically use a medium protein bread flour with high ash content, because minerals in this type of flour are nutrients for the culture's microorganism. Because too much chlorine in some tap water can interfere with yeast and bacteria activity, bottled spring water is a safer choice.

As you will see, a culture takes at least 5 days and up to 2 weeks to become active enough to raise bread. The length of time it takes is no indication of its quality. When you mix your flour and water together on Day 1, incorporating oxygen, you will initiate microbial activity. At this stage, many different types of microorganisms are present in the culture.

On Day 2, you may or may not be able to detect changes in the mixture, including small bubbles or an earthy aroma. In any case, your microorganisms will be getting hungry. In the morning, you'll add flour and water to sustain them. Before going to bed, you'll discard some of the mixture (otherwise you'd have an overflowing bucket of sourdough by the end of the week), and feed the remaining culture again.

You'll continue with this schedule, noticing increasing activity as the days go by. There will be larger bubbles dotting the surface of the culture. It will rise, at first slightly, and later on voluminously. It will develop a tart and fruity flavor. Because of the uniqueness of your starter's environment, it will reach maturity at its own pace. Don't worry if it hasn't doubled by the end of Day 5. Continue to feed it and observe it and you will know when it is ready to use.

Firm Sourdough vs. Liquid Sourdough

By varying the amount of water you use to initiate and then feed your culture, you can cultivate sourdoughs of different consistencies. When I first went to France years ago, a firm starter culture was the norm, simply because temperature-controlled

A SOURDOUGH SOUVENIR

It had been awhile since I'd visited Altamura, so I called food writer Nancy Harmon Jenkins, an expert on Italian food, for some travel tips. She put me in touch with retired journalist and artisan food activist Onofrio Pepe, best known for leading peaceful and ultimately successful protests against the opening of a McDonald's in his hometown. Onofrio has a scholarly demeanor and wears a fashionably tied scarf around his neck, even in July. He served as my escort and guide, translating for me at Pane di Nunzio and several other traditional bakeries.

I must admit, I wasn't enthusiastic when he mentioned Caffetteria del Viale. My focus was on bread, I had a tight schedule, and a pastry shop seemed like a distraction. But Onofrio insisted. "Vincenzo Benvenuto is unbelievably talented, and makes many pastries from *grano duro rimacinata*." He wanted me to taste the baker's famous vegan brioche. Vincenzo greeted us exuberantly and plied us with what were indeed delicious semolina-based pastries. Afterwards, we descended to the basement pastry shop, where Vincenzo opened up a plastic tub of his lievito madre. "My starter was tested by Marco Gobbetti," he told me, dropping the name of the famous sourdough researcher to get my attention. "It has very energetic lactobacilli unique to Altamura."

Vincenzo felt very strongly that the local sourdough made his vegan brioche, along with all other Altamura breads, unique. He was emphatic. "Not only am I telling you, but Marco is too. I really want to give you some to take back so you can see how different it is." I protested, explaining that I was only four days into a twenty-day trip. "Don't worry, I'll assemble everything for you," he said, going back downstairs. He returned with 1½ kilos of semolina flour and an airtight container holding 3 ounces of the lievito madre. "Feed the sourdough every two to three days, put it in the refrigerator when you check into a hotel. It's very vibrant. It won't die." For the next three weeks, as I went from Rome to Genzano to Parma to Milan, I did as he said, unpacking my little box of starter and flour and feeding it in hotel bathrooms in each new city. On my last day in Italy, I prepared the sourdough for flying. I used about 10 percent starter at about 55 percent hydration, kneading it with fresh flour and shaping it into a firm cylinder. Then I wrapped it in plastic, rolled it up inside some of my clothes, and slipped it into my carry-on. A firmer starter wouldn't overferment during the flight, and it wouldn't be confiscated by security, as a liquid starter might be.

When I arrived at Bread Alone I hydrated it to 120 percent. Within 24 hours it took off. Comparing it side by side with the Bread Alone starters, I noticed it fermented more quickly than ours did and had a finer texture, with microbubbles rather than the large and uneven bubbles I was used to. For a few weeks, we baked with it every day, making not only Vincenzo's vegan brioche, which tasted just like the bread I ate in Altamura, but also making some Bread Alone breads to see if they were different with a different starter. The breads made with Vincenzo's starter had a fruity perfume that I had never noticed in my bread before. Their flavor was sweeter and less acidic than our usual breads.

We don't have a lab at Bread Alone, and even if we did, I couldn't verify that the lactobacilli that Marco Gobetti had identified in Vincenzo's starter, *Weissella cibaria* and *Weissella confusa* to be exact, had prevailed in a new location. But I can say, as a baker, that Vincenzo's starter maintained its unique identity, fermenting differently from the other starters in the bakery and producing breads with a singular flavor.

sourdough tanks were not commercially available and it was easier to control the fermentation of a firm starter than a fast-fermenting liquid starter. Both firm and liquid sourdoughs are common in artisan bakeries today. The relative hydration of the starter will affect certain qualities of the dough and of the finished bread. Choose the one more suitable to the type of dough you'd like to work with and the type of bread you want to bake: The higher proportion of water in liquid levain will trigger increased enzyme activity during fermentation. This enzyme activity, and especially the activity of proteases, has some noticeable benefits on the dough extensibility during shaping. For breads with longer forms, such as baguettes, and products that require extensive stretching as part of shaping, including pizza dough and croissant dough, liquid levain is the right choice.

Volume, crust, and crumb characteristics as well as flavor and aroma can also be influenced by the use of liquid or firm levain. Because liquid levain creates better extensibility, these breads will have a nicer volume and more open crumb structure than breads made with a firm levain. Decorative cuts open more beautifully in breads containing liquid levain.

The choice of sourdough also affects the kind of acid produced during fermentation. The extra water in liquid levain promotes the production of mildly flavored lactic acid while a stiff sourdough culture promotes the production of tart acetic acidity. Thus, liquid sourdough will develop a milder acidic flavor in dough that is perfect for mild breads with a high percentage of white flour. The lactic flavor of liquid sourdough is also a good match for the flavor of the butter in sweet breads such as a brioche or croissant. Firmer sourdough has a stronger flavor that complements assertively flavored rye or whole wheat flour in whole grain bread recipes.

My Sourdough Starter, Step-by-Step

The following schedule is a guide for preparing a starter microbial culture, either liquid or stiff, from scratch. Do your best to keep the starter in the 70- to 74-degree range to encourage fermentation. You will see signs of fermentation as early as Day 2. If your schedule prevents you from feeding your culture on schedule every once in a while, don't worry. A missed feeding may slow down the development of your starter culture, but won't harm it. A mature culture will double in volume in 8 to 10 hours. Yours may reach this stage after five days, or may take an additional week or two to achieve peak power. During the process, you will have to discard significant quantities of immature culture. For ways to use this culture instead of throwing it all away, see the recipes in Chapter 9 (page 311).

	LIQUID SOURDOUGH CULTURE	FIRM SOURDOUGH CULTURE
Day 1 Feeding 1	Combine 100 g organic stone-ground whole wheat flour, 100 g Type 65–equivalent bread flour, and 200 g water in a clean, clear, straight-sided 2-quart container. Cover and let stand 24 hours.	Combine 100 g organic stone-ground whole wheat flour, 100 g Type 65–equivalent bread flour, and 130 g water in a clean, clear, straight-sided 2-quart container. Cover and let stand 24 hours.
Day 2 Feeding 1	Stir 100 g Type 65–equivalent bread flour and 100 g water into 100 g of yesterday's culture, discarding the leftover culture. Cover and let stand 12 hours.	Stir 100 g Type 65–equivalent bread flour and 50 g water into 100 g of yesterday's culture, discarding the leftover culture. Cover and let stand 12 hours.

	LIQUID SOURDOUGH CULTURE	FIRM SOURDOUGH CULTURE
Feeding 2	Stir 100 g Type 65–equivalent bread flour and 100 g water into 100 g of yesterday's culture, discarding the leftover culture. Cover and let stand 12 hours.	Stir 100 g Type 65–equivalent bread flour and 50 g water into 100 g of yesterday's culture, discarding the leftover culture. Cover and let stand 12 hours.
Day 3 Feeding 1	Stir 100 g Type 65–equivalent bread flour and 100 g water into 100 g of yesterday's culture, discarding the leftover culture. Cover and let stand 12 hours.	Stir 100 g Type 65–equivalent bread flour and 50 g water into 100 g of yesterday's culture, discarding the leftover culture. Cover and let stand 12 hours.
Feeding 2	Stir 100 g Type 65–equivalent bread flour and 100 g water into 100 g of yesterday's culture, discarding the leftover culture. Cover and let stand 12 hours.	Stir 100 g Type 65–equivalent bread flour and 50 g water into 100 g of yesterday's culture, discarding the leftover culture. Cover and let stand 12 hours.
Day 4 Feeding 1	Stir 100 g Type 65–equivalent bread flour and 100 g water into 100 g of yesterday's culture, discarding the leftover culture. Cover and let stand 12 hours.	Stir 100 g Type 65–equivalent bread flour and 50 g water into 100 g of yesterday's culture, discarding the leftover culture. Cover and let stand 12 hours.
Feeding 2	Stir 100 g Type 65–equivalent bread flour and 100 g water into 100 g of yesterday's culture, discarding the leftover culture. Cover and let stand 12 hours.	Stir 100 g Type 65–equivalent bread flour and 50 g water into 100 g of yesterday's culture, discarding the leftover culture. Cover and let stand 12 hours.
Day 5 Feeding 1	Stir 100 g type 65-equivalent bread flour and 100 g water into 100 g of yesterday's culture, discarding the leftover culture. Cover and let stand 12 hours.	Stir 100 g type 65-equivalent bread flour and 50 g water into 100 g of yesterday's culture, discarding the leftover culture. Cover and let stand 12 hours.
Feeding 2	Stir 100 g Type 65–equivalent bread flour and 100 g water into 100 g of yesterday's culture, discarding the leftover culture. Cover and let stand 12 hours.	Stir 100 g Type 65–equivalent bread flour and 50 g water into 100 g of yesterday's culture, discarding the leftover culture. Cover and let stand 12 hours.
Day 6 Feeding 1	Stir 100 g Type 65–equivalent bread flour and 100 g water into 100 g of yesterday's culture, discarding the leftover culture. Cover and let stand 6 to 8 hours.	Stir 100 g Type 65–equivalent bread flour and 50 g water into 100 g of yesterday's culture, discarding the leftover culture. Cover and let stand 6 to 8 hours.
Evaluate the culture	If the culture has doubled in volume during the previous 6 to 8 hours, if it has a nutty and pleasantly sour flavor, if it has a consistently bubbly structure (look through the clear sides of the container to see this), and if it has a bubbly surface with some little cracks, then it is ready to raise bread. At this stage, the culture becomes a starter. If it hasn't risen enough, feed it again according to schedule and continue to evaluate for signs of readiness.	If the culture has doubled in volume during the previous 6 to 8 hours, if it has a nutty and pleasantly sour flavor, and if it has a consistently bubbly structure (look through the clear sides of the container to see this), then it is ready to raise bread. The bubbles of a firm starter will be smaller than the bubbles of a liquid starter. The surface will dome a little bit and become slightly concave in the center. There might be some cracks on the surface of the sourdough. At this stage, the culture becomes a starter. If it hasn't risen enough, feed it again according to schedule and continue to evaluate for signs of readiness.

Judging the Vitality of Your Sourdough

In the absence of laboratory equipment, sensory clues will reveal whether or not your sourdough is ready to raise bread.

The most important indication is the time it takes to double in volume or reach its peak. It should take 6 to 8 hours. If your sourdough is taking longer, continue to feed on schedule for another day and reevaluate it.

Once a sourdough reaches its peak, it will hold that peak for a certain period of time before collapsing. A well-balanced starter will remain risen for an hour to an hour and a half. It is during this window that you should use it.

Take a look, also, at the sourdough's bubble structure. An immature starter will have tiny, foamy bubbles. A mature starter, in contrast, will have discernable bubbles, from 1/8 to 1/4 inch in diameter.

Finally, taste and smell your starter. A mature starter will have a medium-sour flavor with a detectable sweetness. There will be nutty notes from the wheat. A puckering acidity that obliterates all other flavors indicates a sourdough past its prime.

For extra precision and reassurance, you could test the pH of your starter with a portable pH meter. You want to see a reading in the 4 to 4.3 range. Anything lower indicates an excess of acids that might compromise yeast activity and flavor. Anything higher and the breads will lack depth of flavor and have a shorter shelf life.

From *Chef* to Levain

Now you have the sour ferment or culture—an active microbial culture (or starter culture or, simply, starter). In France, it is called a *chef*. In Germany, it is an *anstellgut*. *Pasta madre* is the Italian equivalent. *Masa madre,* the Spanish term. You are almost, but not quite, ready to bake a loaf of sourdough bread. Think of your *chef* as an ingredient that needs to be prepped before it is used in a recipe, the way a carrot requires peeling or mushrooms are chopped before they are added to soup.

To prepare the sourdough, you are going to mix a portion of it with flour and water and let it ferment

Early morning at
Denise Backerin

for a short period of time. In addition to maintaining the culture's activity, this final backslopping will give you the exact amount of starter you will need for a particular recipe. This exact amount is your *levain*. Because the amount of levain needed varies from recipe to recipe, each recipe in this book contains instructions on how to mix the appropriate amount and type of sourdough.

Influencing Your Culture

Professional bakers have well-established routines for preparing a levain that produces the breads they want. When I spent time in both Lionel Poilâne's and Max Poilâne's boulangeries in Paris in the early 1980s, I admired the simplicity and efficiency with which they perpetuated their starter and crafted their sourdough breads. A large well-used fork mixer was the only piece of equipment, and it was in constant use. After mixing simple levain-risen dough from Type 85 levain dough in the bowl, the bakers would remove enough to shape as many loaves as would fit in the next oven bake, leaving behind about 20 kilos of dough in each bowl. This leftover dough, full of active natural yeast, was fed for the next batch and allowed to ferment. Each day at the oldest bakeries in Altamura, stiff bricks of semolina flour, water, and starter are wrapped in linen and stored in a cool stone chamber to ferment. When the culture is ready, some of it is added to bread dough while the leftovers are used to make new bricks.

Twenty-first-century German and Northern European bakers are more likely to utilize newer technologies, like programmed sourdough fermentation tanks. The Ipeka Sourmatic, a Finnish tank, is a stainless-steel container encased in a water jacket, equipped with a heating element for heating and cooling the culture as necessary. Stainless-steel blades can be programmed to rotate at different speeds and in different directions to keep the sourdough smooth and to incorporate fresh air

on a regular basis. HB-Technik, an Austrian company, makes tanks that can be programmed to follow a 25-step recipe for fermentation. The tanks are 100-percent sealed, guaranteeing that no rogue bacteria floating in the air will contaminate the established culture, a guarantee of uniform bread quality. They are also designed to be cleaned and disinfected very easily. At Bread Alone, we use a sourdough tank manufactured by IsernHager that has temperature, time, and agitation controls. Even with all of our experience and equipment, professional bakers accept that there will always be variations in the flavor of their culture, day to day.

Bakers who do not have access to high-tech equipment can still control the four variables that influence the flavor, texture, and microbial activity of a sourdough. By increasing or decreasing the hydration, percentage of starter you use to build your levain, temperature, and/or fermentation time, you can cultivate a flavor profile and activity level that suits your needs.

Here are some sourdough practices that any baker can follow to control the growth of a sourdough culture:

- For a mild sourdough with medium-sour lactic acid: Reduce the amount of starter to 10 percent, keep hydration at 100 percent, use 70-degree water, and ferment your sourdough 8 to 10 hours at cool room temperature, 70 to 72 degrees.

- For a sourdough with more pronounced acetic acid and much more sour tang: Use 20 percent starter, 100 percent hydration, 75-degree water; ferment at warm room temperature, 75 to 80 degrees, for 3 hours; and refrigerate overnight.

- For a starter with a nice balance of lactic and acetic acids: Use 10 percent starter, 65 percent hydration, 55- to 60-degree water, ferment at cool room temperature, 70 to 72 degrees, overnight.

- For a starter that is the most sour of the four, and with a much higher percentage of acetic acid: Use 20 percent starter, 65 percent hydration, 75-degree water; ferment for 3 hours at cool room temperature, 70 to 72 degrees; and then refrigerate overnight.

Maintaining Your Sourdough over Time

You've spent 5 to 14 days cultivating your sourdough. You certainly don't want to do this every time you bake a loaf of bread, and it won't be necessary if you take care to maintain your culture. It's simple. After you've made the levain from your *chef*, you'll refresh a portion of the leftover *chef* with flour and water, let it ferment for just a couple of hours, and then keep it in the refrigerator to slow its fermentation and keep it in baking shape for several days or up to one week. When you are ready to bake, you'll do the levain feeding (once or several times depending on the activity of the culture; longer refrigeration times with no feeding will require more feedings to get a levain active enough to ferment the final dough) and proceed with your recipe.

	LIQUID SOURDOUGH STARTER	FIRM SOURDOUGH STARTER
Maintenance feeding	Stir 100 g Type 65-equivalent bread flour and 120 g water (80 to 85 degrees) into 30 g of the leftover ripe culture, discarding what remains. Cover and let stand at room temperature for 2 to 3 hours, then refrigerate until ready to use, up to 1 week.	Stir 100 g Type 65-equivalent bread flour and 65 g water (80 to 85 degrees) into 30 g of the leftover ripe culture, discarding what remains. Cover and let stand at room temperature for 2 to 3 hours, then refrigerate until ready to use, up to 1 week.

Building Ancient and Heritage Grain Sourdoughs with Your Starter

You can build an emmer, einkorn, or spelt sourdough, or a Turkey Red or Senatore Cappelli sourdough by simply substituting your flour or flours of choice for the wheat flour in the recipes above. The process will take 5 days to 2 weeks, the same as if you were working with wheat flour. If you are already maintaining a starter (made with any grain), you can hasten the process by adding 15 grams of your ripe sourdough to the new culture on Day 1. If you do this, you will have 200 grams of ripe ancient or heritage grain starter in 6 to 8 hours.

Pane Altamura at
Pane di Nunzio

Rye Sourdough Starter

In Northern Europe, where 100 percent rye breads are popular, every baker I have met initiates and maintains cultures with rye flour. The process is similar to cultivating a wheat starter, but with a couple of significant differences. Because rye flour can be very absorbent and starchy, bakers generally increase hydration to 125 percent. The mixture will ferment more quickly than a sourdough made with wheat flour, because rye is lower in gluten and higher in enzymes than wheat flour.

LIQUID RYE SOURDOUGH STARTER	
Day 1 Feeding 1	Combine 200 g whole rye flour and 250 g water in a clean, clear, straight-sided 2-quart container. Cover and let stand 24 hours.
Day 2 Feeding 1	Stir 100 g rye flour and 125 g water into 50 g of yesterday's culture, discarding the leftover culture. Cover and let stand 8 hours.
Feeding 2	Stir 100 g rye flour and 125 g water into 25 g of yesterday's culture, discarding the leftover culture. Cover and let stand 16 hours
Day 3 Feeding 1	Stir 100 g rye flour and 125 g water into 50 g of yesterday's culture, discarding the leftover culture. Cover and let stand 8 hours.
Feeding 2	Stir 100 g rye flour and 125 g water into 25 g of yesterday's culture, discarding the leftover culture. Cover and let stand 16 hours
Day 4 Feeding 1	Stir 100 g rye flour and 125 g water into 50 g of yesterday's culture, discarding the leftover culture. Cover and let stand 6 to 8 hours.
Evaluate the culture	If the culture has doubled in volume during the previous 6 to 8 hours, if it has a nutty and pleasantly sour flavor, and if it has a consistently bubbly structure (look through the clear sides of the container to see this), then it is ready to raise bread. At this stage the culture becomes a starter. If it hasn't risen enough, feed it again according to schedule and continue to evaluate for signs of readiness.

As with a wheat sourdough, you'll need to nourish your rye sourdough once more before using it:

Anstellgut feeding	Stir 100 g rye flour and 125 g water into 15 to 30 g of the ripe culture, setting the remaining culture aside. Cover and let stand until doubled in volume, 6 to 8 hours.

And as with wheat sourdough, you'll feed some of the leftover sourdough to keep it in baking shape for next time:

Maintenance feeding	Stir 100 g rye flour and 125 g water into 25 g of the leftover ripe culture, discarding what remains. Cover and let stand at room temperature for 2 to 3 hours and then refrigerate until ready to use, up to 1 week.

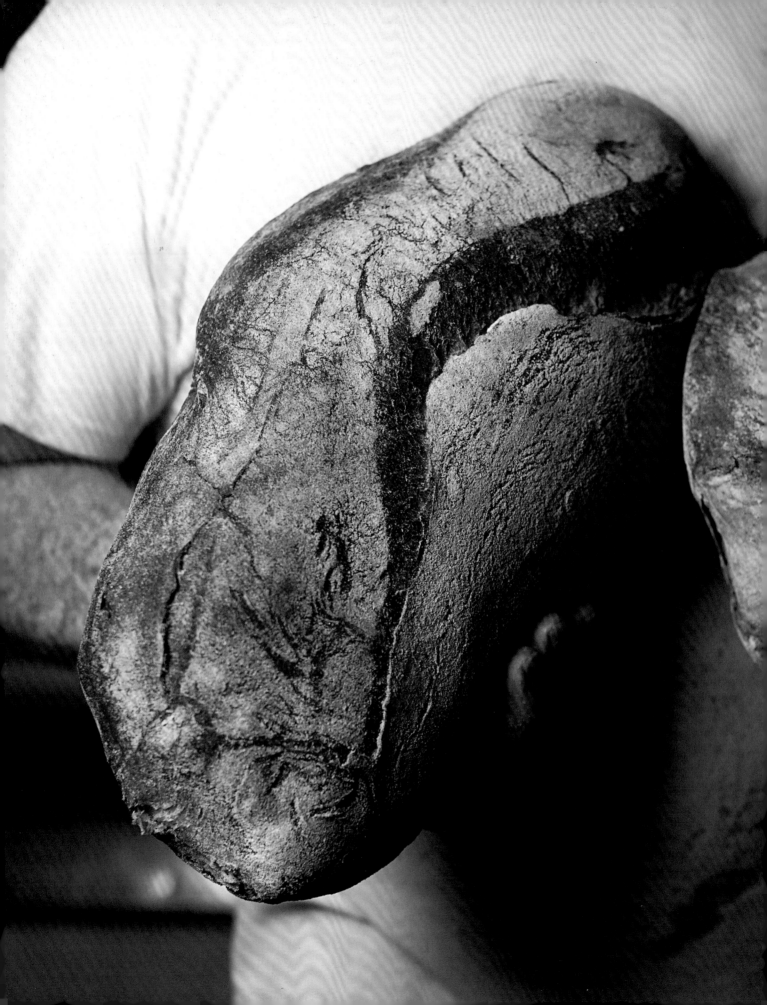

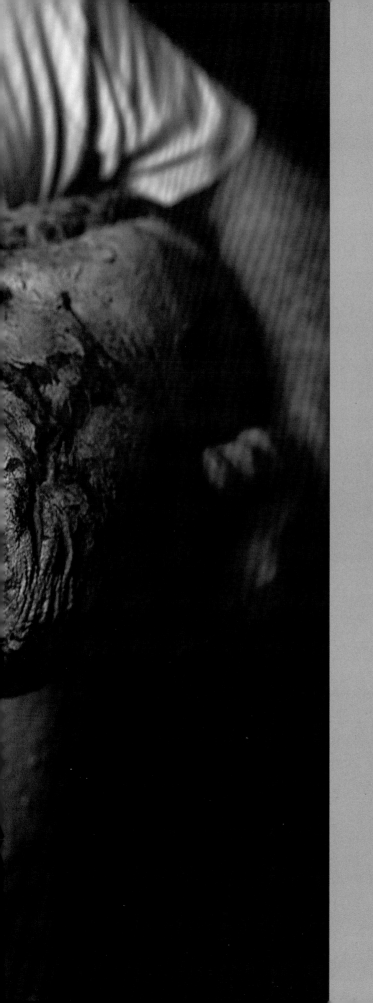

7
SIMPLE
SOURDOUGHS

If you've cultivated a sourdough starter, you've already done most of the time-consuming work necessary to make any of the breads in this chapter. These recipes follow a straightforward pattern: A prescribed amount of sourdough is fed with an exact amount of fresh flour and water and allowed to ferment for 6 to 12 hours. The result is a starter with the right balance of yeast activity and acid development to raise and flavor your bread. This starter is simply mixed with the remaining dough ingredients, and your dough begins to ferment.

PARISIAN ARTISAN-ENTREPRENEUR

RODOLPHE LANDEMAINE, MAISON LANDEMAINE, PARIS, FRANCE

Rodolphe Landemaine's smartly knotted scarf flies behind him as he marches through the streets around his Rue des Martyrs bakery. With his trendy neckwear and closely trimmed beard, the 39-year-old might be taken for a proprietor of a precious, one-man boutique bakery. But as he weaves through the long line of customers leading from the street to the counter, they sense his seriousness and energy. It is clear he is an impatient baker with a larger mission, one that he's well on his way to fulfilling.

Landemaine worked for pastry giant Pierre Hermé, among others, before setting out on his own with the idea of bringing artisan breads to the masses while offering training and opportunity to anyone with a bit of baking ambition and talent. His delicious sourdough breads, made with certified organic French stone-ground flour from Moulin Decollogne in Précy-sur-Marne, northeast of Paris, place him squarely within the tradition of French artisan bakers. His global view of artisan bread as integral to metropolitan life and an engine of economic progress distinguishes him. I wasn't surprised to learn that he was a Campagnon du Devoir, having gone through a rigorous training program for bakers and other artisans that emphasizes the common good along with skill.

Rodolphe was never going to be the village baker in front of the oven or behind the counter. He was always going to be a baker-entrepreneur.

A biology student with a strong interest in business, he became inspired by an observation made by his father. "You want to work with something that is alive, and also be an entrepreneur," said the older man. "Do you know how many opportunities there are in the bakery business?" As he worked his way through apprenticeships and stints in famous kitchens throughout France, he always had an entrepreneurial spirit and the big picture in mind. It wasn't enough to bake good bread. He wanted to bake it in the right places, where a lot of people could easily stop by to get it. He thought about how to display it—on plain shelves, with no baskets. Even though he now owns 13 bakeries in Paris, one in Normandy, and two in Tokyo, he has set up each one with small ovens, so small amounts of fresh bread come out all day long.

It's old-school bread, but sold in a new environment. The shop we sat in as we talked, Rodolphe told me, would serve 2,400 customers that day. I got the sense that he opens shops on instinct, seizing an opportunity in a new location when he sees one and when he has employees he wants to advance.

Rodolphe is committed to baking a certain type of traditional French bread. He works with three types of sourdough: He keeps his liquid levain in a temperature-controlled tank. The soft and batter-like rye sour that he uses for his *tourte de seigle* is kept in a special stone crock near the side of the oven at each bakery to keep it warm. In a cooler spot, he keeps the firm levain, large flecks of bran speckling the dough, in a plastic bin resembling a laundry basket. He regularly rips open the levain and brings it to his nose like a sommelier smelling the cork of

a rare vintage. That's how he evaluates its flavor quality and its readiness to raise his classic *pain au levain*. He laughs at the current fetishization of large holes in a bread's crumb. In French, he calls it *alvéolage exotique* (exotic airholes). "There's a lot more to good bread than big holes." Yes, some of his breads are bubbly. But others, including his *tourte de seigle,* made with 100 percent rye, are purposely dense. With his recipes, he is looking at the whole bread. "It's not about the extra 0.25 percent water you are able to squeeze into the dough," he told me. "It's about the flavor, the texture, the crust." His loaves are rustic and earthy, with an intoxicating fragrance and tremendous solidity.

BAGUETTE DE TRADITION

START TO FINISH:
19½ to 26
hours

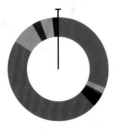

LIQUID LEVAIN STARTER
6 to 8 hours

AUTOLYSE
30 minutes

KNEAD
13 minutes

FIRST FERMENTATION
1 hour

RETARD
8 to 12 hours

WARM UP
1½ to 2 hours

REST
40 minutes

FINAL PROOF
1 hour

BAKE
25 to 30 minutes

MAKES
three 358-gram loaves

With the movement in France toward longer-fermented breads, many bakers are introducing long-fermented baguettes into their repertoire. Rodolphe Landemaine gave me this recipe for his *baguette de tradition*. It's a mix of sweet and sour, with a rich caramelized crust and bubbly but not over-airy crumb. To get this bubbly texture, he uses a liquid levain starter (while preferring a firm starter for his classic miche and other wheat breads). He's keen not to develop too much acidity in his liquid levain, keeping it fairly young by fermenting it for only 6 to 8 hours. Retarding the dough overnight results in a slightly tangy flavor. He puts the baguettes in the oven before they are fully risen to ensure a moistness and denseness to the crumb.

It is very common for bakers making this type of baguette to add an infinitesimal amount of yeast to improve the bread's volume. Yeast is optional; it's up to you. According to the French Bread Law (the Décret Pain) of 1993, this is perfectly legitimate. By law, bakers are allowed to add up to 2 grams per kilo of flour and still call their breads *pain au levain*.

Although a traditional baguette is 22 inches long, most home ovens can't accommodate breads of this length. This recipe will give you three 14-inch baguettes.

INGREDIENTS	BAKER'S %	METRIC WEIGHT
LIQUID LEVAIN STARTER		
Liquid Sourdough Starter (page 182)	16	16 g
Water	100	100 g
Type 65 or equivalent flour (11 to 11.5% protein)	100	100 g
FINAL DOUGH		
Type 65 or equivalent flour (11 to 11.5% protein)	100	545 g
Water	55	300 g
Salt	2.4	13 g
Dry instant yeast (optional)	0.2	1 g
Liquid levain starter	40	216 g

recipe continues

recipe continued from previous page

1. **PREPARE THE LIQUID LEVAIN STARTER**: In a small bowl, dissolve the sourdough starter in the water. Stir in the flour until well incorporated. Cover and let ferment at room temperature (68 to 77 degrees) until doubled in volume, 6 to 8 hours.

2. **AUTOLYSE**: Combine the flour and 280 g of the water in the bowl of an electric mixer fitted with a dough hook. Mix with a rubber spatula just until a dry and shabby dough forms. Cover and let rest 30 minutes.

3. **MAKE THE FINAL DOUGH**: Add the salt, yeast if using, and levain to the bowl. With the dough hook, mix on the lowest setting until the dough comes together, 30 seconds. Turn the mixer to low (2 on a KitchenAid mixer) and mix until the dough is soft and elastic with a velvety texture, and slightly sticky to the touch, 8 minutes. Pull the dough off the hook, and then with the mixer on low, slowly drizzle the remaining 20 g water into the bowl. Continue to mix until the dough is very soft, elastic, and shiny, another 4 minutes.

4. **FIRST FERMENTATION**: Use a dough scraper to transfer the dough to a lightly oiled, clear 4-quart container with a lid. With damp hands, turn the dough over so all sides are oiled. Cover and let stand at room temperature for 1½ hours.

5. **RETARD**: Refrigerate overnight, 8 to 12 hours.

6. **WARM UP**: Remove the dough from the refrigerator and let warm up on the countertop 1½ to 2 hours.

7. **REST**: On a lightly floured countertop, divide the dough into three equal pieces. Gently press them into 4- by 5-inch rectangles. Dust with flour and cover with plastic. Let rest 40 minutes.

8. **FINAL PROOF**: Cover a baker's peel or rimless baking sheet with parchment. Shape each piece of dough into a baguette (see page 78) about 14 inches long. Dust the parchment-covered peel or baking sheet with flour and place the baguettes on the parchment, seam side down, 3 inches apart. Lift the parchment paper between the loaves, making a pleat and drawing the loaves close together. Tightly roll up two kitchen towels and slip them under the parchment paper on the sides of the outer loaves to support each baguette. Alternatively, use baker's linen instead of parchment. Lightly dust the dough with flour and drape with plastic wrap. Let stand 1 hour.

9. **BAKE**: About 1 hour before baking, place a baking stone on the middle rack of the oven and a cast-iron skillet on the lower rack. Preheat the oven to 450 degrees for 1 hour. Uncover the breads, remove the rolled-up towels, and stretch the parchment paper out so that it is flat and the loaves are separated. With a *lame*, a single-edged razor blade, or a serrated knife, make three angled slashes, 2½ inches long and about ½ inch deep, down the length of each loaf. Slide the loaves, still on the parchment, onto the baking stone. Place 1 cup of ice cubes in the skillet to produce steam. Bake until the loaves are golden brown and well risen, 25 to 30 minutes. Slide the loaves, still on the parchment, onto a wire rack. Cool completely. Store in a brown paper bag at room temperature for up to 2 days.

Note for Professional Bakers

After mixing, you can place the dough in dough tubs (scaled at the required weight for a hydraulic dough divider) and leave to ferment overnight at 40 degrees.

CURRY TOMATO CIABATTA

Jochen Gaues's take on Italian ciabatta is as quirky, colorful, and unexpectedly explosive as he is. There's a lot of curry powder in the bread, giving it a spicy aroma and bright golden hue. The chopped walnuts and tomato paste add richness and umami flavor. The texture of this bread is likewise unique. The dough is very soft and baked at a high temperature, so the result is a dark, rigid crust encasing an incredibly moist crumb. Jochen slices it thin and serves it with tart goat cheese or assertively flavored ham or salami.

INGREDIENTS	BAKER'S %	METRIC WEIGHT
RYE SOURDOUGH STARTER		
Whole rye flour	100	30 g
Stale rye bread, coarsely ground	55	17 g
Water	155	47 g
Liquid Sourdough Starter (page 182)	20	6 g
FINAL DOUGH		
Type 65 or equivalent flour (11 to 11.5% protein)	100	500 g
Water	70	350 g
Instant yeast	1	5 g
Sugar	3	15 g
Rye sourdough starter	20	100 g
Salt	2.8	14
Walnuts, toasted and finely chopped	5	25 g
Onion, chopped	5	25 g
Sicilian green olives, pitted and chopped	5	25 g
Tomato paste	5	25 g
Curry powder	5	25 g

recipe continues

START TO FINISH:

20 to 28

hours

RYE SOURDOUGH STARTER
6 to 8 hours

KNEAD
15 minutes

FIRST FERMENTATION
1¾ hours

RETARD
10 to 14 hours

WARM UP
1½ to 2 hours

REST
40 minutes

BAKE
30 minutes

MAKES
two 554-gram loaves

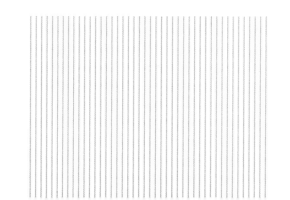

recipe continued from previous page

1. **PREPARE THE RYE SOURDOUGH STARTER**: In a small bowl, stir together the rye flour, ground stale bread, water, and sourdough starter until well incorporated. Cover and let ferment at room temperature (68 to 77 degrees) until doubled in volume, 6 to 8 hours.

2. **MAKE THE FINAL DOUGH**: Combine the flour, water, yeast, sugar, rye sourdough starter, and salt in the bowl of an electric mixer fitted with a dough hook. Mix with a rubber spatula until a rough dough forms. With the dough hook, mix on low (2 on a KitchenAid mixer) for 5 minutes. Turn the mixer to medium-low (4 on a KitchenAid mixer) and mix for 7 more minutes. Turn the mixer back to low, add the walnuts, onion, olives, tomato paste, and curry powder to the bowl and mix until incorporated. Turn back to medium-low and knead until well distributed, another 2 to 3 minutes.

3. **FIRST FERMENTATION**: Transfer the dough to a lightly oiled, clear 4-quart container with a lid. Turn the dough over so all sides are oiled. Cover and let stand 1 hour. Turn the dough out onto a lightly floured counter. Pat into a 6- by 8-inch rectangle and fold like a business letter. Slide both hands under the dough and flip it over so the folds are underneath. Slip it back into the container, cover, and let stand another 45 minutes. Repeat the folding and turning and return to the container.

4. **RETARD**: Cover and refrigerate for 10 to 14 hours.

5. **WARM UP**: Remove the dough from the refrigerator and let stand on the countertop to warm up, 1½ to 2 hours.

6. Line a baker's peel or rimless baking sheet with parchment paper and dust with flour. Place a baking stone on the middle rack of the oven and a cast-iron skillet on the lower rack. Preheat the oven to 450 degrees.

7. **REST**: On a heavily floured countertop, gently press the dough into a rectangle 9 by 11 inches. With a bench scraper or chef's knife, cut into two rectangles 4½ by 11 inches. Transfer to the baker's peel, bottom sides up. Dust with flour and cover with plastic. Let rest for 40 minutes.

8. **BAKE**: Right before they go into the oven, with four fingers of one hand, dimple each ciabatta at 1-inch intervals. Slide the loaves, still on the parchment, onto the baking stone. Place 1 cup of ice cubes in the skillet to produce steam. Bake for 10 minutes. Turn the heat down to 425 degrees and continue to bake until the loaves are nicely browned and puffy, another 20 minutes. Slide the loaves, still on the parchment, onto a wire rack. Cool completely. Curry Tomato Ciabatta is best eaten on the day it is baked, but you can store it in a brown paper bag at room temperature for up to 2 days.

Note for Professional Bakers

The double hydration technique can also be used for this bread. One hour after mixing the dough, fold it, return it to the oiled dough tub, and refrigerate overnight. The dough can then be divided the next day when needed.

BRIOCHE CRÈME FRAÎCHE

START TO FINISH:

24 to 28½
hours

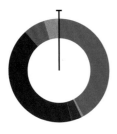

LIQUID LEVAIN STARTER
12 hours

KNEAD
14 minutes

FIRST FERMENTATION
1 hour

RETARD
8 to 12 hours

WARM UP
1½ to 2 hours

FINAL PROOF
1 hour

BAKE
20 minutes

MAKES
twelve 100-gram rolls

It's rare to visit a boulangerie in France that doesn't offer brioche. Often, brioche dough is used to make a wide variety of smaller savory and sweet items. We've always made brioche at Bread Alone, and we make a pecan-caramel bun with brioche dough as its base.

There is no shortage of brioche recipes available to the home baker. But this recipe, developed by my colleague and friend Didier Rosada, is particularly creamy, velvety, and rich. The addition of crème fraîche, milder than sour cream or yogurt but with a similarly tangy taste, creates a unique texture and adds a nutty, gently sour flavor, giving the bread a dimensionality that I love. I particularly enjoy the contrast between the sour tang of the dough and the sweetness of the candied fruit. Another benefit: The added butterfat from the crème fraîche helps the bread hold on to its moisture and freshness for days.

I particularly like it shaped into small rolls for breakfast. You can also bake this dough in two traditional brioche pans. If you have leftovers, freeze them in a zipper-lock bag, then reheat in a 300-degree oven until warmed through.

INGREDIENTS	BAKER'S %	METRIC WEIGHT
LIQUID LEVAIN STARTER		
Type 55 or equivalent flour (11 to 11.5% protein)	100	46 g
Water	100	46 g
Liquid Sourdough Starter (page 182)	20	9 g
FINAL DOUGH		
Type 55 or equivalent flour (11 to 11.5% protein)	100	504 g
Water	10	51 g
Eggs	13	66 g
Sugar	18	91 g
Salt	2	10 g
Dry instant yeast	1.2	6 g
Liquid levain starter	20	101 g
Crème fraîche	25	126 g
Unsalted butter, softened and cut into 8 pieces	25	126 g
Candied orange peel, finely chopped	12	60 g
Candied lemon peel, finely chopped	12	60 g
FINISH		
1 large egg, lightly beaten		57 g
Pearl sugar		150 g

1. **PREPARE THE LIQUID LEVAIN STARTER**: In a small bowl, stir together the flour, water, and sourdough starter until well incorporated. Cover and let ferment at room temperature (68 to 77 degrees) until doubled in volume, about 12 hours.

2. **MAKE THE FINAL DOUGH**: Combine the flour, water, eggs, sugar, salt, yeast, liquid levain starter, and crème fraîche in the bowl of an electric mixer fitted with a dough hook. Stir with a spatula just until a rough dough forms. With the dough hook, mix on low speed (2 on a KitchenAid mixer) for 2 minutes. Turn to medium-low (4 on a KitchenAid mixer) and continue to knead until the dough is elastic and cleans the sides of the bowl, another 5 minutes. With

recipe continues

recipe continued from previous page

the mixer on low (2 on a KitchenAid mixer), add the butter, 1 tablespoon at a time, and then kneading on the lowest speed between each addition to incorporate, about 8 minutes. Knead in the candied orange and lemon peel until evenly distributed.

3. **FIRST FERMENTATION**: Transfer the dough to a lightly oiled, clear 4-quart container with a lid. Turn the dough over so all sides are oiled. Cover and let ferment 1 hour.

4. **RETARD**: Refrigerate overnight, 8 to 12 hours.

5. **WARM UP**: Take the dough out of the refrigerator and let it warm up for 1½ to 2 hours.

6. **FINAL PROOF**: Line a rimmed baking sheet with parchment paper. On a lightly floured countertop, divide the dough into 12 equal pieces. Shape into rounds and/or ovals (see page 78). Place each piece, seam side down, on the prepared pan. Drape with plastic wrap and let stand until increased in volume by 50 percent, about 1 hour.

7. **BAKE**: Preheat the oven to 350 degrees. Brush the top of each roll with egg and sprinkle liberally with pearl sugar. With sharp scissors, make three decorative cuts on the top of each roll. Bake until the rolls are well risen and golden, about 20 minutes. Slide the rolls, still on the parchment, onto a wire rack and let cool completely. Store in a brown paper bag at room temperature for 5 days.

Note for Professional Bakers

In a production environment, this dough could be retarded in bulk or right after shaping. When retarded in bulk in the refrigerator, the dough is a bit easier to work with as the butter isn't as soft and the dough not as sticky. Always let the dough ferment at room temperature for about 1 hour before retarding in bulk, to initiate the fermentation activity.

THE FREE BAKER

ARND ERBEL, BÄCKEREI ERBEL, DACHSBACH, GERMANY

Joerg Lehmann, my partner in *Living Bread,* called me excitedly one day and told me that he had found possibly the best baker in Germany, in a small village outside of Nuremberg. "Dan, this man lives, thinks, works, dreams bread every second of his life." The next time I was in Berlin, I tasted a selection of Arnd's breads that Joerg had brought back to his studio.

Joerg told me that Arnd Erbel works in an old-fashioned bakery in Dachsbach, a tiny town of 600. Unlike most German bakers, who primarily bake German breads, I saw right away that Arnd has been influenced by his travels and studies throughout Europe. His large, golden-crumbed wheat loaves reminded me of the great breads I ate around Lake Como in northern Italy. His sourdough miche is clearly influenced by Poilâne. His *cantucci* are similar to classic Tuscan biscotti but with a Bavarian twist because they are made with local spelt. His richly flavored, compact, dense, chewy, earthy rye sourdough breads were a revelation. When I tasted them, I knew instantly that I needed to meet Arnd and watch him work, so I could reproduce his *Wurzlaib,* a rye with intriguing layers of flavor coming from small amounts of buckwheat and smoked spelt flours, and his *Drescherlaib,* a massive 12-pound whole rye loaf fragrant with Franconian spices like fennel and coriander.

Arnd is a 12th-generation baker running a family business that was founded in 1680. His shop is in a two-story cottage with a sloping red-tiled roof and a hand-lettered sign, spelling out *Arnd Erbel Bäkerei* in gothic letters. In the small-ish workroom, five bakers make bread almost completely by hand. A serious man with a cleanly shaved head and wire-rimmed glasses, Arnd speaks emphatically about his beliefs.

Born in 1969, he was a foodie from the time he could walk, impressed early on by the food-centric culture of the Italian Alps, where his parents took him to ski as a small child. He

learned to bake during a traditional German apprenticeship, where he worked for three years at a bakery, taking classes one day out of every week. Even as an apprentice, he rebelled against his bosses' use of convenience products, trying to eliminate them from recipes without letting anyone know. He told himself, "I work this way or I don't work." He has maintained this philosophy to this day.

He advanced in the culinary world, moving to Vienna to learn to make elaborate pastries, and working at high-end restaurants and hotels as a *chef patissier*. Over the years, luxury foods in luxury settings interested him less and less. "I found the world of the simple things," he said. In 2006, he returned to Dachsbach to bake breads with integrity. "I like to live in the landscape here," he says. "I like to work with my hands and be close to nature with the farmers. That is my passion, that is my life." It is unusual for a baker to work as closely with a farmer as Arnd does. He buys his grain directly from Karl Brehm, a former architect who took over his parents' farm and transitioned to organics, two villages away in Lonnerstadt. "When it is time to harvest, when the grain is on the field, and it comes into the barn, I take it, I mill it, and make very fresh bread. I look forward to this moment all year, to bring this very fresh min-

eral taste into the bakery." He either mills the grain himself, using a small onsite stone mill, or he has miller Michael Litz, also close by in Gremsdorf, mill the grain for him. Each field, every season, produces a different flour with different baking properties. Arnd calls himself a *freibacker* not only because he lives in the Free State of Bavaria, but because he freely adjusts his formulas depending on what the flour needs, and only bakes what the seasons call for. This means that if local buckwheat isn't available, "I wouldn't buy buckwheat from China." Nor is he interested in baking novelty breads. "If we had two hours, we could create a hundred kinds of breads, but I would never add curried ketchup and wurst to a bread just to say I have made a currywurst bread."

He likes to say that there is only one bread recipe: flour, water, salt. Everything else is good local ingredients and craftsmanship. As for measurements, "The flour tells me the hydration." He finds the process endlessly interesting, and he is not alone. "A friend I have is an astrophysics professor. He started baking his own bread years ago. Every day, he looks at the stars with big telescopes. And he said, 'Every day I see things that no other people before me have seen. But the most interesting thing is to bake bread.'"

Bread cooling at Bäckerei Erbel

DRESCHERLAIB

Arnd Erbel makes this loaf in one size—12 kilos—and sells it whole or by the half. The extra-large size means that the fermentation time is very long, allowing for a lot of flavor to develop. Baking time is long, too—close to 2 hours—resulting in an incredibly thick, chewy, rich crust. Arnd's breads are really out of the ordinary. They all have a humble quality, as if they have time-traveled through history and into his shop. Their texture is dense but not at all heavy. Their flavor is rich and complex, but also elementally pleasing.

Of course, you can't make a 12-kilo loaf in a home oven, but you can make a 1½-kilo loaf with a similar character. To approximate Arnd's uniquely soulful bread, you need a high percentage of very active and robust rye starter, whole (not sifted) spelt flour, and the freshest, most fragrant spices. The dough ferments very slowly, and requires a banneton while proofing, to maintain its shape and integrity. Baking the large loaf in a Dutch oven helps contain the soft dough, giving the bread a good shape and encouraging crust development.

START TO FINISH:

13

hours

RYE STARTER
8 hours

AUTOLYSE
30 minutes

KNEAD
15 minutes

FIRST FERMENTATION
2½ hours

FINAL PROOF
1½ hours

BAKE
45 minutes

MAKES
one 1.5-kilo loaf

INGREDIENTS	BAKER'S %	METRIC WEIGHT
RYE STARTER		
Whole rye flour	100	140 g
Water	80	112 g
Rye Sourdough Starter (page 183)	20	28 g
FINAL DOUGH		
Whole rye flour	20	140 g
Whole spelt flour	80	560 g
Water	75	525 g
Salt	2.4	17 g
Rye starter	40	280 g
Fennel seed	1.4	10 g
Coriander seed	1.4	10 g
Caraway seed	1.4	10 g

recipe continues

recipe continued from previous page

1. **PREPARE THE RYE STARTER**: In a small bowl, combine the rye flour, water, and sourdough starter. Cover and let ferment at room temperature for 8 hours.

2. **AUTOLYSE**: In the bowl of an electric mixer fitted with a dough hook, combine the rye flour, spelt flour, and 475 g of the water. Stir with a rubber spatula until a rough dough forms. Cover and let stand 30 minutes.

3. **MAKE THE FINAL DOUGH**: Add the salt, rye starter, fennel, coriander, and caraway to the bowl and stir with a spatula to incorporate. With the dough hook, mix the dough on low speed (2 on a KitchenAid mixer) for 7 minutes, stopping as necessary to pull the dough off the hook. Turn the mixer to medium speed (6 on a KitchenAid mixer) and mix for 2 minutes. Turn the mixer back down to low, slowly drizzle in the remaining 50 g water, and mix until the water is incorporated. Turn the mixer to medium and continue to knead until the dough is well developed, another 4 minutes. The dough will be soft and sticky with a very weak elasticity.

4. **FIRST FERMENTATION**: Transfer the dough to a lightly oiled, clear 4-quart container with a lid. Cover and let rise 1½ hours. Moisten your hands and slide them under the dough, folding it like a business letter. Slide both hands under the dough and flip it over so the folds are underneath. Slip it back into the container, cover, and let stand another 1 hour.

5. **FINAL PROOF**: On a floured countertop, shape the dough into a loose boule (see page 78). Generously and evenly dust the inside of a banneton with rye flour. (Alternatively, line a large bowl with a kitchen towel and dust it with flour.) Place the boule, smooth side down, in the banneton. Lightly dust with flour and cover loosely with plastic wrap. Let stand until pillowy, about 1½ hours.

6. **BAKE**: About 1 hour before baking, position an oven rack in the bottom third of the oven and set a Dutch oven (with the lid on) on the rack. Preheat the oven to 450 degrees for 1 hour. Wearing oven mitts, carefully remove the Dutch oven to a heatproof surface and take off the lid. Tip the dough onto a peel or your hands and put in the Dutch oven (no scoring necessary for this one). Put the lid on and bake for 25 minutes. Turn the heat down to 425 degrees. Remove the lid and bake until a rich caramel brown, about 20 minutes more. Carefully turn the loaf out onto a wire rack. Cool completely. Store in a brown paper bag at room temperature for 3 to 4 days.

Notes for Professional Bakers

As this is a fragile dough, if possible, leave the dough in the mixing bowl after mixing. Then after 1 hour, turn on the mixer for about 30 seconds, in first speed. The gentle mechanical action of the dough hook will duplicate the manual folding of the dough, increasing its strength and making it easier to handle. Depending on the strength of the flour, you can do this once or twice. At the end of the first fermentation, the larger pieces of dough can be directly scaled from the mixing bowl, gently shaped, and placed in bannetons.

REIKALEIPA

As I was putting the finishing touches on this book, Joerg from Tuorilan Kotileipomo called me from his summer vacation in Finland and said he had one more bread we had to include. At a tiny bakery in Porvoo, the second-oldest town in the country, he spotted these traditional doughnut-shaped Finnish rye breads, stacked on a dowel on the counter. Because of its shape, it is lighter and crustier than pan ryes from Germany and the Baltic region. Those heavier ryes often have damp centers because of the grain's starchiness. But this bread, called *reikaleipa* in Finnish, has a high ratio of crust to crumb, more like a moist, rugged cracker than a traditional rye loaf. The bakery's owners, Marjo and Tero Peltonen, bake the cut-out centers alongside the loaves and sell them as rolls. They kindly shared their recipe with Joerg after he snapped some photos of the breads and their adorable cafe, with its mismatched vintage chairs, old-fashioned green-and-white patterned wallpaper, and fresh flowers on the tables.

INGREDIENTS	BAKER'S %	METRIC WEIGHT
RYE SOURDOUGH STARTER		
Whole rye flour, coarsely ground	100	280 g
Water	100	280 g
Liquid Sourdough Starter (page 182)	34	95 g
FINAL DOUGH		
Whole rye flour	100	491 g
Water	58	284 g
Dry instant yeast (optional)	2	10 g
Salt	2.8	14 g
Rye sourdough starter	133	655 g

1. **PREPARE THE RYE SOURDOUGH STARTER**: In a small bowl, stir together the rye flour, water, and sourdough starter until well incorporated. Cover and let ferment at room temperature (68 to 77 degrees) until doubled in volume, 12 hours.

recipe continues

START TO FINISH:
14½
hours

RYE SOURDOUGH STARTER
12 hours

KNEAD
8 minutes

FIRST FERMENTATION
1½ hours

REST
10 minutes

BAKE
40 minutes

MAKES
one 1.4-kilo loaf

recipe continued from previous page

2. **MAKE THE FINAL DOUGH**: Combine the rye flour, water, yeast (if using), salt, and rye sourdough starter in the bowl of an electric mixer fitted with a paddle. Mix with a rubber spatula until a rough dough forms. Mix on low (2 on a KitchenAid mixer) for 4 minutes, stopping two or three times to scrape the sides of the bowl. Continue to mix until very smooth, another 4 minutes.

3. **FIRST FERMENTATION**: Cover and let stand until slightly porous, 1½ hours.

4. One hour before baking, line a baker's peel or rimless baking sheet with parchment paper. Place a baking stone on the middle rack of the oven and a cast-iron skillet on the lower rack. Preheat the oven to 400 degrees.

5. **REST**: Line a rimless baking sheet or baker's peel with parchment paper. Sprinkle with flour. Mound the dough in the center of the parchment. With damp hands, press into a 6-inch disk. Dust with flour and use a rolling pin to roll into a 12-inch round, dusting with more rye flour as necessary. With a floured 2½-inch round biscuit cutter, cut a hole in the center, remove the round dough piece, and set it on a corner of the parchment. Cover both pieces of dough and let rest 45 minutes.

6. **BAKE**: With a pastry wheel or sharp paring knife, make two intersecting lines on the opposite sides of the hole, creating two narrow Xs. Slide the loaf and small round, still on the parchment, onto the baking stone. Place 1 cup of ice cubes in the skillet to produce steam. Bake (the little round as well as the large loaf) until slightly puffed and lightly caramelized, about 40 minutes. Slide the loaves, still on the parchment, onto a wire rack. Cool completely. Store in a brown paper bag at room temperature for up to 4 days.

Note for Professional Bakers

Because this bread is made with 100 percent rye flour, the dough has very little fermentation tolerance. Shaping the bread can be time consuming, so if a large quantity of breads is required in production, it is better to mix several small batches that are faster to process. Otherwise the dough can over-ferment quite rapidly, causing some breads to have lower volume and an excessively acidic flavor.

LAMINATED HONEY RYE

START TO FINISH:

17

hours

LIQUID LEVAIN STARTER
12 hours

KNEAD
10 minutes

FIRST FERMENTATION
2¾ hours

LAMINATION
1½ hours

BAKE
25 minutes

MAKES
three 350-gram loaves

I was introduced to this recipe by Jean-Philippe de Tonnac, the author of *Dictionnaire Universel du Pain* and well known for his close relationships with bakers around the world. He particularly admires the bread of Arnaud Delmontel, who has a way of combining traditional ingredients and techniques to come up with entirely new recipes. This laminated rye is a perfect example of Arnaud's style. A robust, rustic dough made with whole rye flour is given the croissant treatment—layered with butter and folded multiple times—lending richness and a unique texture to the bread. A mixture of herbs, lemon, and honey infuse it with flavor and aroma. I've never seen another baker make anything like it.

To create distinct layers, make sure that your butter is soft and pliable enough to spread easily, but not so warm that it will melt into the dough before baking. The butter should still be cool when the loaves go into the oven. The steam produced by the butter as its water evaporates in the hot oven lifts the layers. For the richest flavor, use a European-style butter with a high fat content.

INGREDIENTS	BAKER'S %	METRIC WEIGHT
LIQUID LEVAIN STARTER		
Water	50	30
Type 55 or equivalent flour (11 to 11.5% protein)	50	30
Liquid Sourdough Starter (page 182)	23	7
FINAL DOUGH		
Whole rye flour	25	112 g
Type 55 or equivalent flour (11 to 11.5% protein)	75	335 g
Salt	2	9 g
Dry instant yeast	2	9 g
Honey	10	45 g
Water	50	224 g
Liquid levain starter	15	67 g
Fresh lemon juice	0.6	3 g
Unsalted butter, softened	50	224 g
Fresh basil, sage, rosemary, and thyme, finely chopped	4	18 g
Grated lemon zest	2	9 g
FINISHING		
Flaky sea salt, such as Maldon		

1. **PREPARE THE LIQUID LEVAIN STARTER**: In a small bowl, stir together the water, flour, and sourdough starter until well incorporated. Cover and let ferment at room temperature (68 to 77 degrees) until doubled in volume, about 12 hours.

2. **MAKE THE FINAL DOUGH**: Combine the rye flour, Type 55 flour, salt, yeast, honey, water, liquid levain starter, and lemon juice in the bowl of an electric mixer fitted with a dough hook. Mix with a rubber spatula just until a rough dough forms. Knead on low speed (2 on a KitchenAid mixer) for 4 minutes. Turn the mixer to medium-low (4 on a KitchenAid mixer) and knead for another 6 minutes. The dough will be smooth and elastic.

recipe continues

recipe continued from previous page

3. **FIRST FERMENTATION**: Transfer the dough to a lightly oiled, clear 4-quart container with a lid. Turn the dough over so all sides are oiled. Cover and let ferment 45 minutes. Turn the dough out onto a lightly floured countertop and roll into an 8- by 12-inch rectangle with a rolling pin. Wrap in plastic, place on a sheet pan, and place in the refrigerator until firm, about 2 hours.

4. **LAMINATION**: While the dough is in the refrigerator, combine the butter, herbs, and lemon zest in the mixer bowl and beat, using the dough hook, until the butter is smooth and the herbs are evenly distributed. Do not overbeat. On top of a piece of parchment, press the butter into a rectangle measuring 8 by 4 inches. Wrap and refrigerate for 5 to 10 minutes.

5. Remove the dough and the butter from the refrigerator. Place the butter rectangle in the center of the dough. Fold the dough on either side of the butter over the butter, with the edges meeting in the middle. On a lightly floured countertop, roll the dough out so it again measures 8 by 12 inches. Fold it as with a letter, making three layers. Wrap and refrigerate for 15 minutes. Roll again into an 8- by 18-inch rectangle, fold each shorter end toward the center, and then fold the piece in half so you have four layers, wrap in plastic, and refrigerate until firm, 15 minutes. Unwrap and place the dough on the countertop with the short side facing you. Roll again into an 8- by 18-inch rectangle. Cut the dough evenly into three triangles and place on a parchment-lined baking sheet. Cover and refrigerate until well chilled, 1 hour.

6 **BAKE**: Preheat the oven to 400 degrees. Slide the baking sheet onto the middle rack of the oven. Sprinkle with flaky sea salt. Bake until the loaves are puffed and brown, about 25 minutes. Transfer to wire racks to cool completely.

Note for Professional Bakers

After the second fold, the slabs of dough can be frozen for up to 5 days, so the baker can offer fresh bread every day without having to mix and laminate every day.

MENHIR AU BLÉ NOIR

Fabrice Guéry made this bread for me on my first visit to the test bakery at Minoterie Suire in Nantes (see page 69). Fabrice is responsible for all research and development and is regularly testing new breads and flours and revisiting old classics. Suire has put a focus on *blé noir*, buckwheat flour, which has an earthy flavor, dark color, and no gluten. Buckwheat isn't actually wheat, but a relative of rhubarb. Its seeds, ground into flour, are rich in complex carbohydrates. France has a long history of growing buckwheat. These days, new-wave artisan bakers are increasingly interested in using buckwheat flour to make distinctive breads with a wonderful aroma and impressive nutritional profile.

This bread, shaped like a *couronne* (doughnut), has enough buckwheat to give it a distinctive flavor and color. The acidity of the firm levain and the earthy, pleasantly bitter notes of *blé noir* make for a well-balanced and even addictive bread. I enjoy it with homemade fruit jam.

START TO FINISH:
18 to 25
hours

FIRM LEVAIN STARTER
6 to 8 hours

AUTOLYSE
30 minutes

KNEAD
25 minutes

FIRST FERMENTATION
1½ hours

RETARD
8 to 12 hours

FINAL PROOF
1 to 1½ hours

BAKE
45 to 50 minutes

MAKES :
one 1-kilo loaf

INGREDIENTS	BAKER'S %	METRIC WEIGHT
FIRM LEVAIN STARTER		
Firm Sourdough Starter (page 182)	22	17 g
Water	65	49 g
Type 65 or equivalent flour (11 to 11.5% protein)	100	75 g
FINAL DOUGH		
Type 65 or equivalent flour (11 to 11.5% protein)	85	400 g
Buckwheat flour	15	71 g
Water	80	376 g
Salt	2.3	11 g
Dry instant yeast	0.1	0.5 g
Firm levain starter	30	141 g

recipe continues

recipe continued from previous page

1. **PREPARE THE FIRM LEVAIN STARTER**: In a small bowl, mash together the sourdough starter and water to loosen the starter. Stir in the flour until well incorporated, then knead by hand in the bowl for a few minutes until smooth. Cover and let ferment at room temperature (68 to 77 degrees) until doubled in volume, 6 to 8 hours.

2. **AUTOLYSE**: Combine the Type 65 flour, buckwheat flour, and 300 g of the water in the bowl of an electric mixer fitted with a dough hook. Mix with a rubber spatula just until a rough dough forms. Cover and let rest 30 minutes.

3. **MAKE THE FINAL DOUGH**: Add the salt, yeast, and starter to the bowl. With the dough hook, mix on the lowest setting (2 on a KitchenAid mixer) until the dough comes together, 30 seconds. Continue to mix on low until the dough is cohesive, 10 minutes. With the mixer on medium-low (4 on a KitchenAid mixer), drizzle in the remaining 76 g water, a couple of grams at a time, about 12 minutes. Continue to mix until the dough is supple and smooth, another 4 minutes.

4. **FIRST FERMENTATION**: Use a dough scraper to transfer the dough to a lightly oiled, clear 4-quart container with a lid. Turn the dough over so all sides are oiled. Cover and let stand at room temperature for 1½ hours.

5. **RETARD**: Refrigerate overnight, 8 to 12 hours.

6. **FINAL PROOF**: On a lightly floured countertop, roll the dough into a smooth, 18-inch-long log. Pinch the ends together to form a doughnut shape, rolling to smooth the connection. Transfer to a floured doughnut-shaped banneton (alternatively, place one small bowl inside a large bowl, line the doughnut shape that is created with a kitchen towel, and dust with flour). Cover and let stand until pillowy, 1 to 1½ hours

7. **BAKE**: About 1 hour before baking, place a baking stone on the middle rack of the oven and a cast-iron skillet on the lower rack. Preheat the oven to 475 degrees for 1 hour. Line a baker's peel or rimless baking sheet with parchment paper. Uncover the loaf and tip out onto the peel or sheet. Slide the loaf, still on the parchment, onto the baking stone. Place 1 cup of ice cubes in the skillet to produce steam. Bake 10 minutes, turn the heat down to 400 degrees, and continue to bake until the loaf is rich caramel brown, 35 to 40 minutes. Slide the loaf, still on the parchment, onto a wire rack. Cool completely. Store in a brown paper bag at room temperature for 3 to 5 days.

Note for Professional Bakers
The gluten needs to be at least 80 percent developed before the second addition of water. This is important to make sure that the dough will be strong enough before the overnight bulk fermentation. If the final dough is strong enough, it could be proofed for the final time on a board covered with flour-dusted linen rather than a banneton.

PAIN À L'AIL DES OURS

Roland Hertzog, who inherited his bakery in Muntzenheim near Colmar from his parents, has an intensely curious spirit and is constantly experimenting with bread. His less traditional loaves include carrot and herb rounds, pain chorizo, and bacon-walnut-mustard bread. A proponent of super-long fermentation, he often slows yeast down by quickly refrigerating or even partially freezing his dough as soon as it is mixed.

For this seasonal bread, he uses local spring onions that grow near his Alsatian bakery, known as *ail des ours*, or "bear's garlic." You can substitute ramps, green garlic, or regular garlic to enjoy the bread year-round, but I prefer to make this with young garlic. In this recipe, long, cool fermentation also allows the garlic to completely infuse the dough with flavor. This subtle, thoughtful combination of ingredients and techniques results in an unusual and delicious product. Try it with charcuterie and cheeses, and Alsatian beer.

INGREDIENTS	BAKER'S %	METRIC WEIGHT
LIQUID LEVAIN STARTER		
Liquid Sourdough Starter (page 182)	40	20 g
Water	100	51 g
Type 65 or equivalent flour (11 to 11.5% protein)	100	51 g
FINAL DOUGH		
Type 65 or equivalent flour (11 to 11.5% protein)	83	506 g
Whole rye flour	17	101 g
Water	60	364 g
Salt	2	13 g
Dry instant yeast	0.5	3 g
Liquid levain starter	20	121 g
Green garlic, ramps, or spring onions, coarsely chopped	15	90 g

recipe continues

START TO FINISH:
15 to 25½
hours

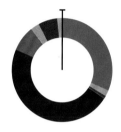

LIQUID LEVAIN STARTER
6 to 8 hours

AUTOLYSE
30 minutes

KNEAD
13 minutes

RETARD
8 to 12 hours

WARM UP
1½ to 2 hours

REST
45 minutes

FINAL PROOF
1½ hours

BAKE
25 minutes

MAKES
two 600-gram loaves

recipe continued from previous page

1. **PREPARE THE LIQUID LEVAIN STARTER**: In a small bowl, dissolve the sourdough starter in the water. Stir in the flour until well incorporated. Cover and let ferment at room temperature (68 to 77 degrees) until doubled in volume, 6 to 8 hours.

2. **AUTOLYSE**: Combine the Type 65 flour, rye flour, and water in the bowl of an electric mixer fitted with a dough hook. Mix with a rubber spatula just until a rough dough forms. Cover and let rest 30 minutes.

3. **MAKE THE FINAL DOUGH**: Add the salt, yeast, and levain starter to the bowl. With the dough hook, mix on the lowest setting until the dough comes together, 30 seconds. Turn the mixer to low (2 on a KitchenAid mixer) and mix for 2 minutes, stopping as necessary to pull the dough from the hook. Turn the mixer to medium-low (4 on a KitchenAid mixer) and mix until the dough is smooth but stiff, another 10 minutes. Add the garlic and mix just until incorporated.

4. **RETARD**: Transfer the dough to a lightly oiled, clear 4-quart container with a lid. Turn the dough over so all sides are oiled, cover, and let stand 1½ hours. Refrigerate 8 to 12 hours.

5. **WARM UP**: Remove the dough from the refrigerator and let stand at room temperature for 1½ to 2 hours to warm up.

6. **REST**: On a lightly floured countertop, divide the dough into two equal pieces. Shape into rounds (see page 78). Drape with plastic wrap and let rest 45 minutes.

7. **FINAL PROOF**: Line a baker's peel or rimless baking sheet with parchment paper. Dust with flour. Shape the dough rounds into bâtards (see page 78) each measuring about 12 by 2 inches. Gently lift the bâtards and place on the parchment, about 2 inches apart from each other. Lift the parchment paper between the loaves, making a pleat and drawing the loaves together. Alternatively, use baker's linen instead of parchment. Tightly roll up two kitchen towels and slip them under the parchment paper on the outer sides of the loaves to support and cradle them. Lightly dust the tops with flour and lightly drape with plastic wrap. Let stand 1½ hours.

8. **BAKE**: About 1 hour before baking, place a baking stone on the middle rack of the oven and a cast-iron skillet on the lower rack. Preheat the oven to 475 degrees for 1 hour. Uncover the breads, remove the rolled-up towels, and stretch the parchment paper out so that it is flat and the loaves are separated. With a *lame*, a single-edged razor blade, or a serrated knife, make a long slash, about ½ inch deep, down the length of each loaf. Slide the loaves, still on the parchment, onto the baking stone. Place ½ cup of ice cubes in the skillet to produce steam. Bake for 10 minutes. Lower the heat to 450 and bake until the loaves are golden brown and well risen, another 15 minutes. Slide the loaves, still on the parchment, onto a wire rack. Cool completely. Store in a brown paper bag at room temperature for up to 2 days.

Note for Professional Bakers

For larger batches of dough, it is better to add the garlic toward the end of the mixing time and incorporate it on low speed until well distributed, since garlic can have a weakening effect on gluten and make a dough that is too slack.

PAIN AU LEVAIN MODERNE

START TO FINISH:

20 to 26½

hours

LIQUID LEVAIN STARTER
6 to 8 hours

AUTOLYSE
30 minutes

KNEAD
17 minutes

FIRST FERMENTATION
3 hours

RETARD
8 to 12 hours

WARM UP
2 to 2½ hours

FINAL PROOF
2¼ hours

BAKE
60 to 65 minutes

MAKES
One 1.5-kilo loaf

This is a large rustic loaf in the tradition of Pain Poilâne, but because it is raised with a liquid rather than firm starter it has a lighter, bubblier texture, more elasticity, and a more subtle sour flavor. A tiny bit of yeast contributes to the dough's liveliness. It is a common technique among the leading bakers in France to add commercial yeast. Generally, they add between 0.25 and 1 gram of yeast to each kilo of flour in the final dough. This is allowed and controlled by French law. The dough ferments at a cool temperature for a long time, allowing for increased lactic acid development. This gives the bread a gentler sour flavor than a standard country sourdough miche made with firm whole wheat levain.

The popularity of this style has grown with the increasing use of modern stainless-steel liquid sourdough tanks in professional bakeries in France. It is easy to cultivate and maintain a liquid sourdough. To mimic the action of a bakery tank, give your fermenting starter a stir every 2 hours. The action will oxygenate the mixture and encourage fermentation and aroma.

INGREDIENTS	BAKER'S %	METRIC WEIGHT
LIQUID LEVAIN STARTER		
Liquid Sourdough Starter (page 182)	20	25 g
Warm water, about 85 degrees	100	125 g
Type 65 flour or equivalent flour (11 to 11.5% protein)	100	125 g
FINAL DOUGH		
Type 65 flour or equivalent flour (11 to 11.5% protein)	90	620 g
Whole rye flour	9	62 g
Water	77	526 g
Salt	2.5	17 g
Dry instant yeast	0.1	1 g
Liquid levain starter	40	275 g

1. **PREPARE THE LIQUID LEVAIN STARTER:** In a small bowl, stir together the sourdough starter and warm water. Stir in the flour until smooth.

recipe continues

recipe continued from previous page

Cover and let ferment at room temperature (68 to 77 degrees) until doubled in volume, 6 to 8 hours, stirring every 2 hours if possible.

2. **AUTOLYSE**: Combine the Type 65 flour, rye flour, and 436 g of the water in the bowl of an electric mixer fitted with a dough hook. Mix just until a rough dough forms. Cover and let rest 30 minutes.

3. **MAKE THE FINAL DOUGH**: Add the salt, yeast, and levain starter to the bowl. Mix with a rubber spatula until a rough dough forms. With the dough hook, mix on low (2 on a KitchenAid mixer) until the dough comes together and begins to smooth out, about 2 minutes. Pull the dough off the hook, then turn the mixer to medium-low (4 on a KitchenAid mixer) and mix for another 4 minutes. With the mixer still on medium-low, slowly drizzle the remaining 90 g water, 10 g at a time, waiting between drizzles until the water is absorbed, about 7 minutes. Continue to mix until the dough is elastic and shiny, another 4 minutes. Turn the dough out onto a lightly floured counter. Pat into a 6 by 8-inch rectangle and fold like a business letter. Slide both hands under the dough and flip it over so the folds are underneath. Slip it back into the container, cover, and let stand another 1½ hours. Repeat the folding and turning, return to the container, and let stand 1½ hours again.

4. **RETARD**: Use a dough scraper to transfer the dough to a lightly oiled, clear 4-quart container with a lid. Turn the dough over so all sides are oiled. Cover and refrigerate overnight, 8 to 12 hours.

5. **WARM UP**: Take the dough out of the refrigerator and let it warm up on the countertop for 2 to 2½ hours.

6. **FINAL PROOF**: On a lightly floured countertop, gently round the dough. Cover and let stand 15 minutes. Shape into a slightly tighter boule (see page 78). Place seam side down in a large, lightly floured banneton. Cover with plastic wrap or a kitchen towel and let rest until pillowy, about 2 hours.

7. **BAKE**: About 1 hour before baking, position an oven rack in the bottom third of the oven and set a Dutch oven (with the lid on) on the rack. Preheat the oven to 450 degrees for 1 hour. Wearing oven mitts, carefully remove the Dutch oven to a heatproof surface and take off the lid. Tip the dough onto a peel or your hands and put in the Dutch oven. With a *lame*, a single-edged razor blade, or a serrated knife, make four slashes in the top of the dough, about ½ inch deep, in a tic-tac-toe pattern. Put the lid on and bake for 30 minutes. Turn the heat down to 425 degrees. Remove the lid and bake until the loaf is a rich golden brown, 30 to 35 minutes more. Carefully turn the loaf out onto a wire rack. Cool completely. Store in a brown paper bag at room temperature for 3 to 4 days.

Notes for Professional Bakers

Due to its relatively high water content, liquid levain encourages protease activity, decreasing the size and binding ability of gluten molecules and smoothing out the dough. Therefore it is a great addition to dough that requires more extensibility, baguette dough for example.

Using liquid levain is also a great way to enhance the flavor of butter in laminated or enriched dough, due to the large amount of lactic acids produced during long fermentation.

PAIN AU SARRASIN AVEC MIEL, PAVOT, ET TOURNESOL

This is my version of one of Marie-Christine's signature breads. Buckwheat is becoming increasingly popular in France. Along with the dark honey, it gives the bread a rugged, earthy aroma. The addition of poppy and sunflower seeds adds layers of texture and flavor. She likes to use a rye sour in her buckwheat breads for the extra acidity. The triangular bread form (I am a fan of the willow baskets from Herbert Birnbaum) gives the bread a charming look to go along with its charming character.

INGREDIENTS	BAKER'S %	METRIC WEIGHT
RYE SOURDOUGH STARTER		
Whole rye flour	100	42 g
Water	125	53 g
Liquid Sourdough Starter (page 182)	20	8 g
FINAL DOUGH		
Type 65 or equivalent flour (11 to 11.5% protein)	78	359 g
Buckwheat flour	22	102 g
Water	61	280 g
Buckwheat honey	18	83 g
Salt	2.2	10 g
Dry instant yeast	0.4	2 g
Rye sourdough starter	23	104 g
Poppy seeds	5	23 g
Sunflower seeds	11	51 g

recipe continues

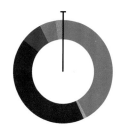

RYE SOUR STARTER
9 to 12 hours

KNEAD
16 minutes

RETARD
8 to 12 hours

WARM UP
1½ to 2 hours

FINAL PROOF
1 to 1½ hours

BAKE
40 minutes

MAKES
one 1-kilo loaf

recipe continued from previous page

1. **PREPARE THE RYE SOURDOUGH STARTER**: In a small bowl, stir together the rye flour, water, and sourdough starter until well incorporated. Cover and let ferment at room temperature (68 to 77 degrees) for 40 minutes, then refrigerate overnight, 8 to 12 hours.

2. **MAKE THE FINAL DOUGH**: Combine the Type 65 flour, buckwheat flour, 239 g of the water, the honey, salt, yeast, and rye sourdough starter in the bowl of an electric mixer fitted with a dough and hook. Mix with a rubber spatula until a rough dough forms. With the dough hook, mix on low (2 on a KitchenAid mixer) for 1 minute. Stop and scrape down the sides. Mix on medium-low (4 on the KitchenAid) for 5 minutes. Turn the mixer back down to low and slowly drizzle in the remaining 41 g water. When the water is fully incorporated, add the seeds, turn the mixer to medium-low, and continue to knead another 10 minutes.

3. **RETARD**: Transfer the dough to a lightly oiled, clear 4-quart container with a lid. Turn the dough over so all sides are oiled, cover, and let stand 1½ hours. Refrigerate 8 to 12 hours.

4. **WARM UP**: Remove the dough from the refrigerator and let stand on the countertop to warm up, 1½ to 2 hours.

5. **FINAL PROOF**: On a floured countertop, shape the dough into a boule (see page 78) and then gently press the sides to form a triangle. Transfer to a floured triangle banneton. Drape with plastic wrap and let stand until pillowy, 1 to 1½ hours.

6. **BAKE**: Place a baking stone on the middle rack of the oven and a cast-iron skillet on the lower rack. Preheat the oven to 450 degrees. Line a baker's peel or rimless baking sheet with parchment paper and tip the dough out onto the peel or sheet. With a *lame,* a single-edged razor blade, or a serrated knife, make three slashes, about ½ inch deep, around the edges of the loaf. Slide the loaf, still on the parchment, onto the baking stone. Place 1 cup of ice cubes in the skillet to produce steam. Bake until the loaf is nicely browned and well risen, about 40 minutes. Slide the loaf, still on the parchment, onto a wire rack. Cool completely. Store in a brown paper bag at room temperature for up to 2 days.

Note for Professional Bakers

If using a more aggressive professional spiral mixer, care should be taken not to overwork the fragile buckwheat and rye dough. Seven minutes on the lower speed, and then 2 minutes on the higher speed will produce dough with the strongest gluten.

PAIN DE CAMPAGNE UTOPISTE

Here's Pierre-Julien Bouniol's signature bread (for more on his bakery, Utopiste, see page 88). Each one of his loaves is slightly different in weight and dimension. For an authentic result, don't fuss with a ruler to make these breads perfectly rectangular or equal to each other in size.

START TO FINISH:

14 to 16

hours

FIRM LEVAIN STARTER
8 to 10 hours

AUTOLYSE
30 minutes

KNEAD
21 minutes

FIRST FERMENTATION
3 hours

FINAL PROOF
2 to 2½ hours

BAKE
40 minutes

MAKES
two 757-gram loaves

INGREDIENTS	BAKER'S %	METRIC WEIGHT
FIRM LEVAIN STARTER		
Firm Sourdough Starter (page 182)	19	16 g
Water	60	50 g
Type 85 or equivalent flour (11 to 11.5% protein)	100	84 g
FINAL DOUGH		
Type 85 flour (11 to 11.5% protein)	90	675 g
Whole rye flour	10	75 g
Water	80	600 g
Salt	2.2	15 g
Firm levain starter	20	150 g

1. **PREPARE THE LEVAIN STARTER:** In a small bowl, dissolve the sourdough starter in the water, breaking it up with the back of a spoon. Stir in the flour until well incorporated, kneading it briefly by hand if necessary. Cover and let ferment at room temperature (68 to 77 degrees) until doubled in volume, 8 to 10 hours.

2. **AUTOLYSE:** Combine the Type 85 flour, rye flour, and 530 g of the water in the bowl of an electric mixer fitted with a dough hook. Mix with a rubber spatula just until a rough dough forms. Cover and let rest 30 minutes.

3. **MAKE THE FINAL DOUGH:** Add the salt and levain starter to the bowl. With the dough hook, mix on the lowest setting for 15 minutes. Pull the dough off the hook, then, with the mixer on low (2 on a

recipe continues

recipe continued from previous page

KitchenAid mixer) slowly drizzle the remaining 55 g water into the bowl. Continue to mix until the dough is very soft, elastic, and shiny, another 6 minutes.

4. **FIRST FERMENTATION**: Use a dough scraper to transfer the dough to a lightly oiled, clear 4-quart container with a lid. Turn the dough over so all sides are oiled. Cover and let stand at room temperature for 1½ hours. Turn the dough out onto a lightly floured counter. Pat into a 6- by 8-inch rectangle and fold like a business letter. Slide both hands under the dough and flip it over so the folds are underneath. Slip it back into the container, cover, and let stand another 1½ hours.

5. **FINAL PROOF**: Sprinkle a baker's couche or clean kitchen towel with whole rye flour. Repeat the folding and turning and transfer the dough to the couche. Dust with flour and cover with another towel. Let stand until the dough is very pillowy, 2 to 2½ hours.

6. **BAKE**: About 1 hour before baking, place a baking stone on the middle rack of the oven and a cast-iron skillet on the lower rack. Preheat the oven to 450 degrees for 1 hour. Cover a baker's peel or rimless baking sheet with parchment and dust with flour. Turn the dough onto the parchment and gently pat into a rough rectangle about 10 inches by 5 inches. Cut the rectangle into two 5-inch squares and separate, leaving 4 inches between the loaves. Slide the loaves, still on the parchment, onto the baking stone. Place 1 cup of ice cubes in the skillet to produce steam. Bake for 25 minutes. Turn the heat down to 425 degrees and continue to bake until the loaves are golden brown and well risen, about 15 minutes more. Slide the loaves, still on the parchment, onto a wire rack. Cool completely. Store in a brown paper bag at room temperature for up to 2 days.

Notes for Professional Bakers

Not every baker will want to charge for this bread by the gram as Pierre-Julien does. For the sake of consistency, the dough can be divided once fermentation is complete using a 20-part hydraulic divider. Then, after a quick 30-minute final proof, the loaves can be baked. This technique will ensure efficiency and consistency in production.

PAIN À LA FARINE DE KHORASAN

Khorasan, an ancient precursor to wheat, is named for the region in modern-day Iran where it was originally grown and has been consistently cultivated across centuries. Trademarked under the name Kamut when introduced to the U.S., it continues to grow in popularity because of its particular nutritional and baking qualities. Rich in protein, vitamins, and minerals, it is increasingly embraced by health-minded consumers. Khorasan, although technically a type of wheat, has a very digestible type of gluten that is well tolerated by many people with gluten sensitivity.

Fabrice Guéry, of Minoterie Suire in France, has become an expert on developing recipes with unusual grains, including this one. His *pain à la farine de khorasan* dough requires extremely high hydration, often up to 100 percent. But don't hesitate to try this recipe for fear of working with such a wet dough. Khorasan is unusually absorbent and the dough is soft but not impossible to work with. It does require a gentle touch. When Fabrice shapes a loaf, he carefully folds the sides into the center to create a loose round, and then flips the round into a floured banneton, smooth side down.

INGREDIENTS	BAKER'S %	METRIC WEIGHT
FIRM LEVAIN STARTER		
Firm Sourdough Starter (page 182)	40	12 g
Water	60	18 g
Whole khorasan flour	100	29 g
FINAL DOUGH		
Whole khorasan flour	100	555 g
Very hot water, 140 degrees	95	527 g
Salt	2.1	12 g
Firm levain starter	10	59 g
Dry instant yeast	0.5	3 g

recipe continues

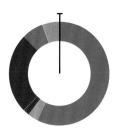

START TO FINISH:
12 to 14
hours

FIRM LEVAIN STARTER
6 to 8 hours

AUTOLYSE
30 minutes

KNEAD
16 minutes

FIRST FERMENTATION
3½ hours

FINAL PROOF
1 hour

BAKE
45 minutes

MAKES
one 1.2-kilo loaf

recipe continued from previous page

1. **PREPARE THE FIRM LEVAIN STARTER**: In a small bowl, mash together the sourdough starter and water to loosen the starter. Stir in the flour until well incorporated, then knead by hand in the bowl for a few minutes until smooth. Cover and let ferment at room temperature (68 to 77 degrees) until doubled in volume, 6 to 8 hours.

2. **AUTOLYSE**: Combine the khorasan flour and 477 g of the very hot water in the bowl of an electric mixer fitted with a dough hook. Mix with a rubber spatula until a rough dough forms. Cover and let stand 30 minutes.

3. **MAKE THE FINAL DOUGH**: Add the salt, levain starter, and yeast to the bowl. Turn the mixer to low (2 on a KitchenAid mixer) and mix for 2 minutes. Increase the speed to medium-low (4 on a KitchenAid mixer) and mix for 5 minutes. Pull the dough off the hook, and then, with the mixer on medium-low, slowly drizzle in the remaining 50 g hot water, 10 g at a time, waiting between drizzles until the water is absorbed, about 5 minutes. After the water has been absorbed, continue to mix for 4 minutes.

4. **FIRST FERMENTATION**: Use a dough scraper to transfer the dough to a lightly oiled, clear 4-quart container with a lid. Turn the dough over so all sides are oiled. Cover and let stand at room temperature for 1½ hours.

5. Turn the dough out onto a lightly floured counter. Pat into a 6- by 8-inch rectangle and fold like a business letter. Slide both hands under the dough and flip it over so the folds are underneath. Slip it back into the container, cover, and let stand 2 hours.

6. **FINAL PROOF**: On a lightly floured countertop, gently round the dough (see page 78). Place in a lightly floured banneton, seam side up. Cover with a kitchen towel and let rest until pillowy, 1 hour.

7. **BAKE**: About 1 hour before baking, position an oven rack in the bottom third of the oven and set the Dutch oven (with the lid on) on the rack. Preheat the oven to 450 degrees for 1 hour. Wearing oven mitts, carefully remove the Dutch oven to a heatproof surface and take off the lid. Tip the dough onto a peel or your hands and put in the Dutch oven. With a *lame*, a single-edged razor blade, or a serrated knife, make four slashes, about ½ inch deep, in a starburst shape: If the round is a clock face, slash from 12 o'clock to 6 o'clock, 9 to 3, 1 to 7, and 11 to 4. Cover and bake for 25 minutes. Turn the heat down to 425 degrees, uncover, and bake until the loaf is golden brown and well risen, another 20 minutes longer. Slide the loaf, still on the parchment, onto a wire rack. Cool completely. Store in a brown paper bag at room temperature for up to 1 week.

Notes for Professional Bakers

Due to difference in water absorption in khorasan flour from crop to crop, you must pay attention to the hydration. To start, 85 percent of the water can be used, but keep in mind that the water could go up to 105 percent to reach the desired dough consistency. When working with khorasan, softer dough will always provide better bread quality.

ROME'S NEIGHBORHOOD BAKER

PIERLUIGI ROSCIOLI, ANTICO FORNO ROSCIOLI, ROME, ITALY

With its vibrant outdoor vegetable market and famous Forno Campo de' Fiori, producing 6-foot stretches of pizza bianca all day long, Campo de' Fiori is my favorite Roman neighborhood and my home base when I'm in Rome. When I set out from here to visit Antico Forno Roscioli, the well-known artisan bakery on Via dei Chiavari, I didn't have to walk very far. The bakery is down a narrow, crooked cobblestone street, a few blocks from the piazza. Jewelry and leather goods boutiques are interspersed with outdoor cafes. The walls of the buildings are clad in varying shades of red and yellow plaster that make Roman streets like this glow with flattering light. Although the Via dei Chiavari twists so you can't see more than one block ahead of you, I knew I was approaching the shop when I saw bicycles with bread delivery baskets lined up along the sidewalk, right next to two tiny delivery vehicles—scooters with little trailers to hold bread. Hanging two stories above the entrance is a large iron sign: "Forno."

The atmosphere inside was chaotic in that joyful Italian way. Customers, bakers, and a mixed bag of counter people scurried around the small but high-ceilinged room. Pierluigi's wife, Giusy Di Fede, greeted customers from behind the counter. There was no side door or loading dock. Delivery men came in and out through the front with everyone else, carrying large bags full of warm bread, loading their bikes or scooters, and rushing to nearby cafes and restaurants. The bakery supplies dozens of local spots with their daily bread. Completely lacking was that sense of precision that you get in a French or German establishment, where products are perfectly lined up on neat shelves. Instead, there were piles of biscotti, overlapping pizzas, haphazardly arranged loaves.

Pierluigi Roscioli, whose father, Marco, founded this bakery in the 1970s, has baking in his blood. His grandmother had eleven brothers, all of them bakers. But he is also a man of the world, someone who travels, who reads widely, and who brings plenty of new ideas back into the business, which also includes a revered salumeria/restaurant and a bar. That's why panettones sit alongside apple pies, grissini are stacked next to pita breads, and *pane di casa* shares shelf space with khorasan loaves. At Antico Forno Roscioli, you can buy the most traditional *pane di Lariano* in the city, but you can also get a bagel with egg and cheese. Traditional methods and impeccable ingredients are the common denominators.

When I arrived for my tour, the nighttime bakers were just leaving, their eyelashes, eyebrows, the hair on their arms covered in flour as if it had been snowing all night. On entering the oven room, you walk into a wall of heat. Cesare Agostini, an Italian-Canadian baker who came from Ottawa to apprentice with Pierluigi and never left, manages the bakery in the daytime. He led me from the shop up a few steps and then down a series of corridors as crooked as the street. Suddenly, the space opened up a little into a 6- by 4-foot delivery staging area, with baskets of bread piled up all over the place, a scale for weighing them (the bread here is sold by weight), bakery bags, and a little desk with a computer for keeping track of orders. Moving down another narrow corridor, we arrived at the bakery itself, a room that couldn't have been more than 10 feet wide and 14 feet deep, with a massive deck oven built into a wall. There was a mixer and a worktable, some shelving. I was thinking, "*This* is where all of the bread comes from?" There was a disconnect between the number of loaves I saw in the anteroom and the modest size of this workroom. He laughed when he saw my incredulous expression, and then took me around a corner and into the pastry room, which was the size of a walk-in closet.

During the Christmas season, he said, they sell a crazy number of sweets, and panettones by the thousands.

I found at least a partial explanation for this production magic in the room where the sourdough is kept. I am used to bakeries with giant vats of the stuff. But here, there was a teeny little closet fitted with a walk-in refrigerator about 3 feet wide and 6 feet deep. It was filled with stainless-steel bins about 3 feet tall, each one filled with lievito madre that was rock hard, like clay. Cesare explained that the compact, cold mixture, used in relatively small quantities, was responsible for raising all of the natural sourdough breads I had seen. The bakery gets so hot, especially in the summertime, that a liquid sourdough would be difficult to control. And anyway, there was no room for a less dense starter. Fermented at a cool temperature for 24 hours, its acetic acid flavor was intense. In casual Italian style, there were no pH meters at Roscioli. To test the acidity of the dough, a baker would simply tear off a small piece and taste it before pronouncing it properly fermented. I finally understood the unique aroma that permeated the place. It was this concentrated sourdough, which left its traces everywhere, from the wooden proofing boards to the linen couches to the cooling baskets.

Pierluigi and his wife, Giusy Di Fede, outside of their bakery

PANE AI FICHI

When I first walked into Antico Forno Roscioli in Rome, I was completely charmed by the rustically shaped breads. My eye was drawn to these fig loaves in particular. Some of them were split in half so you could see the interiors, dense with large pieces of moist figs and chunks of walnuts. Spending the night working alongside the overnight team, I watched the bakers casually shape the *pane ai fichi* at breakneck speed. Each log was obviously handmade and seemed to have its own individual character and personality. When I tasted one, the rich, nutty, sweet fragrance did not disappoint. I discovered how addictively delicious it was, as I devoured chunks of it all the way back to my hotel. The recipe below is adapted from the one they use at the bakery.

INGREDIENTS	BAKER'S %	METRIC WEIGHT
LIEVITO MADRE		
Tipo 00 flour with W value of 250 to 260	100	74 g
Water	65	48 g
Liquid Sourdough Starter (page 182)	20	15 g
FINAL DOUGH		
Tipo 00 flour with W value of 250 to 260	100	600 g
Water	85	510 g
Lievito madre	23	136 g
Sugar	3.3	20 g
Almond paste, broken into small pieces	3.3	20 g
Grated zest of 1 lemon	0.6	3.5 g
Dried figs, stemmed and coarsely chopped	70	420 g
Toasted walnuts, chopped	30	180 g
Salt	2.5	15 g

recipe continues

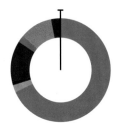

LIEVITO MADRE
12 to 16 hours

AUTOLYSE
30 minutes

KNEAD
16 to 18 minutes

FIRST FERMENTATION
3 hours

REST
30 minutes

FINAL PROOF
2 to 2½ hours

BAKE
40 minutes

MAKES
two 952-gram loaves

recipe continued from previous page

1. **PREPARE THE LIEVITO MADRE**: In a small bowl, stir together the flour, water, and sourdough starter until well incorporated. The mixture will be very stiff. Cover and let ferment at room temperature (68 to 77 degrees) for 4 hours, then refrigerate overnight, 8 to 12 hours. It will double in size.

2. **AUTOLYSE**: Combine the 00 flour and water in a large bowl. With a spatula, mix until a rough dough forms. Cover and let stand 30 minutes.

3. **MAKE THE FINAL DOUGH**: Add the lievito madre, sugar, almond paste, and lemon zest to the bowl. With the dough hook, mix on medium-low (4 on a KitchenAid mixer) for 5 minutes. Scrape the sides of the mixer. Continue to mix on medium-low for 8 minutes more. Add the figs, walnuts, and salt and mix on low until the nuts and figs are evenly incorporated, 3 to 5 minutes.

4. **FIRST FERMENTATION**: Transfer the dough to a lightly oiled, clear 4-quart container with a lid. Turn the dough over so all sides are oiled. Cover and let stand until the dough has doubled in volume, 3 hours.

5. **REST**: On a lightly floured countertop divide the dough into two equal pieces. Pre-shape into rounds (see page 78). Dust with flour and cover with plastic wrap. Let rest 30 minutes.

6. **FINAL PROOF**: Shape the dough into squat, snub-nosed batards (called *filones* in Italy), about 8 inches long and 4½ inches wide. Line a baker's peel or rimless baking sheet with parchment paper or linen and dust generously with flour. Place the filones seam side up in the middle. Lift the parchment paper between the loaves, making a pleat and drawing the loaves close together. Tightly roll up two kitchen towels and slip them under the parchment paper or linen on the sides of the breads to support them. Generously dust with flour and drape with plastic wrap. Alternatively, place loaves in two 8- by 4-inch floured bannetons. Let rise until pillowy, 2 to 2½ hours.

7. **BAKE**: About 1 hour before baking, place a baking stone on the middle rack of the oven and a cast-iron skillet on the lower rack. Preheat the oven to 450 degrees for 1 hour. Pick up one side of the parchment or linen and gently roll the dough onto the middle of the peel. Slide the loaves onto the baking stone. Place 1 cup of ice cubes in the skillet to produce steam. Bake for 25 minutes. Lower the oven temperature to 400 degrees and bake until the loaves are golden brown and well risen, another 15 minutes. Cool completely. Store in a brown paper bag at room temperature for 3 to 4 days.

Note for Professional Bakers

After shaping, this bread can easily be retarded overnight at 40 to 45 degrees F. The extra acidity that develops will enhance the delicate flavor combination of the almond, lemon, fig, and walnuts.

PANE CON FARINA DI FARRO

U.S. food writers have been arguing whether Italian farro and spelt are one and the same for at least 20 years. It's something of a trick question. The answer is that all spelt is farro, but not all farro is spelt. According to Markus Buerli, a Swiss expert on Italian farming traditions, farro is an ethnobotanical term, meaning that it describes three cultivated ancient wheat species—einkorn, emmer, and spelt—that are viewed as similar across Italy. The three are genetically related but not identical, and have different flavor and texture profiles. What they have in common is the fact that their berries retain their hulls during harvest. In Italy, einkorn is known as *farro piccolo*, emmer is *farro medio*, and spelt is *farro grande*.

Italian millers have taken up a renewed interest in all three types of farro, grinding them into flour to be used in pasta and bread. Pierluigi uses emmer for his *pane con farina di farro*, so that's what I've use here. Spelt flour will also work.

INGREDIENTS	BAKER'S %	METRIC WEIGHT
LIEVITO MADRE		
Tipo OO flour with W value of 250 to 260	100	125 g
Water	60	75 g
Liquid Sourdough Starter (page 182)	10	12 g
FINAL DOUGH		
Tipo OO flour with W value of 250 to 260	59	286 g
Whole emmer flour	41	196 g
Water	67	324 g
Salt	2.9	14 g
Dry instant yeast	0.6	3 g
Lievito madre	44	212 g

recipe continues

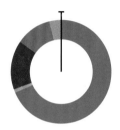

START TO FINISH:
13½ to 18
hours

LIEVITO MADRE
8 to 12 hours

KNEAD
10 minutes

FIRST FERMENTATION
2 hours

REST
40 minutes

FINAL PROOF
1½ to 2 hours

BAKING
40 minutes

MAKES
two 517-gram loaves

recipe continued from previous page

1. **PREPARE THE LIEVITO MADRE**: In a small bowl, stir together the flour, water, and sourdough starter until well incorporated. Cover and let ferment at room temperature (68 to 77 degrees) until doubled in volume, 8 to 12 hours.

2. **MAKE THE FINAL DOUGH**: Combine the 00 flour, emmer flour, water, salt, yeast, and lievito madre in the bowl of an electric mixer fitted with a dough hook. With a spatula, mix until a rough dough forms. With the dough hook, mix on low (2 on a KitchenAid mixer) for 5 minutes, turn the mixer to medium (6 on a KitchenAid mixer) and mix for 5 more minutes.

3. **FIRST FERMENTATION**: Transfer the dough to a lightly oiled, clear 4-quart container with a lid. Cover and let stand until the dough has doubled in volume, about 2 hours.

4. **REST**: On a lightly floured countertop, divide the dough in half and pre-shape into two loose rounds (see page 78). Dust with flour and cover with plastic wrap. Let rest 40 minutes.

5. **FINAL PROOF**: Cover a baker's peel or rimless baking sheet with parchment. Shape the dough into two snub-nosed *bâtards* (see page 78), about 12 inches long and 3 inches wide. Line a baker's peel or rimless baking sheet with parchment paper or linen and dust with flour. Place the *bâtards* on the parchment, seam sides down, 3 inches apart. Lift the parchment paper between the loaves, making a pleat and drawing the loaves close together. Alternatively, use baker's linen instead of parchment. Tightly roll up two kitchen towels and slip them under the parchment paper on the sides of the outer loaves to support each *bâtard*. Lightly dust with flour and drape with plastic wrap. Let rise until pillowy, 1½ to 2 hours.

6. **BAKE**: About 1 hour before baking, place a baking stone on the middle rack of the oven and a cast-iron skillet on the lower rack. Preheat the oven to 425 degrees for 1 hour. Uncover the breads, remove the rolled-up towels, and stretch the parchment paper out so that it is flat and the loaves are separated. Gently flip the loaves over so they are seam side up and 2 inches apart. Slide the loaves, still on the parchment, onto the baking stone. Place ½ cup of ice cubes in the skillet to produce steam. Bake until the loaves are golden brown and well risen, about 40 minutes. Cool completely. Store in a brown paper bag at room temperature for 3 to 4 days.

Note for Professional Bakers

Because emmer and spelt have relatively little gluten, and the gluten that they do have is fragile, doughs made with these flours have to be mixed gently and for shorter periods of time. Overmixing will tear fragile gluten strands, compromising the volume and crumb texture of the bread.

PANE GIRANDOLA AL GRANO DURO

START TO FINISH:

12 to 17

hours

LIEVITO MADRE

12 hours

KNEAD

15 minutes

FIRST FERMENTATION

2 to 3 hours

REST

45 minutes

FINAL PROOF

¾ to 1 hour

BAKE

45 to 50 minutes

MAKES

one 1-kilo loaf

Heading away from Altamura towards Matera, another famous bread town, I made a stop at a farmstand, where I saw this bread. It was made from local durum wheat flour and shaped beautifully into a pinwheel. Its yellow color and unusual geometry reminded me of the sunflowers growing in the adjacent field. Here is my version, which I developed to preserve the memory.

INGREDIENTS	BAKER'S %	METRIC WEIGHT
LIEVITO MADRE		
Liquid Sourdough Starter (page 182)	40	21
Water	60	32
Extra-fancy durum flour (*semolina rimacinata*)	100	52
FINAL DOUGH		
Extra-fancy durum flour (*semolina rimacinata*)	100	512 g
Lievito madre	20	105 g
Water	70	358 g
Barley malt syrup	2	10 g
Salt	2	10 g
Dry instant yeast	1	5 g

1. **PREPARE THE LIEVITO MADRE:** In a small bowl, dissolve the sourdough starter in the water. Stir in the flour until well incorporated. Cover and let ferment at room temperature (68 to 77 degrees) until doubled in volume, 12 hours.

2. **MAKE THE FINAL DOUGH:** Using a rubber spatula, combine the flour, lievito madre, water, barley malt syrup, salt, and yeast in the bowl of an electric mixer fitted with a dough hook. Mix just until a rough dough forms. With the dough hook, mix on the lowest setting until smooth and very elastic, about 15 minutes.

recipe continues

recipe continued from previous page

3. **FIRST FERMENTATION**: Use a dough scraper to transfer the dough to a lightly oiled, clear 4-quart container with a lid. Turn the dough over so all sides are oiled. Cover and let stand at room temperature for 2 to 3 hours.

4. **REST**: On a lightly floured countertop, divide the dough into two equal pieces and pre-shape into rounds (see page 78). Cover and let rest 30 minutes.

5. **FINAL PROOF**: Cover a baker's peel or rimless baking sheet with parchment. Shape each piece of dough, adding additional flour to the work surface as needed, into a 10-inch bâtard. Cover and let rest 15 minutes. With a ¾-inch dowel, press lengthwise down the center of each loaf to create a deep channel. With the dowel, press down crosswise in the center of each loaf to create a perpendicular channel where they will be joined. Set the loaves together at those channels and twist together at the center to create one large X-shaped loaf with the sides with the indentations facing up. Dust the parchment-covered peel or baking sheet with flour and place the loaf on the parchment. Lightly dust with flour and drape with plastic wrap. Let rise until pillowy, 45 to 60 minutes.

6. **BAKE**: About 1 hour before baking, place a baking stone on the middle rack of the oven and a cast-iron skillet on the lower rack. Preheat the oven to 425 degrees for 1 hour. Slide the loaf, still on the parchment, onto the baking stone. Place 1 cup of ice cubes in the skillet to produce steam. Bake until the loaf is golden brown and well risen, 45 to 50 minutes. Slide the loaf, still on the parchment, onto a wire rack. Cool completely. Store in a brown paper bag at room temperature for up to 2 days.

Note for Professional Bakers

The dough should be proofed upside down on semolina flour–dusted linen. Once ready to bake, a round and rigid cake board (diameter similar to the shape of the bread) could be used to quickly and efficiently transfer the dough from the linen to the loader or oven peel.

PROFILE:

UNBROKEN BAKING TRADITION IN ALTAMURA

NUNZIO NINIVAGGI, IL PANE DI NUNZIO, ALTAMURA, ITALY

As you drive from Puglia's capital, Bari, toward Altamura, the scenery consists of olive, fig, apricot, and plum trees as well as wheat fields. The olive trees in this part of Italy are broader and more vibrant than what you see in Umbria or Tuscany. The wheat, planted in patchwork fields and featuring heritage Appulo and Senatore Cappelli varieties, along with a dozen others, comes in a full range of colors from moss to sage to fern to hunter and in heights from knee-high to LeBron. The closer you get to Altamura, as the landscape becomes a series of rolling hills, the more wheat you see. Altamura itself sits on a high plateau, as if it is watching over its agricultural domain. There's a long tradition of wheat farming in this area as well as a long tradition of milling. Neolithic settlements in Puglia show evidence of well-developed agriculture techniques and a wide variety of cereal crops, including einkorn, emmer, and durum wheat likely used in bread making. Municipal records from as early as 1600 show 26 mills operated in or on the outskirts of town.

These days, both farming and milling are key to the economy in Altamura. Immediately outside the town's historic center are at least a dozen high-tech mills that process 2 million kilos of durum wheat daily, servicing pasta and bread makers across Italy and around the world. Barilla, the pasta giant and largest user of durum wheat in the world, has a factory nearby.

And yet, traditional bread-baking technology has not been forsaken in the charming town's historical center. This is a place where residents still take part in the nightly *passeggiata* (stroll), greeting each other as they stroll the tile-paved streets and piazzas and past the Romanesque cathedral, stopping for drinks or espressos at 19th-century cafes. Coexisting with some of the most advanced milling facilities in the world are several dozen bakeries producing 60,000 kilos of traditional Altamura bread daily, each loaf made by hand and according to narrow restrictions mandated by the government. Visiting a traditional Altamura bakery is like going back in time. Centuries-old techniques and recipes are utterly respected. Bread has been baked continuously for hundreds of years in a certain way, and there is every indication that it will be baked this way far into the future. I first wrote about Altamura bread in *Local Breads*. It is such a singular example of bread-baking tradition that I wanted to present it, along with some very traditional variations, to a new generation of home bakers.

To be labeled *DOP* (Denomination of Protected Origin), all phases of bread production must take place within a specified geographic area and carry the characteristics of the local environment. Rugged Altamura loaves are made with a natural sourdough starter called *acidi madre* and finely milled local semolina

profile continues

wheat, called *grano duro semola rimacinata*. They are shaped in one of several traditional ways and baked in wood-fired ovens. To satisfy DOP rules, their crusts must be between 3 and 5 millimeters thick. While all Altamura breads have similar rough and rustic shapes, a sweet and sunny yellow crumb, and a chewy amber crust, every bakery produces unique breads within these parameters. Some are lighter, some are darker. The flour used is more or less refined. Naturally, every resident of Altamura has an opinion on which bakery makes the best bread. It is a beautiful phenomenon that this ancient bread-baking industry thrives alongside the modern mills. In fact, Altamura bread is an important part of the local economy. Only 20 percent of it is consumed by residents. The rest is shipped across the country for the rest of Italy to enjoy.

Il Pane di Nunzio, a small shop on Via Torino, is one of the best and most respected of the traditional Altamura bakeries. Nunzio Ninivaggi is a fourth-generation baker who resembles an Altamura loaf: short, stocky, and bulging with muscle. His place is as simple a bakery as I've ever seen. There's a mixer, a worktable, some boxes to put the dough in, and a wood-fired oven. With this equipment, he and three employees produce 400 kilos (about 1,000 pounds) of bread a day.

This bread begins with a mildly acidic sourdough typical of the area, teeming with local lactobacilli *W. cibaria* and *W. confusa*. Nunzio doesn't have refrigeration in his bakery, so he prepares a very stiff, slow-fermenting culture every evening before closing up shop, and lets it sit at room temperature overnight. In the morning, he stokes the fire in his oven with twisted branches of very dry oak. Then he mixes his dough. The sourdough, extra-fancy semolina flour, water, and sea salt all go into the giant bowl of an old Pietroberto mixer, covered in cream-color enamel with ocean-blue dials. This mixer, an absolute classic, is to bakers what a pristine vintage Ford pickup truck would be to a car collector. For 25 minutes, the two arms of the mixer move slowly up, around, and down, as the bowl rotates. It is a hypnotically beautiful process. After kneading, the dough is divided, loosely rounded, put into long wooden boxes, and left to ferment for 2 to 3 hours.

Here comes the unusual part of the time-honored process: Instead of shaping the loaves and then letting them proof again, Altamura bakers sweep the hot coals from the oven floor, shape their breads, and immediately slide them into the white-hot ovens. Because the dough

profile continues

profile continued from previous page

hasn't had a chance to rise a second time, the resulting breads have that characteristically dense and moist crumb. The breads are famously bumpy because they rise explosively in the oven. There's no steam, so the crusts are rough and unrefined.

At Il Pane di Nunzio, there's a whole ballet involved in getting 100 kilos of bread into the 12-foot-deep oven. Four men (this is an all-male shop) work together and around each other to load the shaped loaves into the blisteringly hot oven. Each type has its place. The larger loaves go in first and the smaller ones last, in a swirling seashell pattern. A heavy iron door seals the oven closed, and there's no peeking while the breads bake. All of a sudden, there is a complete calm in the bakery. The bakers sweep up, have a coffee, and relax. Many of the breads stick together as they rise. They are pulled from the oven on long narrow peels and broken apart. Their crusts are so thick that the breads remain intact and uncrushed as they are piled on top of each other in the cooling baskets.

PANE DI ALTAMURA

Semolina is a very sweet-tasting grain. Even when fermented it has a sweet-sour flavor. The silky texture of the very refined flour (*rimacinata* means "twice-milled") produces an exceptionally smooth dough. If possible, seek out imported durum wheat flour to replicate Altamura bread.

It's not unusual to see outstanding Altamura bakers adding a minute amount of yeast, 0.1 percent, to their dough. For bakeries mixing 100 kilos of flour, that means adding 10 grams of yeast. Yeast speeds up fermentation slightly, and is a bit of an insurance policy against a less active sourdough. When I asked Nunzio about his use of yeast, he told me that he's been making dough this way for his entire career, and a small amount of yeast in no way compromises the integrity of the bread. Nunzio shapes his bread in all seven classic Altamura shapes. In the following recipe, I shape the dough in the most common, called *pane accavallato,* or "overlapped bread."

INGREDIENTS	BAKER'S %	METRIC WEIGHT
LIEVITO MADRE		
Fine semolina flour (*semolina rimacinata*)	100	106 g
Water	69	73 g
Liquid Sourdough Starter (page 182)	20	21 g
FINAL DOUGH		
Extra-fancy durum flour (*semolina rimacinata*)	100	500 g
Water	70	350 g
Salt	2.6	13 g
Lievito madre	40	200 g
Dry instant yeast (optional)	0.2	1 g
FINISHING		
Extra-fancy durum flour (*semolina rimacinata*)		20 g

recipe continues

START TO FINISH:
10 to 12
hours

LIEVITO MADRE
6 to 8 hours

KNEAD
15 minutes

FIRST FERMENTATION
2½ hours

REST
30 to 40 minutes

BAKE
30 to 35 minutes

MAKES
one 1,084-gram loaf

recipe continued from previous page

1. **PREPARE THE LIEVITO MADRE**: In a small bowl, stir together the flour, water, and sourdough starter until well incorporated. Cover and let ferment at room temperature (68 to 77 degrees) until doubled in volume, 6 to 8 hours.

2. **MAKE THE FINAL DOUGH**: Combine the semolina flour, water, salt, lievito madre, and yeast if using in the bowl of an electric mixer fitted with a dough hook. Mix with a spatula just until a rough dough forms. With the dough hook, mix on medium-low (4 on a KitchenAid mixer) until the dough is velvety, soft, shiny, and elastic, about 15 minutes.

3. **FIRST FERMENTATION**: Transfer the dough to a lightly oiled, clear 4-quart container with a lid. Turn the dough over so all sides are oiled. Cover and let stand 45 minutes. Turn the dough out onto a lightly floured counter. Pat into a 6- by 8-inch rectangle and fold like a business letter. Slide both hands under the dough and flip it over so the folds are underneath. Slip it back into the container, cover, and let stand another 45 minutes. Repeat the folding and turning, return to the container, and let stand until the dough is very pillowy, 1 hour longer. (If making Altamura Focaccia or Panzanella, skip to directions in the following variations at this point.)

4. **REST**: On a lightly floured countertop, pre-shape into a round (see page 78). Dust with flour and cover with a towel or plastic wrap. Let rest 30 to 40 minutes.

5. **BAKE**: Right after pre-shaping, place a baking stone on the middle rack of the oven and a cast-iron skillet on the lower rack. Preheat the oven to 425 degrees. Dust a parchment-covered peel or baking sheet with about 15 g of the semolina flour and place the dough on the parchment, seam side up. Flatten into an 11- to 12-inch round and fold almost in half. Push down on the edge with the heel of your hand to seal the edge. Turn the folded dough in the semolina to coat on all sides, sprinkling with the remaining 5 g as needed. Slide the loaf, still on the parchment, onto the baking stone. Place 1 cup of ice cubes in the skillet to produce steam. Bake until the loaf is reddish brown and well risen, 30 to 35 minutes. Slide the loaf, still on the parchment, onto a wire rack. Cool completely. Store in a brown paper bag at room temperature for 5 to 6 days.

Note for Professional Bakers

To duplicate the kick of the hot brick oven used by the bakers in Altamura, preheat the deck oven up to 500 degrees and drop the temperature to 460 degrees once the loaves have been loaded.

recipe continued from previous page

VARIATION:
ALTAMURA FOCACCIA

Altamura bakers use their dough for flatbreads and calzones as well as traditionally shaped breads. If you'd like, bake a half-size loaf and use half of your dough to make a focaccia:

Brush the bottom and sides of a 12-inch round baking pan with 1 tablespoon olive oil. Gently deflate the dough after its first fermentation, divide into two equal pieces, and press one piece into the pan, setting aside the second piece of dough for another use. You won't be able to press the dough to the edges. Cover, let it rest 20 minutes, and press again so the dough reaches the edges. Scatter 142 g sliced tomatoes and ½ cup pitted and chopped black olives over the dough. Sprinkle with salt and pepper and ½ teaspoon dried oregano. Drizzle with a little more olive oil. Bake at 425 degrees for 25 to 30 minutes. Let stand 5 to 10 minutes. Run a knife around the edges to loosen from the pan and pop out the focaccia onto a cutting board. Serve warm or at room temperature.

VARIATION:
PANZANELLA (FRIED CALZONE)

Here's another popular use for Altamura dough:

After its first fermentation, roll 270 g of dough (about one-fourth of a recipe) into a 6-inch round. Spread 3 tablespoons tomato sauce on one-half of the dough, stopping an inch from the edge. Sprinkle with ¼ cup grated mozzarella cheese and a tablespoon or two of chopped ham. Fold the round in half and seal the edges by crimping with the tines of a fork. While the calzone is resting, heat 2 inches vegetable oil to 350 degrees in a deep pot over medium-high heat. Fry the calzone until golden brown, turning once, about 3 minutes per side. Drain on a wire rack set over a baking sheet for a few minutes before serving. Alternatively, bake in a 425-degree oven for 30 minutes.

PANE NERO DI CASTELVETRANO

START TO FINISH:
11¼ to 13¼
hours

LIEVITO MADRE
6 to 8 hours

KNEAD
10 minutes

FIRST FERMENTATION
2½ to 3 hours

REST
10 minutes

FINAL PROOF
1 hour

BAKE
45 minutes

MAKES
one 1.1-kilo loaf

Ottavio Guccione worked at Eataly in Turin before returning to Palermo, his birthplace, to open L'Antico Forno San Michele. Fulfilling a long-held dream, he makes breads that showcase his creativity, including poppy seed, bacon and cheese, and almond and olive loaves. He works exclusively with Sicilian grain, and his pride and joy is his version of the most traditional of Sicilian breads, Pane Nero di Castelvetrano.

The bread is made with local Tumminia flour, one of the wheat varieties that Sicilian farmers are growing in larger yields at the request of bakers like Ottavio. He also uses local Russello flour, a heritage variety of durum wheat. You can substitute extra-fancy durum flour for the Russello if you'd like. Or you can use a blend of Sicilian flours from Molini Riggi (see Resources, page 347) that includes Tumminia, Russello, and durum wheat flour. There's nothing unusual about this recipe in terms of technique. What makes it very special is the quality of the Sicilian flour. Make the effort to seek out Tumminia and Russello flour, or a blend of the two, and you will be rewarded with a bread with a unique texture and captivating aroma.

Working with these old wheat variety flours takes practice. With gluten that is more fragile than modern varieties, the dough needs to be handled with care. Ottavio gives his dough multiple folds to develop strength. If you are baking this bread at home, give the bread two folds. When I visited Molino Riggi, I was surprised to see them milling just a few tons at a time. Such small-batch milling makes blending for consistency difficult. Ottavio adjusts his recipe depending on the characteristics of each batch of flour.

INGREDIENTS	BAKER'S %	METRIC WEIGHT
LIEVITO MADRE		
Firm Sourdough Starter (page 182)	20	20 g
Water	60	60 g
Russello wheat flour	100	100 g
FINAL DOUGH		
Russello wheat flour	80	392 g
Tumminia flour	20	98 g
Water	76	373 g
Lievito madre	37	180 g
Salt	2	10 g
FINISHING		
Sesame seeds	10	50 g

1. **PREPARE THE LIEVITO MADRE**: In a small bowl, mash together the sourdough starter and water to loosen the starter. Stir in the Russello flour until well incorporated, then knead by hand in the bowl for a few minutes until smooth. Cover and let ferment at room temperature (68 to 77 degrees) until doubled in volume, 6 to 8 hours.

2. **MAKE THE FINAL DOUGH**: Combine the Russello flour, Tumminia flour, water, lievito madre, and salt in the bowl of an electric mixer fitted with a dough hook. Stir with a spatula just until a rough dough forms. With the dough hook, mix on low (2 on a KitchenAid mixer), scraping the dough from the hook once or twice as necessary, until the gluten is developed but not overworked (the dough will be not too stretchy, and a little bit gritty from the flour), about 10 minutes.

3. **FIRST FERMENTATION**: Transfer the dough to a lightly oiled, clear 4-quart container with a lid. Turn the dough over so all sides are oiled. Cover and let stand 45 minutes. Pat into a 6 by 8-inch rectangle and fold like a business letter. Slide both hands under the dough and flip it over so the folds are underneath. Slip it back into the container, cover, and let stand another 45 minutes. Fold again. Cover and let stand until the dough is relaxed and increased in volume by about 50 percent, another 1½ hours.

recipe continues

recipe continued from previous page

4. **REST**: On a lightly floured countertop, pre-shape the dough into a loose round (see page 78). Dust with flour and cover with plastic. Let rest for 10 minutes.

5. **FINAL PROOF**: Line a baker's peel or rimless baking sheet with parchment. Shape the dough into a snub-nosed torpedo, about 12 inches long, and transfer to the parchment. Brush all over with water and sprinkle with the sesame seeds. Drape with plastic wrap and let stand 1 hour.

6. **BAKE**: About 1 hour before baking, place a baking stone on the middle rack of the oven and place a cast-iron skillet on the lower rack. Preheat the oven to 400 degrees for 1 hour. Slide the dough, still on the parchment, onto the baking stone. Place 1 cup of ice cubes in the skillet to produce steam. Bake until the crust is a caramel brown and the sesame seeds are toasted, about 45 minutes. Slide the loaf, still on the parchment, onto a wire rack. Cool completely. Store in a brown paper bag at room temperature for up to 6 days.

Note for Professional Bakers

Because of the weaker characteristics of the Russello and Tumminia flour, it is very important to control the strength of the dough through the folding process during the first fermentation. For larger batches, the dough should be divided in bulk and fermented in a well-oiled container to make sure it won't stick and ensure a proper folding process without having to take the dough out of the tub. This will ensure precision and efficiency during this process.

CIABATTA CON SEGALE

Although rye isn't associated with Roman baking, it is increasingly used by Italian bakers across the country looking to incorporate a variety of whole grains into their breads. This bread was inspired by the rye ciabatta I saw at Antico Forno Roscioli in Rome (page 232). The breads there are a mix of the very traditional along with the new and novel.

Italian bakers don't maintain a rye sourdough, so when they want to bake with rye they simply build one from the wheat starter they already have, which is what I've done here. To wind up with a rye-flavored ciabatta that is characteristically bubbly and light, I've limited the use of rye to the starter, using wheat flour in the final dough.

START TO FINISH:

8 to 14

hours

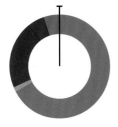

RYE SOURDOUGH STARTER
6 to 8 hours

KNEAD
10 minutes

FIRST FERMENTATION
2½ hours

REST
40 minutes

BAKE
35 minutes

MAKES
two 509-gram loaves

INGREDIENTS	BAKER'S %	METRIC WEIGHT
RYE SOURDOUGH STARTER		
Whole rye flour	100	45 g
Water	100	45 g
Liquid Sourdough Starter (page 182)	22	10 g
FINAL DOUGH		
Tipo 00 flour with W value of 250 to 260	100	500 g
Water	80	400 g
Salt	2.8	14 g
Dry instant yeast	1	5 g
Rye sourdough starter	20	100 g

1. **PREPARE THE RYE SOURDOUGH STARTER**: In a small bowl, stir together the rye flour, water, and liquid sourdough starter until well incorporated. Cover and let ferment at room temperature (68 to 77 degrees) until doubled in volume, 6 to 8 hours.

2. **MAKE THE FINAL DOUGH**: Combine the flour, 300 g of the water, the salt, yeast, and rye sourdough starter in the bowl of an electric mixer fitted with a dough hook. Mix with a rubber spatula until a rough dough forms. With the dough hook, mix on low (2 on a KitchenAid mixer)

recipe continues

recipe continued from previous page

for 5 minutes. Turn the mixer to medium-low (4 on a KitchenAid mixer) and slowly drizzle the remaining 100 g water into the bowl, pausing every 10 g to allow the dough to absorb the water. Once the water is incorporated, continue to mix on medium-low for 5 minutes more.

3. **FIRST FERMENTATION**: Transfer the dough to a lightly oiled, clear 4-quart container with a lid. Turn the dough over so all sides are oiled. Cover and let stand 1 hour. Turn the dough out onto a lightly floured counter. Pat into a 6- by 8-inch rectangle and fold like a business letter. Slide both hands under the dough and flip it over so the folds are underneath. Slip it back into the container, cover, and let stand another 1½ hours.

4. One hour before baking, line a baker's peel or rimless baking sheet with parchment paper. Place a baking stone on the middle rack of the oven and a cast-iron skillet on the lower rack. Preheat the oven to 450 degrees.

5. **FINAL PROOF**: On a lightly floured countertop, gently press the dough into a rectangle measuring 9 by 11 inches. With a bench scraper or chef's knife, cut into two rectangles, 4½ by 11 inches. Transfer the two rectangles to the baker's peel, bottom sides up. Dust with flour and cover with plastic wrap. Let rest 40 minutes.

6. **BAKE**: Right before they go into the oven, with the four fingers of one hand, dimple each ciabatta at 1-inch intervals. Slide the loaves, still on the parchment, onto the baking stone. Place 1 cup of ice cubes in the skillet to produce steam. Bake for 10 minutes. Turn the heat down to 425 degrees and continue to bake until nicely browned and puffy, about 25 minutes. Slide the loaves, still on the parchment, onto a wire rack. Cool completely. Ciabatta con Segale is best eaten on the day it is baked, but can also be stored in a brown paper bag at room temperature for up to 2 days. Leftover loaves can be wrapped in plastic and then aluminum foil and frozen for up to 1 month.

Note for Professional Bakers

The double hydration technique can be used to skip the second folding of the dough. Mix the dough with the first portion of water until the gluten is about 80 percent developed. Then add the remaining water and mix the dough until full gluten development is achieved. One hour after mixing, fold the dough just once, place in an oiled tub, cover, and refrigerate.

SEELE

Florian Domberger says that this is his second-favorite bread, right behind his signature rye loaf (page 278). It's a hybrid. When he was putting together his product list, he remembered from his childhood a style of rye bread popular in his town, long and thin with a shatteringly crispy crust. Reluctant to offer a second rye that might draw customers away from the first one, he substituted wheat dough for rye, dipping the fermented dough in water and placing it directly in the oven to get the crust style he was searching for. "At first it was a big mess, with water everywhere. We learned to work quickly, dunking the breads in water and then baking them immediately without a final proof." At home, I found that this dough needed a 30-minute rest before baking. The cumin seed and flaky sea salt sprinkled on the dough make these breads an irresistible savory treat.

INGREDIENTS	BAKER'S %	METRIC WEIGHT
RYE STARTER		
Rye Sourdough Starter (page 183)	30	15
Water	125	65
Whole rye flour	100	50
FINAL DOUGH		
Type 55 or equivalent flour (11 to 11.5% protein)	100	504 g
Water	65	328 g
Salt	2.4	12 g
Dry instant yeast	0.6	3
Rye starter	26	130 g
FINISHING		
Cumin seed		11 g
Flaky sea salt		14 g

recipe continues

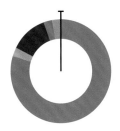

START TO FINISH:
18½ to 25
hours

RYE STARTER
15 hours

AUTOLYSE
30 minutes

KNEAD
16 minutes

FIRST FERMENTATION
2 hours

REST
30 minutes

BAKE
30 minutes

MAKES
three 325-gram loaves

recipe continued from previous page

1. **PREPARE THE RYE STARTER**: In a small bowl, dissolve the sourdough starter in the water. Stir in the rye flour until well incorporated. It will have the consistency of thick pancake batter. Cover and let ferment at room temperature 68 to 77 degrees) until it rises and is very puffy, about 15 hours.

2. **AUTOLYSE**: Combine the flour and water in the bowl of an electric mixer fitted with a dough hook. Mix just until a dry and shaggy dough forms. Cover and let rest 30 minutes.

3. **MAKE THE FINAL DOUGH**: Add the salt, yeast, and rye starter to the bowl. Mix with a rubber spatula until a rough dough forms. With the dough hook, mix on medium-low (4 on a KitchenAid mixer) setting until the dough is soft and elastic with a velvety texture, and slightly sticky to the touch, 12 minutes, stopping to scrape down the bowl as needed. Pull the dough off the hook. Turn the mixer to medium (6 on a KitchenAid mixer) and mix until shiny and elastic, another 4 minutes.

4. **FIRST FERMENTATION**: Use a dough scraper to transfer the dough to a lightly oiled, clear 4-quart container with a lid. With damp hands, turn the dough over so all sides are oiled. Cover and let stand until pillowy, about 2 hours.

5. **FINAL PROOF**: Preheat the oven to 425 degrees. Line a baking sheet with a silicone baking mat. On a lightly floured countertop, divide the dough into four equal pieces. Shape each piece of dough into a baguette (see page 78) about 10 inches long. Fill a small rimmed baking sheet with ½ inch of water. Spread the cumin seed and sea salt on another rimmed baking sheet. Working quickly, roll each seele in the water to coat, then roll the top in the seed and salt

mixture, and transfer to the lined baking sheet, arranging the loaves 2 inches apart. Cover and let rest 30 minutes.

6. **BAKE**: Bake the loaves until deep brown and shiny, about 30 minutes. Immediately transfer the loaves to a wire rack. Cool completely. Seele are best eaten on the day they are baked.

Note for Professional Bakers

When working with a deck oven, it is important to line the loader with parchment paper, or the wet dough will stick to the canvas. If working with an oven peel in a wood-fire oven, cover the peel with parchment to facilitate the transfer from the peel to the oven deck. After baking, the parchment is easily swept from the bake chambers.

VARIATION:
KAISER ROLLS

You can use this same dough and technique to make delicious Kaiser rolls. After the first fermentation, divide the dough into ten pieces, 95 to 100 g each. On a well-floured work surface, shape each into a square (see page 79), cover, and let rest for 20 minutes. Press to flatten into 4-inch squares. Working with one square at a time, fold in one quarter toward the center. Make an indentation in the center of this folded piece. Make a second fold to match up with the indentation just made. Repeat the indentation, now in the center of the second folded piece. Continue around the dough. On the final fold, tuck the dough to the outside edge. Turn the dough over to be folded side down. Repeat with the remaining squares. Dip each one in water, roll tops in the seed and salt mixture, and bake on Silpat-lined baking sheets for 20 minutes, until golden brown.

TOURTE DE MEULE

START TO FINISH:

13 to 15

hours

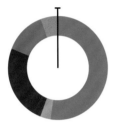

FIRM LEVAIN STARTER
6 to 8 hours

AUTOLYSE
30 minutes

KNEAD
22 minutes

FIRST FERMENTATION
3½ hours

FINAL PROOF
2 hours

BAKE
50 minutes

MAKES
one 1.5-kilo loaf

Thirty years ago, the only bakers making this classic French country bread ("millstone bread") were the Poilâne brothers and a handful of others trying to keep bread traditions alive in an era of increasing industrial bread production. This bread was generally made with a firm levain starter, which fermented slowly and reliably at cool room temperature (these bakeries were often at basement level). This starter gave breads a more pronounced sour flavor because of the predominance of acetic acids produced during fermentation. The Poilânes and their cohort were successful to such a degree that today you can see large miches almost everywhere in France. I myself was an early adopter, producing a Poilâne-style loaf at Bread Alone from the very beginning of my business.

With the renewed popularity of big country breads, there has naturally been some experimentation. One of the most important realizations has been that today's artisan flour, because of careful wheat selection and improved milling practices, can absorb more water than the flours used 30 years ago, especially if the water is added in a particular way. Younger French bakers like Rodolphe Landemaine are more likely than their predecessors to employ the technique of *bassinage,* in which extra water is slowly added to the dough after autolyse. The result is similar to the classic miche, but with a moister, softer crumb and a larger cell structure. After watching Fabrice Guéry, the head baker at Minoterie Suire, employ bassinage in the mill's test bakery, I revised my own recipe and this is how we make pain au levain at Bread Alone today.

INGREDIENTS	BAKER'S %	METRIC WEIGHT
FIRM LEVAIN STARTER		
Firm Sourdough Starter (page 182)	20	20 g
Water	65	65 g
Type 85 or equivalent flour (11 to 11.5% protein)	100	100 g
FINAL DOUGH		
Type 85 or equivalent flour (11 to 11.5% protein)	100	726 g
Water	80	580 g
Salt	2.5	18 g
Firm levain starter	25	185 g

1. **PREPARE THE FIRM LEVAIN STARTER**: In a small bowl, mash together the sourdough starter and water to loosen the starter. Stir in the flour until well incorporated, then knead by hand in the bowl for a few minutes until smooth. Cover and let ferment at room temperature (68 to 77 degrees) until doubled in volume, 6 to 8 hours.

2. **AUTOLYSE**: Combine the flour and 525 g of the water in the bowl of an electric mixer fitted with a dough hook. Mix just until a rough dough forms. Cover and let rest 30 minutes.

3. **MAKE THE FINAL DOUGH**: Add the salt and levain starter to the bowl. With the dough hook, mix on the low speed (2 on a KitchenAid mixer) until the dough comes together and begins to smooth out, about 5 minutes. Pull the dough off the hook. With the mixer still on low, slowly drizzle the remaining 50 g water, about 10 g at a time, waiting between drizzles until the water is absorbed, about 15 minutes. Turn the mixer to medium-low speed (4 on the KitchenAid) and continue to mix until the dough is soft, elastic, and shiny, another 2 minutes.

4. **FIRST FERMENTATION**: Use a dough scraper to transfer the dough to a lightly oiled, clear 4-quart container with a lid. Turn the dough over so all sides are oiled. Cover and let stand until the dough is pillowy, 2 to 3 hours. Turn the dough out onto a lightly floured counter. Pat into a 6- by 8-inch rectangle and fold like a business letter. Slide

recipe continues

recipe continued from previous page

both hands under the dough and flip it over so the folds are underneath. Slip it back into the container, cover, and let stand another 1½ hours.

5. **FINAL PROOF**: On a lightly floured countertop, gently round the dough. Place in a lightly floured banneton, seam side up. Cover with plastic wrap or a kitchen towel and let rest until pillowy, about 2 hours.

6. **BAKE**: About 1 hour before baking, place a baking stone on the middle rack of the oven and a cast-iron skillet on the lower rack. Preheat the oven to 425 degrees for 1 hour. Cover a baker's peel or rimless baking sheet with parchment. Tip the loaf onto the parchment-lined peel. With a *lame*, a single-edged razor blade, or a serrated knife, make four slashes, about ½ inch deep, to form a square. Make two small cuts in the center of the loaf to form a small X. Place 1 cup of ice cubes in the skillet to produce steam. Bake until the loaf is golden brown and well risen, about 50 minutes. Slide the loaf, still on the parchment, onto a wire rack. Cool completely. Store in a brown paper bag at room temperature for up to 1 week.

Notes for Professional Bakers

In order to maintain a consistent level of acidity and a balanced flavor in the levain, and therefore in the finished breads, it is very important to be consistent in the feeding process: the proportion of the ingredients (especially starter), water temperature, maturation time, and temperature. At Bread Alone, we scale our levain into 15-kilo pieces, store them in a temperature-controlled environment, and check the development at precise times, measuring the increase in volume and the pH as well. We also taste the levain frequently, to make sure that it is meeting our flavor expectations.

Miches can be retarded overnight after shaping, allowing you some flexibility in your production schedule. At Bread Alone, we hold our miches at 48 degrees for 12 hours, then proof them at 73 degrees until ready for the oven.

VARIATION:

WALNUT MICHE

Add 250 g toasted and cooled walnut pieces to the dough after the bassinage at the end of step 3 and before the final 2 to 3 minutes of mixing. Blend slowly, stopping the mixer in 30-second intervals until the walnuts are incorporated.

TOURTE DE SEIGLE

I first saw this rye bread, also known as *tourte Auvergnate,* at Pierre Nury's bakery in Loubeyrat. The rye flour he uses is ground from the rye grown in the fields that ring the town. His large, gnarled breads weigh in at 4 kilos, and fit comfortably in the muscled arms of the farmers who shop there.

I had the unique privilege of being tutored by Pierre Nury on how to make this Auvergne specialty. Pierre showed me how bakers use very hot water, 140 degrees, which spurs fermentation in the starter, ensuring a vibrant and active culture teeming with warm wild yeast and energetic enzymatic activity. The culture is responsible for the bread's volcanic rise in the oven. Pierre was careful when kneading the dough, blending it on low speed for up to 10 minutes, but no longer, to safeguard the rye's fragile structure while incorporating oxygen for the best rise. Properly blended, it has a thick, porridge-like texture. This recipe has a hydration of 90 percent. Depending on the flour's ability to absorb water, Pierre will go up to 100 percent if necessary. As the dough sits in the banneton it begins to hold its shape on its own so it can be turned onto the baker's peel. Then it must sit on the peel for another 5 to 10 minutes to begin to develop the cracks that characterize the final bread.

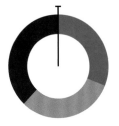

START TO FINISH:
6 to 6½
hours

FIRM RYE STARTER
2 hours

FIRST FERMENTATION
1½ to 2 hours

FINAL PROOF
1½ hours

BAKE
50 to 55 minutes

MAKES
one 1.2-kilo loaf

INGREDIENTS	BAKER'S %	METRIC WEIGHT
FIRM RYE STARTER		
Whole rye flour	100	130 g
Very hot water, 140 degrees	62	80 g
Rye Sourdough Starter (page 183)	50	65 g
FINAL DOUGH		
Whole rye flour	100	500 g
Very hot water, 140 degrees	90	450 g
Salt	3	15 g
Instant yeast	0.2	1 g
Firm rye starter	55	275 g

recipe continues

recipe continued from previous page

1. **PREPARE THE FIRM RYE STARTER**: In a medium bowl, combine the rye flour and very hot water. With a rubber spatula, blend for 1½ minutes, to incorporate and cool slightly. Add the sourdough starter and continue to mix until thick but smooth, about 3 minutes. Cover and let ferment at room temperature (68 to 77 degrees) until it becomes porous with small bubbles on the surface, about 2 hours.

2. **MAKE THE FINAL DOUGH**: Add the flour, very hot water, salt, and yeast to the firm rye starter. Mix with a rubber spatula until smooth, about 4 minutes.

3. **FIRST FERMENTATION**: Cover the mixing bowl with plastic wrap and let stand until the dough increases in volume by about 20 percent, becoming porous and with small bubbles on the surface, 1½ to 2 hours.

4. **FINAL PROOF**: Gently scrape the dough from the bowl onto a well-floured countertop. Get your hands slightly wet (this will make the dough easier to handle) and gently form the dough into a ball, shaping it like clay. Generously flour a cloth-lined banneton and put the dough in, smooth side down. Cover with a clean kitchen towel and let stand for 1½ hours.

5. **BAKE**: About 1 hour before baking, position an oven rack in the bottom third of the oven and set the Dutch oven (with the lid on) on the rack. Preheat the oven to 450 degrees for 1 hour. Wearing oven mitts, carefully remove the Dutch oven to a heatproof surface and take off the lid. Tip the dough directly into the Dutch oven. Put the lid on and bake for 25 minutes. Turn the heat down to 400 degrees, remove the lid, and bake until the loaf is dark brown, another 25 to 35 minutes. Carefully turn the loaf out onto a wire rack. Cool completely. Store in a brown paper bag at room temperature for 3 to 4 days.

Notes for Professional Bakers

The dividing and shaping of this bread must be done by hand. There's no way to streamline the process. The best way to divide the dough is by keeping a digital scale by the mixer and portioning it directly from the mixing bowl to the bannetons, previously heavily dusted with flour. The handling of the dough will be easier with wet hands, so a bucket of water by the scale is essential.

Because these breads have an excellent shelf life, they could be baked at the end of the day to be sold first thing in the morning. Their texture and flavor will be even better after they sit overnight.

VEGAN BRIOCHE

Even in a very traditional place like Altamura, there's a growing vegan community and bakers who want to serve them. Vincenzo Benvenuto of Caffetteria del Viale, a classically trained pastry chef who has made just such a foray into vegan baking, gave me this recipe during my most recent visit. He shapes his brioche dough into tapered bâtards. Perfumed with olive oil and semolina, they were really yummy. He uses fructose, a natural plant sugar. I've substituted more easily available agave syrup, which can be found in natural foods stores and most supermarkets. If you are not strictly vegan, you can use substitute granulated sugar and get the same result.

Because of the quantity of olive oil in this recipe, it is important to add it slowly and in stages to the final dough. This gradual incorporation will ensure a strong structure and a better development and volume for the finished bread. I've shaped Vincenzo's dough into rolls. Leftovers can be frozen in a zipper-lock bag in the freezer and defrosted whenever the need for brioche arises.

INGREDIENTS	BAKER'S %	METRIC WEIGHT
LIEVITO MADRE		
Extra-fancy durum flour (*semolina rimacinata*)	100	85 g
Water	70	59 g
Liquid Sourdough Starter (page 182)	20	17 g
FINAL DOUGH		
Extra-fancy durum flour (*semolina rimacinata*)	100	618 g
Agave syrup	10	62 g
Water	61	377 g
Salt	2.1	13 g
Lievito madre	26	161 g
Dry instant yeast	0.5	3 g
Extra-virgin olive oil	15	93 g

recipe continues

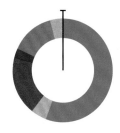

START TO FINISH:
10½ to 11
hours

LIEVITO MADRE
6 hours

KNEAD
32 minutes

FIRST FERMENTATION
2 hours

REST
20 minutes

FINAL PROOF
1½ hours

BAKE
25 minutes

MAKES
twelve 110-gram rolls

recipe continued from previous page

1. **PREPARE THE LIEVITO MADRE**: In a small bowl, stir together the flour, water, and sourdough starter until well incorporated. Cover and let ferment at room temperature (68 to 77 degrees) until doubled in volume, about 6 hours.

2. **MAKE THE FINAL DOUGH**: Combine the flour, agave, water, salt, lievito madre, and yeast in the bowl of an electric mixer fitted with a dough hook. Stir with a spatula just until a rough dough forms. With the dough hook, mix on lowest setting for 2 minutes. Turn to low (2 on a KitchenAid mixer) and continue to knead until the dough is elastic and pulls away from the sides of the bowl, another 10 minutes. With the mixer on, drizzle the olive oil into the bowl about one-fourth at a time, allowing the oil to be absorbed between drizzles, about 20 minutes more.

3. **FIRST FERMENTATION**: Transfer the dough to a lightly oiled, clear 4-quart container with a lid. Turn the dough over so all sides are oiled. Cover and let ferment 1 hour.

4. Turn the dough out onto a lightly floured counter. Pat into a 6- by 8-inch rectangle and fold like a business letter. Slide both hands under the dough and flip it over so the folds are underneath. Slip it back into the container, cover, and let stand another hour.

5. **REST**: On a lightly floured countertop, divide the dough into nine equal pieces. Cover and let rest 20 minutes.

6. **FINAL PROOF**: Line a baker's peel or rimless baking sheet with parchment paper. Roll each dough piece into a 10-inch-long strip. Loop one end of each strip toward the bottom, draping the tip over the other end, leaving two inches of the bottom of each end hanging. Twist the loop over itself once. Loop the 2-inch end piece underneath and through the center of the roll. Place on prepared peel. Cover loosely with a towel or plastic wrap. Let rest until pillowy, 1½ hours.

7. **BAKE**: About 1 hour before baking, place a baking stone on the middle rack of the oven and a cast-iron skillet on the lower rack. Preheat the oven to 350 degrees for 1 hour. Place 1 cup of ice cubes in the skillet to produce steam. Slide the rolls, still on the parchment, onto the baking stone. Bake the rolls until risen and golden, about 25 minutes. Slide the rolls, still on the parchment, onto a wire rack. Cool completely. Store in a brown paper bag at room temperature for 2 to 3 days.

Notes for Professional Bakers

The vegan brioche dough could also be used to make delicious pan bread or as a base for vegan cinnamon rolls. After refrigeration, simply use as you would for pan bread or laminate for cinnamon rolls.

Use only the first speed of the mixer when mixing this bread. A warmer dough temperature, between 80 and 85 degrees, is recommended to trigger faster fermentation activity.

8

COMPLEX
SOURDOUGHS

The recipes that follow are "complex," in that they are built in several stages. Bakers take these multiple steps for good reasons.

Florian Domberger's traditional German rye requires a starter that must be refreshed not once but twice before the dough is mixed. The culture develops tasty acidity during the first stage, and lively yeast activity during the second. Jochen Gaues soaks toasted rye bread crumbs at the same time that he prepares his starter. This soaker adds smoky, caramel flavor to the finished bread. *Pane giallo,* a traditional Italian bread made with cornmeal, calls for a cornmeal soaker as well as a sourdough starter. Soaking the grain unlocks its flavor and ensures a bread with a moist crumb.

None of the steps in these recipes is difficult, but success does depend on being organized and prepared. Before plunging in, read your recipe carefully, several times over, so you understand the timing of the steps and all starters and soakers are ready to go when you need them.

A BAKER'S DREAM, FULFILLED

FLORIAN DOMBERGER, DOMBERGER BROT-WERK
BERLIN, GERMANY

Florian Domberger was not born to be a baker, although bread has always been part of his life. "I could almost live off bread alone, with a little butter, beer, and sausage." His great-grandfather, grandfather, and father all worked in the family business, freight forwarding. He's driven trucks, repaired engines, and managed the logistics of a large moving company. "I have diesel fuel in my veins," he says. But after a stint in the German Air Force, he felt that Augsburg, his hometown in Bavaria, was too small. A job with a transport company in Hong Kong, where he was responsible for business in 17 Asian countries, allowed him to discover another part of the world. He met his wife, Vanessa See, and they moved to Indonesia. "I was a shipping person, so naturally I arranged for my favorite German rye bread to be delivered to me every two weeks, wherever we were living. Because in the end, everything is logistics."

After a move to Australia with Vanessa and their infant daughter, he enrolled in an MBA program and took a life-changing class in entrepreneurship. His class project, a business plan for a craft bakery, won first prize and enthusiastic praise from his teacher. The idea was to bake pure, simple, German rye sourdough bread, inspired by the loaves baked by nuns at a monastery outside of Augsburg. A medical emergency brought him and his family back to Germany just as he was on the verge of implementing his plan. Bakery on the back burner, he took a job in sourcing at Johnson & Johnson in Europe and stayed for ten years.

In the meantime, he set out to become a home baker, making sourdough bread in his own kitchen, experimenting with feeding schedules and visiting regularly with small craft bakers. "When I first started working with dough, I was almost afraid to touch it, afraid I would damage it." With experience came more confidence.

On a whim, Florian and Vanessa bought a camouflage-painted mobile bakery, built in 1968 for the Swiss Army, that they saw on the side of the road in Switzerland and towed it

back to Germany. In 2015, Florian apprenticed with master baker Björn Meadow, owner of a craft bakery in Eberswalde, developing recipes for what would become Domberger's signature breads. With Björn, he began to bake rustic sourdough rye loaves in the mobile bakery at various locations between Eberswalde and Berlin. In 2016, with the help of Björn, he opened Domberger Brot-Werk in the lovely residential neighborhood of Alt Moabit, where it has become a gathering spot for a diverse group of locals hungry for old-style German bread.

Florian and Björn combined their business and baking experience to produce exemplary bread. Ingredients are organic. They bake just 200 to 250 loaves a day, using the traditional German two-stage sourdough method. "The mobile bakery turned out to be one of the best things that happened to us, because it forced us to think small and work with discipline."

The product list is capped at ten. An expert at sourcing, Florian works with just two mills, one for spelt and wheat and another for rye. With a small materials portfolio and a small product portfolio, there is little to no waste. He would like to expand the business by opening more bakeries in the city. But each one would follow the model of the original, baking a limited menu of breads on the premises to control quality and eliminate waste. Even though his bakery is young, he has already won awards for baking some of Berlin's best sourdough.

And with the continuing operation of the mobile bakery, he hopes to teach, train, and inspire young bakers in and around Berlin. He regularly visits elementary schools, giving workshops meant to get kids excited about the craft. His business is proof that you can do something with your hands, make a living, and go home satisfied at night.

DOMBERGER RYE BREAD

START TO FINISH:

22 to 29

hours

FIRST STAGE STARTER
16 to 24 hours

SECOND STAGE STARTER
3 to 4 hours

FIRST FERMENTATION
1 hour

FINAL PROOF
1 hour

BAKE
50 to 60 minutes

MAKES
one 1.76-kilo loaf

Florian Domberger graciously let me use his bakery in the afternoons and evenings to bake the breads that we photographed for this book. When I arrived at the end of his workday, I admired these large, rustic rounds. It is Domberger's signature bread, and each loaf is dramatically scored with a large "D." He only bakes a few each day, and they sell out right away. Towards the end of my week there, I made sure to reserve one. When I tried it, I fell for its distinctively pungent flavor and rugged, old-world look. Florian graciously shared his recipe with me, and I am sharing it now with you.

Florian follows a very traditional two-stage sourdough build. The first stage (*grundsauerteig*) is a stiff dough and contributes acidic flavor. The second stage (*schaumsauerteig*) is much warmer and softer than the first, and encourages lively yeast activity. Florian uses a vintage diving arm mixer. The mixer's gentle movement is favored by northern European bakers who primarily bake rye breads. These rye breads do not get kneaded in the same manner as wheat breads. Let the sourdough do the work and handle this dough as little as possible.

INGREDIENTS	BAKER'S %	METRIC WEIGHT
GRUNDSAUERTEIG (First Stage Rye Starter)		
Rye Sourdough Starter (page 183)	10	16 g
Water	100	160 g
Whole rye flour	100	160 g
SCHAUMSAUERTEIG (Second Stage Rye Starter)		
Grundsauerteig	140	336 g
Warm water, 90 degrees	133	320 g
Whole rye flour	100	240 g
FINAL DOUGH		
Schaumsauerteig	149	896 g
Whole rye flour	100	600 g
Salt	3.3	20 g
Warm water, 90 degrees	41	250 g

recipe continues

recipe continued from previous page

1. **PREPARE THE GRUNDSAUERTEIG (first stage rye)**: In a small bowl, dissolve the sourdough starter in the water and stir vigorously. Stir in the rye flour until well incorporated. It will have the consistency of thick pancake batter. Cover and let ferment at room temperature (68 to 77 degrees) for 16 to 24 hours.

2. **PREPARE THE SCHAUMSAUERTEIG (second stage rye)**: Preheat the oven to 200 degrees for 5 minutes. Turn off the oven. In a small bowl, combine the grundsauerteig, warm water, and rye flour in a medium bowl. Stir to combine. Cover and let ferment in the warm oven until bubbly and soft, 3 to 4 hours.

3. **MAKE THE FINAL DOUGH**: Combine the schaumsauerteig, rye flour, salt, and warm water in a medium bowl. Mix with a rubber spatula until well blended, about 4 minutes.

4. **FIRST FERMENTATION**: Cover the mixing bowl with plastic wrap and let stand until the dough increases in volume by about 50 percent, about 1 hour. It will become porous, with a few small bubbles on the surface.

5. **FINAL PROOF**: On a well-floured countertop (use rye flour here), shape the dough into a loose boule (see page 78). Dust the inside of a banneton generously with rye flour. (Alternatively, use a bowl lined with a kitchen towel and dusted with rye flour.) Place the boule, smooth side down, in the banneton. Lightly dust with more flour and cover loosely with plastic wrap. Let stand until puffy, 1½ to 2 hours.

6. **BAKE**: About 1 hour before baking, position an oven rack in the bottom third of the oven and set the Dutch oven (with the lid on) on the rack. Preheat the oven to 450 degrees for 1 hour. Wearing oven mitts, carefully remove the Dutch oven to a heatproof surface and take off the lid. Tip the dough directly into the Dutch oven. Put the lid on and bake for 25 minutes. Turn the heat down to 400 degrees. Remove the lid and bake until the loaf is dark brown, another 35 to 40 minutes. Carefully turn the loaf out onto a wire rack. Cool completely. Store in a brown paper bag at room temperature for 3 to 4 days.

Note for Professional Bakers

This bread can also be baked in a regular deck oven. For optimum results, it is best to start at a high temperature (480 to 500 degrees) with a lot of steam to maximize the oven spring, then decrease the temperature to 425 to achieve the proper baking of the bread. Leave the door open the last 10 minutes of the bake to provide better crust characteristics.

REBEL IN THE BACKSTUBE

JOCHEN GAUES, BÄCKER GAUES, LACHENDORF, GERMANY

Jochen Gaues describes his childhood self as unruly in school and a mystery to his father, a respected chemist, and his mother, a medical technician. "At school, I began sketching large balls of fire and loose, prehistoric-looking breads that could easily be mistaken for small boulders. You see, I had visited my uncle, a master baker in Wolfsburg, many times growing up. The ovens, the sweaty bakers, the masses of dough left a strong impression on me. But my parents were disturbed by my pictures of ovens and fire. My parents took me for some psychological testing. 'Is our son intelligent?' they asked the psychologist. 'Well, it's not that he's not intelligent. He just wants to be a baker!' was the reply."

Inside his immaculate bakery, he crafts his bubbly loaves, unique in a country that has a tradition of dense rye breads. Jochen gives his small staff directions in a voice loud enough to fill a concert hall. "The bakery is my theater more than it is my laboratory. The first thing I do in the morning is set the stage. There are not too many props. I have two big wooden work-tables, a mixer, some buckets, and a sourdough machine. I spend thirty minutes organizing

profile continues

profile continued from previous page

and oiling pans, getting measuring equipment ready, getting the buckets of ice, getting the buckets for dough ready. Then it is showtime." His baritone can be heard from the street, barking instructions as well as his thoughts on the government and the health department. His run-ins with both the tax man and German health officials (some inspectors didn't understand that his well-fermented sourdough starters were teeming with only healthy bacteria) have earned him his nickname: Rebel in the Backstube. He has equally nonconformist beliefs about baking.

He has a large grinder to grind stale bread, which he mixes together with rye flour and starter to build his dark, pungent sourdough. This sourdough is in constant motion inside two vintage stainless-steel dairy tanks. The caramelized starches in the ground bread, along with a smaller quantity of fresh rye flour, produce a starter with a dark caramel flavor, almost smoky, that is completely unique.

Jochen mixes his dough in an extremely unorthodox way. At the beginning of the 30-minute

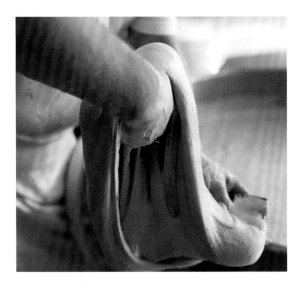

process it may look like any other bread dough, stiff and easy to handle. After additions of water, then ice, and then more water, it looks more like a bubbling porridge. "I don't like to analyze or quantify. Bakers have to learn by feel. I do everything by hand here. That's strange in Germany. Most German bakers love their machinery for dumping, cutting, and scaling dough. I hardly use a scale. I know by sight how many buckets of water, scoops of salt, and tubs of sourdough to put in the mixer with a 25 kilogram bag of flour. That's strange too, because other bakers weigh each ingredient down to the gram." Jochen, in contrast, must "feel the energy of the dough, feel its texture, to know when the moment is right to move to the next step."

The stretchy, flowing mixture would slip through most bakers' hands, but Jochen has figured out how to wrangle the dough. He cuts it, then deposits it into small plastic tubs to ferment for up to 8 hours. During this period, he folds the dough three times, to develop gluten and thus build its strength. Jochen casually shapes the slack dough, using large handfuls of flour, into manageable blobs. He doesn't give the "shaped" loaves too much time to proof (or spread). Instead he puts them almost immediately into his beloved Heuft thermal oil-heated oven, where they get a huge rise. You can see from the photos that his breads are richly caramelized, almost black. The finished bread is crudely formed, baked dark, with a supermoist and aromatic crumb.

The contrast in Jochen's breads between the dense, moist crumb and the thick crust is striking and unique. So is his use of ingredient combinations like tomato and curry. And who bakes bread inside a cabbage leaf? These are like no other breads I've ever seen or tasted.

KOHL-SPECK BROT

This dark, moist rye loaf is one of Jochen's signature breads. Setting a piece of dough atop a cabbage ("kohl") leaf and a slice of ham ("speck") is a technique he picked up as a young apprentice. It makes for an unusual-looking bread, embraced by a blackened, roasted cabbage leaf that is oozing with fat from the ham, which also bakes into the bottom crust. The cabbage prevents the ham from sticking to the baking sheet. The ham's flavor permeates the bread.

The bread itself is raised with a simplified version of Jochen's very aromatic toasted bread sourdough starter. The caramelized crumbs that he stirs into the sourdough give the bread a rugged rye flavor with some sweetness and smoke.

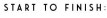

START TO FINISH:

12

hours

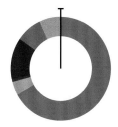

INGREDIENTS	BAKER'S %	METRIC WEIGHT
RYE STARTER		
Whole rye flour	100	140 g
Water	125	175 g
Rye Sourdough Starter (page 183)	14	20 g
OLD BREAD SOAKER		
Stale rye bread, coarsely ground and lightly toasted	100	200 g
Water	125	250 g
FINAL DOUGH		
Bread soaker	82	450 g
Whole wheat flour	45	250 g
Type 65 or equivalent flour (11 to 11.5% protein)	55	300 g
Cool water, 60 degrees	50	275 g
Dry instant yeast	2.4	13 g
Salt	2.4	13 g
Rye starter	60	335 g
Two 4-inch-round green cabbage leaves, blanched		—
Two ⅛-inch-thick slices country ham, about 5 inches in diameter each		30 to 40 g

RYE STARTER AND BREAD SOAKER
8 hours

AUTOLYSE
30 minutes

KNEAD
9 minutes

FIRST FERMENTATION
1½ hours

FINAL PROOF
¾ to 1 hour

BAKE
50 minutes

MAKES
two 830-gram rounds

recipe continues

recipe continued from previous page

1. **PREPARE THE RYE STARTER**: In a small bowl, stir together the rye flour, water, and sourdough starter until well incorporated. Cover and let ferment at room temperature (68 to 77 degrees) until doubled in volume, 8 hours.

2. **MAKE THE BREAD SOAKER**: Combine the ground bread and water in a small bowl and let stand, stirring occasionally, for 8 hours. Drain excess water from the bread soaker.

3. **AUTOLYSE**: Combine the bread soaker, whole wheat flour, Type 65 flour, and cool water in the bowl of an electric mixer fitted with a dough hook. Cover the bowl with plastic wrap and let rest 30 minutes.

4. **MAKE THE FINAL DOUGH**: Add the yeast, salt, and rye starter to the bowl and mix on medium-low speed for 9 minutes. At this point you'll have a smooth dough with some small flecks and pieces of the old bread.

5. **FIRST FERMENTATION**: Cover the bowl and let the dough rise until almost doubled in volume, about 1½ hours.

6. **FINAL PROOF**: Brush a rimmed baking sheet lightly with olive oil. Place the cabbage leaves on the baking sheet and top with the ham. Turn the dough onto a lightly floured countertop. Divide into two equal pieces and shape each into a round (see page 78). Place the dough rounds on the ham. Cover with plastic wrap and let stand until the dough springs back when pressed with a fingertip, 45 to 60 minutes.

7. **BAKE**: About 1 hour before baking, place a baking stone on the middle rack of the oven and a cast-iron skillet on the lower rack. Heat the oven to 425 degrees for 1 hour. When ready to bake, turn the oven temperature down to 375 degrees. Transfer the baking sheet to the oven. Place ½ cup of ice cubes in the skillet to produce steam. Bake until the loaves are a rustic brown and well risen, about 50 minutes. Remove from the oven and transfer to a wire rack. Cool completely. Store in a brown paper bag at room temperature for 5 to 7 days.

Notes for Professional Bakers

After mixing, place the dough in an oiled tub and give it two folds during the first fermentation. This will increase the strength of the dough and the volume of the finished products. It is easy to overproof this dough. Because of the delicate gluten structure, the final proof must be short and carefully monitored.

The dough is very soft and sticky. Keep a small pail of warm water beside you so you can work the dough with wet hands during folding.

PANE GIALLO

I've seen *pane giallo* (yellow bread) in various shapes and sizes in bakeries in Puglia as well as in southern Tuscany and northern Umbria, places where polenta often appears on the dinner table. To make this bread, bakers don't simply stir cornmeal into their dough. Instead, they take the extra step of preparing polenta—stirring until it has a velvety, creamy texture with no trace of grit—that becomes the flavor and texture base of the bread. Once the polenta is cooled, it is combined with fine semolina flour. The result is a loaf with a delicate corn flavor; golden yellow hue; unique, moist crumb; and bronzed crust.

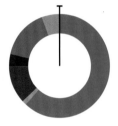

START TO FINISH:

13

hours

LIEVITO MADRE AND POLENTA
8 hours

KNEAD
10 minutes

FIRST FERMENTATION
1 to 1½ hours

REST
30 minutes

FINAL PROOF
2 hours

BAKE
45 minutes

MAKES
two 710-gram loaves

INGREDIENTS	BAKER'S %	METRIC WEIGHT
LIEVITO MADRE		
Fine semolina flour (*semolina rimacinata*)	100	100 g
Water	75	75 g
Liquid Sourdough Starter (page 182)	25	25 g
POLENTA		
Water	112	149 g
Milk	112	149 g
Stone-ground yellow cornmeal	75	100 g
Salt	2.7	2 g
FINAL DOUGH		
Fine semolina flour (*semolina rimacinata*)	100	500 g
Polenta	60	300 g
Water	72	360 g
Olive oil	5	25 g
Salt	2.8	14 g
Dry instant yeast	0.4	2 g
Lievito madre	40	200 g

recipe continues

recipe continued from previous page

1. **PREPARE THE LIEVITO MADRE**: In a small bowl, stir together the flour, water, and sourdough starter until well incorporated. Cover and let ferment at room temperature (68 to 77 degrees) until doubled in volume, about 8 hours.

2. **PREPARE THE POLENTA**: In a small pot, bring the water and milk to a boil over medium-high heat. Slowly whisk in the cornmeal and then the salt, then whisk continually until the mixture thickens, 2 to 3 minutes. Turn the heat to low, switch to a spoon, and continue to cook, stirring often, until the grains are swollen and taste cooked, about 15 minutes. Scrape into a bowl and let cool to room temperature. (The polenta can be prepared at the same time as the lievito madre and refrigerated overnight. Let it come to room temperature before using.)

3. **MAKE THE FINAL DOUGH**: Combine the flour, polenta, 300 g of the water, the olive oil, salt, yeast, and lievito madre in the bowl of an electric mixer fitted with a dough hook. Mix with a spatula just until a rough dough forms. With the dough hook, mix on low (2 on a KitchenAid mixer) for 2 minutes. Pull the dough off the hook and then, with the mixer on medium-low (4 on a KitchenAid mixer), slowly drizzle in the remaining 60 g water, 10 g at a time, waiting between drizzles until the water is absorbed, about 5 minutes. Continue to knead until elastic and shiny, about 3 minutes more.

4. **FIRST FERMENTATION**: Transfer the dough to a lightly oiled, clear 4-quart container with a lid. Cover and let stand until the dough has doubled in volume, 1 to 1½ hours.

5. **REST**: On a lightly floured countertop, divide the dough into two equal pieces and pre-shape into loose rounds (see page 78). Dust with flour and cover with plastic wrap. Let rest 30 minutes.

6. **FINAL PROOF**: Shape each round into a boule (see page 78). Place each boule, smooth side down, in a floured banneton or floured kitchen towel–lined bowl. Lightly dust with flour and cover loosely with plastic wrap. Let stand until pillowy, about 2 hours.

7. **BAKE**: About 1 hour before baking, place a baking stone on the middle rack of the oven and a cast-iron skillet on the lower rack. Preheat the oven to 425 degrees for 1 hour. Lightly flour a baker's peel or rimless baking sheet. Uncover the loaves. With a *lame*, a single-edged razor blade, or a serrated knife, score with three parallel cuts. Slide the loaves, still on the parchment, onto the baking stone. Place 1 cup of ice cubes in the skillet to produce steam. Bake until golden brown and well risen, about 45 minutes. Slide the loaves, still on the parchment, onto a wire rack. Cool completely. Store in a brown paper bag at room temperature for 3 to 5 days.

Note for Professional Bakers

Flour the bannetons with fine durum, or use a blend of durum and cornmeal to give the crust a more rustic appearance and crisp texture.

DUSSELDORF'S BELOVED BAKER

JOSEF HINKEL, BÄCKEREI HINKEL, DUSSELDORF, GERMANY

When I was considering getting a thermal oil-heated oven, the German oven manufacturer Heuft arranged for me to bake for a night at Bäckerei Hinkel. I had never used one, and I wanted to experience the quality of the bake in a busy German shop. I was told that Josef Hinkel, a fifth-generation Dusseldorf baker, had been using a Heuft oven for years, and was experienced with thermal oil technology, which requires special knowledge.

I arrived at the Dusseldorf address at midnight. The bakery was on the ground floor of an older, elegant apartment building on one of the city's nicest shopping streets. The head baker, a strong, young guy, was expecting me. At this point, he was alone in the mixing room with at least 15 large mixing bowls on wheels, each one containing a different amount of dark rye sourdough. The bowls were uncovered and the sourdough was slowly bubbling from the activity of the culture. The air was thick with the essence of fermenting rye, alive the way the air in a brewery or distillery is. He went to work, adding flour, ground and soaked bread crumbs,

profile continues

profile continued from previous page

seed soakers, water, and salt in precise amounts to each bowl, one by one, mixing each dough in a mixer and lining up each successive bowl of completed dough in the workroom.

At 1:15 a.m. a team of six bakers came in to begin dividing and shaping the dough. A mixing bowl was placed on a hydraulic lift, which dumped 200 kilos of dough, a massive amount, onto a worktable fitted with a flexible plastic bumper to prevent the soft mixture from oozing onto the floor. Two bakers scaled the dough and threw the pieces onto a conveyor belt running along an adjacent worktable. Bakers on either side of that table took the dough pieces off the conveyor belt, quickly shaped them, and placed the shaped loaves on boards above the worktable. Those boards of shaped breads were placed on rolling racks and quickly moved into proofing boxes. Using this semi-automated system, the bakers told me they could shape 2,400 breads in an hour.

I observed their speed and dexterity with awe, but was most amazed that they were shaping dozens of varieties of rye bread, which ranged from earthen tan to dark chocolate brown, from lightly grainy to 100 percent whole grain. There were rounds, ovals, logs, rolls, pan loaves. Just the way that "cheese" can encompass hundreds of different varieties, rye bread at Hinkel means many different things.

Mid-shift, Josef Hinkel himself arrived to check on what seemed to me to be barely controlled chaos. At this point, different teams of bakers were mixing, shaping, and baking breads all at once, not to mention the pastry-making that was going on in the corner of the room. Tall and thin, dressed in a perfectly white baker's shirt with his trademark yellow suspenders and starched white soda jerk's hat, he was obviously the baker in charge. When the breads started coming out of the oven, I saw how dark and rugged they were. "It takes a serious oven," he said, "to bake breads like this." Like two car enthusiasts discussing the way the electricity-powered BMW i8 coupe holds the road at high speed, we dove deep into the characteristics and functioning of his high-performance, clean-energy oven as the work continued around us.

At 5 a.m. a handful of shop clerks arrived and spent 2½ hours carefully arranging pyramids, columns, and basketfuls of bread in the large plate glass windows of the shop and on shelves behind the counters. Hinkel's commitment to supplying Dusseldorf with a dazzling array of classic German breads is astonishing. Since my night at Hinkel I have sent dozens of colleagues to his shop. For its diversity of breads, their complexity of flavor, and the sheer abundance on display, Hinkel should be on every bread lover's travel itinerary.

SCHWARZBROT

Although this multi-step dough takes time and is very sticky, the result—a dense, dark, chewy, and pungent rye—is worth the effort. Germans slice it very thin and eat it with strong cheeses and sausages, and good beer. Josef uses rye malt syrup, from malted rye berries, to give the bread dark color. I use molasses in my version because I like the sweetness and caramel color it lends to the dough.

Josef Hinkel shapes this bread into a log, and you can, too. Just make sure your Dutch oven is at least 12 inches in diameter to accommodate the dough.

recipe continues

START TO FINISH:

12

hours

RYE STARTER AND SOAKERS
8 hours

KNEAD
12 minutes

FIRST FERMENTATION
1½ hours

FINAL PROOF
1½ hours

BAKE
50 minutes

MAKES
one 1,080-gram loaf

INGREDIENTS	BAKER'S %	METRIC WEIGHT
RYE STARTER		
Rye Sourdough Starter (page 183)	14	25 g
Water	114	200 g
Medium rye flour	100	175 g
RYE FLOUR SOAKER		
Dark rye flour	100	50 g
Water	130	65 g
Salt	20	10 g
OLD BREAD SOAKER		
Stale rye bread, ground	100	50 g
Water	100	50 g
COOKED RYE SOAKER		
Medium rye flour	100	35 g
Water	286	100 g
FINAL DOUGH		
Medium rye flour	100	280 g
Rye starter	143	400 g
Rye flour soaker	45	125 g
Old bread soaker	36	100 g
Cooked rye soaker	48	135 g
Black strap molasses or rye malt	14	40 g

recipe continued from previous page

1. **PREPARE THE RYE STARTER**: In a small bowl, dissolve the sourdough starter in the water. Stir in the rye flour until well incorporated. It should have the consistency of thick pancake batter. Cover and let ferment at room temperature (68 to 77 degrees) until it increases in volume by about 30 percent, about 8 hours.

2. **MAKE THE RYE FLOUR SOAKER**: In a small bowl, combine the flour, water, and salt. Cover and let stand at room temperature for about 8 hours.

3. **MAKE THE OLD BREAD SOAKER**: In a small bowl, combine the ground bread and water. Cover and let stand at room temperature for about 8 hours.

4. **MAKE THE COOKED RYE SOAKER**: In a small pot, combine the flour and water. Bring to a simmer over medium-high heat. Cook, stirring, for 5 minutes. Scrape into a bowl and let stand to cool.

5. **MAKE THE FINAL DOUGH**: Combine the rye flour, rye starter, flour soaker, old bread soaker, cooked rye soaker, and molasses or rye malt in the bowl of an electric mixer fitted with paddle. Mix on the low (2 on the KitchenAid mixer) for 1 to 2 minutes. Turn the mixer to medium-low (4 on the KitchenAid mixer) and mix for 10 minutes, stopping to scrape down the sides of the bowl every 2 minutes. Scrape down the sides of the bowl and gather the dough into a ball.

6. **FIRST FERMENTATION**: Cover the mixing bowl with plastic wrap and let stand until the dough increases in volume by about 20 percent, about 1½ hours. If you touch the surface of the dough, you will feel that it has become softer underneath.

7. **FINAL PROOF**: On a lightly floured countertop, shape the dough into an 8- by 3-inch log (see page 78). Line a rimmed baking sheet with parchment, dust with rye flour, and place the log, seam side down, on the sheet. Cover loosely with plastic wrap. Let stand another 1½ hours.

8. **BAKE**: About 1 hour before baking, position an oven rack in the bottom third of the oven and set the Dutch oven (with the lid on) on the rack. Preheat the oven to 425 degrees for 1 hour. Wearing oven mitts, carefully remove the Dutch oven to a heatproof surface and take off the lid. Tip the dough onto a peel or your hands and put in the Dutch oven. Put the lid on and bake 25 minutes. Remove the lid and continue to bake until the dough is a rich caramel brown and very dense (this bread isn't going to rise a lot), another 25 minutes. Carefully turn the loaf out onto a wire rack. Immediately use a pastry brush to brush the surface liberally with water while it is still very hot to create a shiny crust. Cool completely. Store in a brown paper bag at room temperature for 3 to 4 days.

Notes for Professional Bakers

For the old bread soaker in this bread and the others, it is important to use only breads that have been kept in optimum hygiene conditions to avoid the growth of undesirable microorganisms that could spoil the final products.

As with any rye dough, a lot of care should be paid to the mixing process: long enough to ensure thorough incorporation of the ingredients, but not so long that the structure of the dough is compromised.

VARIATION:
WALNUSS-SCHWARZBROTSTANGE

Add 100 g toasted and chopped walnuts to
the kneaded dough and mix to incorporate.
After the first fermentation, turn the dough
onto a floured countertop and shape into a
3-inch-thick, 8-inch-long log. Place on a
parchment-lined baker's peel or rimless baking sheet, cover with plastic, and let stand
1 hour. Bake as directed.

ROGGENMISCHTEIG

There aren't many bakers who continue to follow the tradition of building a rye sour in several stages. Josef Hinkel organizes his bakery around a mixing room where he has large mixing bowls of *sauerteig* at different stages of development. It's hard to tell from looking, but the bakers know exactly which bowl is ready at which moment. Because the bowls are all open, the air is thick with the powerful, pungent aroma.

This particular bread is Hinkel's go-to everyday loaf. He makes hundreds of them a day, selling them exclusively at his two shops, both on the same busy shopping street in Dusseldorf. For people who are new to 100 percent rye breads, this is a great gateway recipe.

START TO FINISH:

21 to 22
hours

FIRST STAGE STARTER
AND OLD BREAD SOAKER
15 hours

SECOND STAGE STARTER
3 to 4 hours

KNEAD
12 minutes

FIRST FERMENTATION
1½ hours

FINAL PROOF
1 hour

BAKE
50 to 60 minutes

MAKES
one 1-kilo loaf

INGREDIENTS	BAKER'S %	METRIC WEIGHT
GRUNDSAUERTEIG **(First Stage Rye Starter)**		
Rye Sourdough Starter (page 183)	30	9 g
Room-temperature water, 75 degrees	87	26 g
Whole rye flour	100	30 g
OLD BREAD SOAKER		
Stale rye bread, ground	33	25 g
Water	100	75 g
SCHAUMSAUERTEIG **(Second Stage Rye Starter)**		
Grundsauerteig	42	65 g
Warm water, 90 degrees	200	310 g
Whole rye flour	100	155 g
FINAL DOUGH		
Schaumsauerteig	154	530 g
Whole rye flour	36	125 g
Type 55 or equivalent flour (11 to 11.5% protein)	64	220 g
Old bread soaker	29	100 g
Salt	4.4	15 g
Dry instant yeast	3.5	12 g

recipe continues

recipe continued from previous page

1. **PREPARE THE GRUNDSAUERTEIG (first stage rye starter)**: In a small bowl, dissolve the sourdough starter in the water. Stir in the rye flour until well incorporated. Cover and let ferment at room temperature (68 to 77 degrees), about 15 hours.

2. **MAKE THE OLD BREAD SOAKER**: In a small bowl, combine the ground bread and water. Cover and let stand at room temperature for 6 to 8 hours. Drain away excess water.

3. **PREPARE THE SCHAUMSAUERTEIG (second stage rye starter)**: Preheat the oven to 200 degrees for 5 minutes. Turn off the oven. In a small bowl, combine the grundsauerteig, warm water, and rye flour. Stir to combine. Cover and let ferment in the warm oven until bubbly and soft, like a poolish, 3 to 4 hours.

4. **MAKE THE FINAL DOUGH**: Combine the schaumsauerteig, rye flour, Type 55 flour, old bread soaker, salt, and yeast in the bowl of an electric mixer fitted with a dough hook. Stir with a rubber spatula a few times to combine. Mix on the low speed (2 on the KitchenAid) for 2 minutes. Scrape the sides and bottom of the bowl. Turn the mixer to medium-low (4 on the KitchenAid) and mix for 10 minutes. Scrape down the sides of the bowl and gather the dough into a ball.

5. **FIRST FERMENTATION**: Cover the mixing bowl with plastic wrap and let stand until the dough increases in volume by about 50 percent, becoming porous and with small bubbles on the surface, 1½ hours.

6. **FINAL PROOF**: On a lightly floured countertop, shape into a loose boule (see page 78). Dust the inside of a 10-inch round banneton with rye flour. (Alternatively, use a bowl lined with a kitchen towel and dusted with flour.) Place the boule, smooth side down, in the banneton.

Lightly dust with more flour and cover loosely with plastic wrap. Let stand until very active and puffy, another hour.

7. **BAKE**: About 1 hour before baking, position an oven rack in the bottom third of the oven and set the Dutch oven (with the lid on) on the rack. Preheat the oven to 450 degrees for 1 hour. Wearing oven mitts, carefully remove the Dutch oven to a heatproof surface and take off the lid. Tip the dough onto a peel or your hands and put in the Dutch oven. Put the lid on and bake for 25 minutes. Remove the lid and bake until the loaf is a warm brown, another 25 to 35 minutes. Carefully turn the loaf out onto a wire rack. Cool completely. Store in a brown paper bag at room temperature for 3 to 4 days.

Note for Professional Bakers

Because of the large amount of rye flour used in this recipe, it is important to carefully monitor the length of the first fermentation. You need to divide the dough as soon as it starts to become porous. A first fermentation that is too long will generate an excess of acidity and some dough degradation that will create a bread with lower volume.

VARIATION:

MEHRKORNBROT

Combine 65 g sunflower seeds, 65 g flax seeds, 45 g sesame seeds, 35 g pumpkin seeds, 100 g barley flakes, 100 g oat flakes, 30 g rye flakes, and 400 g water. Cover and let stand 1 hour. Add to the dough after kneading, stirring for a few minutes until well incorporated. After the first fermentation, divide the dough into two equal pieces, shape into logs, place in loaf pans, cover, and let stand 1 to 1½ hours. Bake as directed above.

THE BAREFOOT BAKER

DENISE PÖLZELBAUER, DENISE BÄCKERIN
BRUNN AN DER PITTEN, AUSTRIA

When I first spoke to Denise Pölzelbauer, I felt like I already knew her. Living in Woodstock, I am surrounded by free spirits and Denise clearly is one. When I told her that one of Bread Alone's locations is in Woodstock, she immediately said she wanted to visit. "It's perfect, because I am a hippie."

She says she always knew she would follow in her grandfather's footsteps. The small village bakery, in a 200-year-old farmhouse, had been in the family for generations. When she was only 21, after working beside him for four years, she had acquired the skill to run it on her own. It delights her grandfather to see her carrying on the family tradition and bringing her special gifts to the bakery. She has guided the business in a new direction, following her instincts and the stars.

She has great respect for the traditional rye bread recipes passed down to her from her grandfather, the ones that he had learned when he was young. "It's very special to inherit a bakery from your grandparents." She's making his traditional *volkornbrot*, his rye with sunflower seeds, a rye with spices, and two others. Her sourdough is a descendent of the one her grandfather used his whole life. She has switched to organic grain and eliminated the commercial yeast and additives that he sometimes used. She prefers biodynamic flour, which she mills herself from local wheat that is grown organically and also according to the spiritual and mystical beliefs of Rudolf Steiner. Not only does her grandfather appreciate the improved flavor, texture, and beauty of the breads due to Denise's artistic touch, but he also values the relationships she has forged with local organic farmers. Her grandfather's legacy combined with Steiner's philosophy define her breads. She is grounded and spiritual at the same time.

She lives in her grandparents' farmhouse. The building also houses the bakery, which is unchanged except for her Waldner stone mill. She uses her grandfather's vintage brick oven in the rear of the shop and displays her breads on the same green counter and simple wooden shelves where he sold his breads. She bakes

profile continues

profile continued from previous page

about 200 kilos of bread just two days a week, and when she opens for business you can find her at the cash register. She is always barefoot, even in the workroom, because she is more comfortable without shoes.

The response to her line of wine crackers made with grape seed flour and flavored with different combinations of spices has been enthusiastic. She grinds the seeds, which come from a local farmer who grows wine grapes. The flavors, based on the Chinese theory of five elements, are a balance of sour, bitter, sweet, spicy, and salty. On the days when she isn't making bread, she's producing these specialty crisps, which are sold at gourmet shops throughout Switzerland, Germany, and Austria. I asked her where she got the idea, and she laughed. "It happened. I'm not a big planner."

VOLKORNBROT

In northern Germany and Austria, *volkornbrot* is as common as baguettes are in France. This isn't to say that the dense, chewy rye bread is taken for granted. Instead, it is savored for its substantial flavor and rugged texture. The dough is a pungent, coarse batter with no elasticity that is scooped into loaf pans. Rising just slightly in the oven, it is very moist and dense. Cool the bread for 12 to 16 hours before slicing, so it can fully set. It is a natural match for the rich, hearty foods of the region. Thinly sliced and topped with mustard, ham, and cheese, it is a beloved and popular breakfast.

This bread is one of Denise Pölzelbauer's specialties and fits well with her low-tech, handmade philosophy. She mixes the same dough that her grandfather did, in the same ancient mixer, and bakes it in the brick oven that he built.

INGREDIENTS	BAKER'S %	METRIC WEIGHT
GRUNDSAUERTEIG **(First Stage Rye Starter)**		
Rye Sourdough Starter (page 183)	25	20 g
Water	100	125 g
Coarse rye flour	100	125 g
SCHAUMSAUERTEIG **(Second Stage Rye Starter)**		
Whole rye flour	50	246 g
Rye chops	50	246 g
Salt	4.9	24 g
Water	81	400 g
Grundsaurteig	55	275 g
FINAL DOUGH		
Coarse rye flour	100	340 g
Rye malt syrup	4.4	15 g
Water	84	285
Schaumsauerteig	350	1,191
FINISHING		
Rye chops		20 g

recipe continues

FIRST STAGE STARTER
8 hours

SECOND STAGE STARTER
18 to 24 hours

FINAL PROOF
1½ to 2 hours

BAKE
1½ hours

MAKES
two 915-gram loaves

recipe continued from previous page

1. **PREPARE THE GRUNDSAUERTEIG (first stage rye starter):** In a small bowl, dissolve the sourdough starter in the water. Stir in the rye flour until well incorporated. It will have the consistency of thick pancake batter. Cover and let ferment at room temperature (68 to 77 degrees) until it increases in volume by about 30 percent, about 8 hours.

2. **PREPARE THE SCHAUMSAUERTEIG (second stage rye starter):** In a medium bowl, combine the rye flour, rye chops, salt, water, and grundsauerteig. Mix thoroughly. Cover and let stand at room temperature for 18 to 24 hours.

3. **MAKE THE FINAL DOUGH:** Combine the rye flour, malt syrup, water, and schaumsauerteig in a large bowl and stir with a spatula until a soft batter is formed, 3 to 4 minutes.

4. **FINAL PROOF:** Oil two 9- by 5-inch loaf pans and line with parchment paper to avoid sticking. Scrape the batter into the pans and smooth the top with a spatula. (It will come just below the top of the pans.) Sprinkle with additional rye chops, drape with plastic wrap, and let rise until the dough has expanded 25 to 30 percent (about ¼ inch over the top of the pans) and the texture has become porous, with little bubbles visible underneath the surface, 1½ to 2 hours.

5. **BAKE:** Preheat the oven to 375 degrees. Place the loaves on the middle rack of the oven. Bake until they pull away from the sides of the pan, their crusts are deep brown, the internal temperature registers 190 degrees, and a cake tester inserted into the middle of the bread comes out clean, about 1½ hours. Let cool in the pans on a wire rack for 15 minutes. Invert the loaves onto a wire rack and then flip right side up. Cool for at least 12 hours before slicing. Store in a brown paper bag at room temperature for a week or more. The breads actually improve in texture and flavor with a little age.

VARIATION:

VOLKORNBROT MIT SONNENBLUMEN

Cover 260 g sunflower seeds with boiling water and let stand 1 hour. Drain and stir into the dough after it is mixed in step 3. Sprinkle a mix of sunflower seeds and rye chops on top of the bread before final proof.

START TO FINISH:

14 to 17

hours

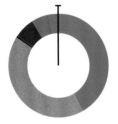

RYE STARTER
8 hours

BREAD SOAKER
10 to 12 hours

KNEAD
11 minutes

FIRST FERMENTATION
1 hour 50 minutes

FINAL PROOF
1½ hours

BAKE
50 to 60 minutes

MAKES
one 1.2-kilo loaf

Arnd Erbel is becoming one of Germany's most admired bakers. He has just one shop, in Dachsbach, northwest of Nuremberg, where he devotes himself to practicing the finest German baking traditions. It was at this bakery where I first saw bread made with *grünkern,* spelt that has been harvested while still green and then smoked over a fire to preserve it. This old technique (it's been in use since at least the 1600s) was originally a hedge against bad weather later in the season. These days, German farmers and bakers have become fans of grünkern because of its health properties and taste. Grünkern flour has 12 grams of protein and 9 grams of fiber per 100-gram serving. Grain harvested early is slightly sweet, because sugars in the endosperm have not yet been converted into complex carbohydrates. Drying the grain adds a pleasing smoky flavor.

Arnd employs a bread soaker, a traditional technique for economizing that also lends flavor and moisture to the dough. A combination of anise, fennel, coriander, and caraway gives the bread a familiar German aroma. He bakes his bread in large, rectangular rattan baskets but a round basket or Dutch oven, which I prefer, will also work.

INGREDIENTS	BAKER'S %	METRIC WEIGHT
RYE STARTER		
Coarse rye flour	100	100
Water	100	100
Rye Sourdough Starter (page 183)	10	10
OLD BREAD SOAKER		
Stale dark rye bread, ground	100	39 g
Water	100	39 g
FINAL DOUGH		
Anise seed, toasted	2	10 g
Fennel seed, toasted	2	10 g
Coriander seed, toasted	2	10 g
Caraway seed, toasted	2	10 g
Whole rye flour	30	156 g
Whole spelt flour	40	208 g
Grünkern flour	10	52 g
Einkorn flour	10	52 g
Buckwheat flour	10	52 g
Bread soaker	15	78 g
Salt	3.6	19 g
Dry instant yeast	0.4	2 g
Rye starter	40	210 g
Water	64	333 g

1. **PREPARE THE RYE STARTER**: In a small bowl, combine the rye flour, water, and sourdough starter. Cover and let ferment at room temperature for 8 hours.

2. **MAKE THE BREAD SOAKER**: In a small bowl, stir together the ground bread and water until the bread is well moistened. Cover and let stand at room temperature (68 to 77 degrees) for 10 to 12 hours.

3. **MAKE THE FINAL DOUGH**: In a spice grinder, combine the toasted seeds: anise, fennel, coriander, and caraway. Pulse several times to coarsely grind. In the bowl of an electric mixer fitted with a dough hook, combine the rye flour, spelt flour, grünkern flour, einkorn

recipe continues

recipe continued from previous page

flour, buckwheat flour, bread soaker, salt, yeast, rye starter, water, and half of the seed mixture. With the dough hook, mix the dough on low speed (2 on a KitchenAid mixer) for 7 minutes. Scrape the dough down. Turn the mixer to medium (6 on a KitchenAid mixer) and continue to knead until the dough is well developed, another 4 minutes. The dough will be soft and sticky with a very weak elasticity.

4. **FIRST FERMENTATION**: Transfer the dough to a lightly oiled, clear 4-quart container with a lid. Turn the dough over so all sides are oiled. Cover and let rise 1½ hours. Turn the dough out onto a lightly floured counter. Pat into a 6- by 8-inch rectangle and fold like a business letter. Slide both hands under the dough and flip it over so the folds are underneath. Slip it back into the container, cover, and let stand another 20 minutes.

5. **FINAL PROOF**: Gently scrape the dough onto a well-floured countertop. Get your hands slightly wet (this will make the dough easier to handle) and gently form the dough into a ball, shaping it like clay. Generously flour a cloth-lined banneton and put the bread in, smooth side down. Cover with a clean kitchen towel and let stand for 1½ hours.

6. **BAKE**: About 1 hour before baking, position an oven rack in the bottom third of the oven and set the Dutch oven (with the lid on) on the rack. Preheat the oven to 450 degrees for 1 hour. Wearing oven mitts, carefully remove the Dutch oven to a heatproof surface and take off the lid. Tip the dough directly into the Dutch oven. Poke with a fork, making four parallel rows for a decorative pattern. Put the lid on and bake for 25 minutes. Turn the heat down to 400 degrees. Remove the lid and bake until the loaf is dark brown, another 25 to 35 minutes. Carefully turn the loaf out onto a wire rack. Cool completely. Store in a brown paper bag at room temperature for 3 to 4 days.

Notes for Professional Bakers

You can easily slice old rye bread for the soaker using a mechanical slicer. Slice the loaves in one direction, gently rotate 90 degrees, and slice in the other direction. The cubes of bread will be of even size, creating a soaker with a consistent texture that will incorporate easily into the dough.

The poking can be done with a dough docker just before baking.

9
SPROUTED
BREADS

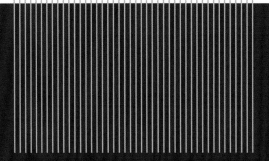

When you open up a bag of flour, it is easy to forget that before wheat berries and other whole grains are milled, they are essentially the seeds of cereal grasses. Each whole grain, consisting of germ, endosperm, and bran, has the potential to become a new plant. The germ is the plant embryo, the endosperm contains the food that the embryo needs to grow, and the bran provides additional nutrients in addition to protecting the embryo before germination. When seeds are exposed to water, they will sprout.

Grain sprouts naturally in damp conditions. Farmers and millers generally go to great lengths to make sure that grain doesn't sprout before it is milled, storing it in temperature- and humidity-controlled bins. But recently, sprouted grains, both whole and milled, have become increasingly popular with bakers for their nutritional value and flavor. Sprouts have long been touted as "health food." When a grain sprouts, enzymes break down complex carbohydrates in the endosperm into easier-to-digest molecules, allowing the germ to feed on these carbohydrates and grow.

Proponents of sprouted grains believe that sprouting renders grains more easily digestible for humans as well, making more of the grain's nutrients available to us. It's only in recent years that new technology has allowed for sprouted grain to be ground into flour. Humidity is introduced into large quantities of grain, which is allowed to just sprout. Then it is dried to 16 percent humidity and ground like regular flour. Sprouted wheat flour is sold by artisan mills like Central Milling, and at retail by King Arthur Flour. Today, to give their breads a nutritional boost, bakers can use flour ground from sprouted grains, as well as adding whole sprouted grains directly to bread dough.

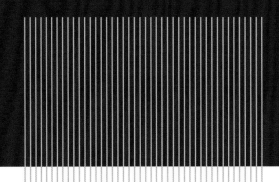

100 PERCENT EINKORN BREAD

START TO FINISH:

2 days for sprouting plus 19 hours

SPROUT EINKORN
2 days

EINKORN SOURDOUGH
STARTER
12 hours

FIRST FERMENTATION
4 hours

REST
20 minutes

FINAL PROOF
1½ to 2 hours

BAKE
45 to 50 minutes

MAKES
two 870-gram pan loaves

My Bread Alone partner Sharon Burns-Leader has taken the lead in seeking out local farmers who grow alternative wheat varieties to develop bread for our customers who are interested in ancient grains and those with gluten sensitivity. She learned about einkorn from Klaas Martens, a pioneer in organic grain farming who has had a lot of success with it. Klaas's farm is in central New York, but he's of German descent and was familiar with einkorn from old German recipes. It is a particularly beautiful plant: Each spikelet resembles an intricate herringbone weaving and contains one seed, sheathed in a tough husk that must be removed before grinding. "Covered" wheats, which include einkorn, emmer, and spelt, fell out of favor during industrialization, because their husks made them difficult to mill. But their comparative genetic simplicity (einkorn has 14 chromosomes; modern hybridized wheat, which is uncovered or naked, has 42) may make them easier to digest.

This 100 percent einkorn bread is one result of Sharon's research. With a wonderfully malty, nutty flavor, it's very good toasted and for sandwiches and has become a bakery bestseller. To customers unfamiliar with einkorn, she points them toward spelt. "Were you familiar with spelt fifteen years ago? In fifteen years," she promises, "you will be familiar with einkorn."

Einkorn dough is sticky and not very elastic, due to its particular protein content and structure. Sharon has found that it helps to use moistened hands rather than extra flour when folding and shaping the dough. In addition to einkorn flour, she adds sprouted einkorn berries and cracked and toasted einkorn to the dough for wholesome flavor and texture. To crack and toast the einkorn, measure out 97 grams of einkorn berries and place them in a zipper-lock bag. Pound the bag with the bottom of a cast-iron skillet to lightly crush. Toast the cracked berries on a baking sheet in a 350-degree oven for 10 minutes.

INGREDIENTS	BAKER'S %	METRIC WEIGHT
SPROUTED WHOLE EINKORN		
Einkorn berries		40 g
Water		60 g
EINKORN SOURDOUGH STARTER		
Rye Sourdough Starter (page 183) or Liquid Levain Starter (page 182)	6	8 g
Water	75	100 g
Whole einkorn flour	100	133 g
FINAL DOUGH		
Sprouted einkorn	10	76 g
Einkorn sourdough starter	32	241 g
Water	73	555 g
Salt	2.2	17 g
Cracked, toasted einkorn	13	97 g
Whole einkorn flour	100	756 g

1. **SPROUT THE EINKORN BERRIES**: Combine the einkorn berries and water in a small bowl. Cover and let stand 24 hours. Let stand for another 6 hours, rinsing them three times in a fine-mesh sieve during the 6-hour period. Place in a bowl, cover with a damp paper towel, and let stand at room temperature until sprouted, overnight. Kernels should be soft with small sprouts (radicle) appearing at the root end. Drain away excess water. At this point you can keep the sprouted berries, covered with a damp cloth, in your refrigerator for 1 week, or freeze in a zipper-lock bag for up to 1 month.

2. **PREPARE THE EINKORN SOURDOUGH STARTER**: In a small bowl, stir together the sourdough and water. Stir in the einkorn flour until smooth. Cover and let ferment at room temperature (68 to 77 degrees) until doubled in volume, 12 hours.

3. **MAKE THE FINAL DOUGH**: If refrigerated or frozen, let the sprouted kernels come to room temperature. In a large bowl, combine the sprouted einkorn, einkorn sourdough starter, water, salt, toasted einkorn, and einkorn flour. Stir with a spatula until smooth. Use a dough scraper to transfer the dough to a lightly oiled, clear 4-quart

recipe continues

recipe continued from previous page

container with a lid. Turn the dough over so all sides are oiled. Cover and let stand 30 minutes. Moisten your hands and slide them under the dough, folding it like a business letter. Slip it back into the container, cover, and let stand another 30 minutes. Repeat three times, until the dough is very pillowy.

4. **REST**: Turn the dough onto a moistened countertop. Divide into two equal pieces. Gently shape into blunt-ended *bâtards*, sprinkle with flour, cover with plastic wrap, and let stand another 20 minutes.

5. **FINAL PROOF**: Oil two 9- by 5-inch loaf pans and line with parchment. Gently place each dough piece into a prepared pan, stretching it gently to fit. Sprinkle with einkorn flour, gently drape with plastic wrap, and let stand until the loaves begin to bubble up, 1½ to 2 hours.

6. **BAKE**: About 1 hour before baking, place a cast-iron skillet on the lower rack of the oven. Preheat the oven to 450 degrees for 1 hour. Place the pans on the middle rack of the oven. Place 1 cup of ice cubes in the skillet to produce steam. Bake for 15 minutes. Turn the heat down to 400 degrees and bake until the loaves are golden brown and well risen, 30 to 35 minutes. Transfer the loaves, still in the pans, to a wire rack to cool for 20 minutes. Invert the loaves onto the wire rack, re-invert, and let cool for 12 hours before slicing and serving. Store in a brown paper bag at room temperature for 5 to 7 days.

Notes for Professional Bakers

When working with dough made with einkorn flour, first generously sprinkle water on the table and then dip your hands in water before attempting to touch the dough. Continue to dip your hands every time you approach this dough and you will have an easier clean-up and better final results.

After the sprouting process, the einkorn berries can be run through a meat grinder to get an einkorn mash that can then be scaled (to the amount needed for one batch of final dough) and then frozen in a plastic bag. Sprouted berries can also be frozen whole. The frozen berries will keep for up to 3 months in the freezer. The berries should be left in the refrigerator overnight to defrost before being added to the final dough the next day.

100 PERCENT SPROUTED WHEAT PAN BREAD

START TO FINISH:

2 days for sprouting plus 16 hours

SPROUT WHEAT BERRIES
2 days

SPONGE
12 hours

KNEAD
11 minutes

FIRST FERMENTATION
80 minutes

REST
20 minutes

FINAL PROOF
1 hour

BAKE
45 to 50 minutes

MAKES
two 769-gram loaves

Five or ten years ago, you couldn't get sprouted flour. Today, it's easily available online (see Resources, page 347). I developed this recipe for people who are looking for a delicious and satisfying bread made with sprouted wheat flour, which is sweeter and nuttier than regular wheat flour. Whole sprouted wheat berries contribute texture and additional sweet flavor.

INGREDIENTS	BAKER'S %	METRIC WEIGHT
SPROUTED WHEAT BERRIES		
Wheat berries		75 g
Water		75 g
SPONGE		
Sprouted whole wheat flour	100	210 g
Water	70	147 g
Salt	0.2	.5 g
Dry instant yeast	1	2 g
FINAL DOUGH		
Sprouted wheat berries	12	75 g
Sponge	59	360 g
Sprouted whole wheat flour	100	615 g
Water	65	400 g
Salt	2.1	13 g
Dry instant yeast	1	6 g
Honey	3	20 g
White grape juice	8	50 g

recipe continues

recipe continued from previous page

1. **SPROUT THE WHEAT BERRIES**: Combine the wheat berries and water in a small bowl. Cover and let stand 24 hours. Let stand for another 6 hours, rinsing them three times in a fine-mesh sieve during the 6-hour period. Place in a bowl, cover with a damp paper towel, and let stand until sprouted, overnight. Kernels should be soft with small sprouts (radicle) appearing at the root end. At this point you can keep the sprouted seeds, covered with a damp cloth, in your refrigerator for 1 week, or freeze in a zipper-lock bag for up to 1 month.

2. **MAKE THE SPONGE**: In a small bowl, stir together the sprouted wheat flour, water, salt, and yeast until smooth. Cover and let ferment at room temperature (68 to 77 degrees) until doubled in volume, about 12 hours.

3. **MAKE THE FINAL DOUGH**: If refrigerated or frozen, let the sprouted kernels come to room temperature. In the bowl of an electric mixer fitted with a dough hook, combine the sprouted wheat berries, sponge, sprouted whole wheat flour, water, salt, yeast, honey, and grape juice. Stir with a spatula until a rough dough forms. Knead on low speed (2 on a KitchenAid mixer) for 3 minutes. Turn the mixer to medium-low (4 on the KitchenAid) and knead an additional 8 minutes.

4. **FIRST FERMENTATION AND FOLDING**: Use a dough scraper to transfer the dough to a lightly oiled, clear 4-quart container with a lid. Turn the dough over so all sides are oiled. Cover and let stand 30 minutes. Turn the dough out onto a lightly floured counter. Pat into a 6- by 8-inch rectangle and fold like a business letter. Slide both hands under the dough and flip it over so the folds are underneath. Slip it back into the container, cover, and let stand for another 30 minutes. Repeat the folding and turning, return to the container, and let stand until the dough is very pillowy, about 20 minutes longer.

5. **REST**: Turn the dough onto a lightly floured countertop. Divide into two equal pieces. Gently round, sprinkle with flour, cover with plastic wrap, and let stand another 20 minutes.

6. **FINAL PROOF**: Shape each round into a pan loaf (see page 79) and place, seam sides down, in each of two 9- by 5-inch loaf pans. Sprinkle with flour, gently drape with plastic wrap, and let stand until the loaves begin to crown in the pans, about 1 hour.

7. **BAKE**: About 1 hour before baking, place a cast-iron skillet on the lower rack of the oven. Preheat the oven to 375 degrees for 1 hour. Lightly dust the loaves with flour. With a *lame*, a single-edged razor blade, or a serrated knife, make diagonal slashes, about ½ inch deep and 1½ inches long, in two parallel rows. Place the pans on the middle rack of the oven. Place 1 cup of ice cubes in the skillet to produce steam. Bake until the loaves are golden brown and well risen, 45 to 50 minutes. Invert the loaves onto a wire rack, re-invert, and let cool completely. Store in a brown paper bag at room temperature for 5 to 7 days.

Note for Professional Bakers

The sprouted wheat flour could be replaced with sprouted wheat. In this case, it is important to select a wheat with a high protein content in order to have sufficient strength in the final dough. Alternatively, gluten could be added to the formula for strength.

1 day for sprouting plus 3½ hours

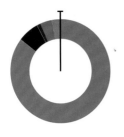

SPROUT SEEDS
1 day

KNEAD
8 minutes

FIRST FERMENTATION
110 minutes

REST
20 minutes

FINAL PROOF
1 hour

BAKE
45 to 50 minutes

MAKES
two 645-gram loaves

SPROUTED MULTIGRAIN "S"

Bäckerei Beumer & Lutum in Berlin is a medium-scale certified organic bakery that delivers bread daily to a multitude of small natural foods stores that have proliferated in the changing city in recent years. Antonius Beumer has developed a line of sprouted grain products using a high-tech Owisan seed sprouting machine that holds the whole berries at the ideal temperature and humidity for sprouting, rinsing them periodically to prevent bacteria from multiplying during the process.

I was impressed by the uniformity of his sprouted seeds, an important issue when you want to produce breads in larger quantities at a consistent quality. Antonius's breads, packed with sprouted seeds and grains, are chewier and sweeter—and more interesting—than multigrain breads made with soaked but not sprouted seeds.

It's easy to sprout a small quantity of seeds safely in a bowl at home. For passionate sprout enthusiasts, small sprouting machines are available online (see Resources, page 347).

INGREDIENTS	BAKER'S %	METRIC WEIGHT
SPROUTED SEEDS		
Flax seeds		30 g
Millet seeds		30 g
Sunflower seeds		30 g
Rolled oats		30 g
Quinoa		30 g
Room-temperature water		207 g
FINAL DOUGH		
Sprouted seeds	30	192 g
Sprouted whole wheat flour	100	639 g
Water	60	384 g
Salt	2.3	15 g
Dry instant yeast	0.9	6 g
Honey	3	20 g
Dark molasses	3	20 g
Canola oil	2.5	16 g

recipe continues

recipe continued from previous page

1. **SPROUT THE SEEDS**: Combine the flax seeds, millet seeds, sunflower seeds, rolled oats, quinoa, and water in a small bowl. Cover and let stand, rinsing them three times in a fine-mesh sieve, for 6 hours. Place in a bowl, cover with a damp paper towel, and let stand until sprouted, overnight (some seeds may take longer to sprout than others). Seeds should be soft with small sprouts (radicle) appearing at the root end. At this point you can keep the sprouted seeds, covered with a damp cloth, in your refrigerator for 1 week, or freeze in a zipper-lock bag for up to 1 month.

2. **MAKE THE FINAL DOUGH**: If refrigerated or frozen, let the sprouted kernels come to room temperature. In the bowl of an electric mixer fitted with a dough hook, combine the drained sprouted seeds, sprouted whole wheat flour, water, salt, yeast, honey, molasses, and canola oil. Stir with a spatula until a rough dough forms. Knead on low speed (2 on a KitchenAid mixer) for 3 minutes. Turn the mixer to medium (6 on a KitchenAid mixer) and knead an additional 5 minutes.

3. **FIRST FERMENTATION**: Use a dough scraper to transfer the dough to a lightly oiled, clear 4-quart container with a lid. Turn the dough over so all sides are oiled. Cover and let stand 30 minutes. Turn the dough out onto a lightly floured counter. Pat into a 6- by 8-inch rectangle and fold like a business letter. Slide both hands under the dough and flip it over so the folds are underneath. Slip it back into the container, cover, and let stand for another 60 minutes. Repeat the folding and turning, return to the container, and let stand until the dough is very pillowy, about 20 minutes longer.

4. **REST**: Turn the dough onto a lightly floured countertop. Gently divide and shape into two logs (see page 78). Sprinkle with flour, cover with plastic wrap, and let stand another 20 minutes.

5. **FINAL PROOF**: Line a baker's peel or rimless baking sheet with parchment. Shape the dough into two 16-inch-long bâtards and place on the peel 4 inches apart. Curl one end of each loaf one way and the other end the other way to form an S. Gently drape with plastic wrap and let stand until the loaves relax and become slightly pillowy, about 1 hour.

6. **BAKE**: About 1 hour before baking, place a baking stone on the middle rack of the oven and a cast-iron skillet on the lower rack. Preheat the oven to 375 degrees for 1 hour. Slide the loaves, still on the parchment, onto the baking stone. Place 1 cup of ice cubes in the skillet to produce steam. Bake until the loaves are golden brown and well risen, 45 to 50 minutes. Slide the breads, still on the parchment, onto a wire rack and let cool completely. Store in a brown paper bag at room temperature for 5 to 7 days.

Note for Professional Bakers

After sprouting, you can drain the seeds and run them through a meat grinder to obtain a mash, which can then be frozen in blocks scaled at the quantity to be used in the final dough. When needed, defrost the blocks overnight in the refrigerator to use the next day. This way, the seeds only have to be sprouted once a month.

SPROUTED VOLKORNBROT

During my visit with Antonius Beumer at his bakery in Berlin, I wondered what a traditional *volkornbrot* (whole grain bread) would taste like if made with 100 percent sprouted rye berries. After seeing how easy it was for him to make large quantities of sprouted grain, I immediately went to work developing this recipe. Using sweet sprouted grains solved a problem that some people have with *volkenbrot*, which can be very sour-tasting. This sprouted version has a balanced flavor profile with sweet overtones that I find particularly pleasing.

Due to its high natural sugar content, this dough ferments only once. Two fermentations might cause it to break down. Cold ground berries will slow down the fermentation. If you sprout your rye berries in advance, refrigerate them. Note that the rye berries must be put through a meat grinder to get the proper texture; a food processor will chop them too finely.

INGREDIENTS	BAKER'S %	METRIC WEIGHT
SPROUTED RYE BERRIES		
Rye berries		700 g
Water		700 g
RYE SOURDOUGH STARTER		
Rye Sourdough Starter (page 183)	21	23 g
Water	100	95 g
Medium rye flour	100	95 g
FINAL DOUGH		
Sprouted rye berries	100	895 g
Water	20	179 g
Salt	2	18 g
Molasses	3	27 g
Rye Sourdough Starter (page 183)	23	210 g

recipe continues

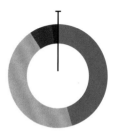

START TO FINISH:

1 day for sprouting, plus 22 to 29 hours

SPROUT RYE BERRIES
1 day

SOURDOUGH
18 to 24 hours

FINAL PROOF
3 to 4 hours

BAKE
1 hour

MAKES
one 1.3-kilo pan loaf

recipe continued from previous page

1. **SPROUT THE RYE BERRIES**: Combine the rye berries and water in a small bowl. Cover and let stand, rinsing them in a fine-mesh strainer three times, for 6 hours. Place in a bowl, cover with a damp paper towel, and let stand at room temperature until sprouted, overnight. Berries should be soft with small sprouts (radicle) appearing at the root end. At this point you can keep the sprouted berries, covered with a damp cloth, in your refrigerator for 1 week, or freeze in a zipper-lock bag for up to 1 month.

2. **PREPARE THE RYE SOURDOUGH STARTER**: In a small bowl, vigorously stir together the sour-dough and water. Stir in the flour until smooth. Cover and let ferment at room temperature (68 to 77 degrees) until doubled in volume, 8 to 12 hours.

3. **MAKE THE FINAL DOUGH**: If refrigerated or frozen, let the sprouted berries come to room temperature. Process them in a meat grinder as you would sausage meat. The finer the grind, the finer the crumb. I prefer to grind the mash on the medium screen. Scrape into a large mixing bowl. Add the water, salt, molasses, and sourdough. Stir with a spatula until smooth.

4. **FINAL PROOF**: Coat a 9- by 5-inch loaf pan with vegetable oil. Scrape the dough into the pan and smooth the top with a spatula. Cover with plastic wrap. Let stand at room temperature until it is porous and slightly risen, 3 to 4 hours.

5. **BAKE**: Preheat the oven to 350 degrees. Place the pan on the middle rack of the oven. Bake until the loaf is caramel brown and a thermometer inserted into the center registers 190 degrees, about 1 hour. Immediately invert the loaf onto a wire rack, re-invert, and let cool completely. Store in a brown paper bag at room temperature for 5 to 7 days.

Note for Professional Bakers

Professional bakers can use rye malt in place of molasses. Because of the quantity of pento-sans naturally occurring in rye flour, it is better to let this bread cool down and mature at least 12 hours before serving to allow a proper mois-ture distribution within the loaf. The baking could easily be done at the end of the day, so the bread is ready to sell the following morning.

10
USING
LEFTOVER
STARTER

As you cultivate your sourdough, you will inevitably have some undeveloped culture that must be discarded when it is time to feed only a portion of the culture as part of the process. If it takes two weeks or more for your sourdough to take off, that's a lot of leftover dough to throw in the compost pile. In a bakery setting, leftover starter is not an issue. We throw a little undeveloped sourdough into whatever breads we are mixing, so it doesn't go to waste. In relatively small proportions, leftover undeveloped sourdough won't throw off the recipe.

Home bakers, too, can add their leftover culture to any dough they are making. In general, the leftover sourdough should not be more than 20 percent of the total weight of the flour in the recipe you are using. To help you get comfortable with the idea, I've developed the following breads, with some leftover built into the formula, to demonstrate how it's done. If you are using a firm starter, you can increase the hydration by 5%.

In each case, commercial yeast helps the bread rise, because the young culture is not ready to do this on its own. It might, however, add flavor and good texture to the bread, depending on how developed it is.

CHOCOLATE SOURDOUGH BABKA

While it's not in our regular rotation at Bread Alone, we make chocolate babka on special occasions. Customers are always happy when it appears, because real babka—rich and chocolatey and chewy—is not that easy to find anymore. The addition of some leftover levain helps the babka stay fresh longer. I personally like the tangy flavor of a little sourdough along with the mascarpone and chocolate.

START TO FINISH:

11 to 16

hours

KNEAD
5 minutes

FIRST FERMENTATION
9 to 13 hours

FINAL PROOF
1 to 2 hours

BAKE
40 minutes

MAKES
two 675-gram loaves

INGREDIENTS	BAKER'S %	METRIC WEIGHT
FINAL DOUGH		
Whole milk, room temperature	35	148 g
Mascarpone cheese, room temperature	6	25 g
Sugar	24	102 g
Eggs, room temperature	23	100 g (about 2 large)
Egg yolk, room temperature		20 g (about 1 large)
Pure vanilla extract	1	4 g
Salt	1	4 g
Type 55 or equivalent flour (11 to 11.5% protein)	100	425 g
Unused Liquid Sourdough Starter (page 182)	15	65 g
Dry instant yeast	1.4	6 g
Unsalted butter, cut into small pieces and softened	34	143 g
FILLING		
Bittersweet chocolate, finely chopped	50	213 g
Sugar	24	102 g
EGG WASH		
Egg yolk		20 g
Heavy cream	7	30 g

recipe continues

recipe continued from previous page

1. **MAKE THE FINAL DOUGH**: Combine the milk, mascarpone, sugar, eggs, egg yolk, vanilla, and salt in the bowl of an electric mixer. Stir with a rubber spatula to combine. Add the flour, sourdough starter, and yeast and stir a few times until a rough dough forms. Mix on the lowest speed for 1 minute. With the mixer running, add the butter, one piece at a time, until it is all incorporated. Turn the mixer to medium (6 on a KitchenAid mixer) and knead until it comes together in a sticky but cohesive mass, 4 to 5 minutes.

2. **FIRST FERMENTATION**: Use a dough scraper to transfer the dough to a lightly oiled, clear 4-quart container. Cover the bowl with plastic wrap. Let stand at room temperature for 1 hour, then refrigerate overnight, 8 to 12 hours.

3. **MAKE THE FILLING**: Combine the chocolate and sugar in a medium bowl.

4. **FINAL PROOF**: Grease two 9- by 5-inch loaf pans. Deflate the dough by gently pressing down on it with your palms. Turn it onto a lightly floured countertop and divide into two equal pieces. Roll each piece into a rough 8- by 16-inch rectangle, with the long side facing you. Sprinkle half of the filling over each dough rectangle, leaving a ½-inch border on all sides. Starting with the long sides closest to you, roll each piece, like a jelly roll, into a snug log. Pinch the outside edges to seal. Fold the logs in half and twist them once in the center (giving them a shape like an awareness ribbon). Gently place the folded and twisted doughs into the prepared pans, tucking the ends under. Lightly drape with plastic wrap and let rise until increased in volume by 50 percent, 1 to 2 hours.

5. **BAKE**: Preheat the oven to 350 degrees. Whisk together the egg yolk and cream in a small bowl. Brush the tops of the babkas with the egg wash. Bake until the tops are deep golden brown, about 30 minutes. Tent with foil and continue to bake 10 minutes more. Let sit in the pans on a wire rack for 10 minutes. Run a paring knife around the edges of each pan. Very gently overturn the loaves onto a wire rack and re-invert. Let cool completely before slicing and serving. Chocolate Babka will keep, wrapped in plastic at room temperature, for up to 3 days.

Note for Professional Bakers

For the production of large quantities of babka, the dough can be refrigerated after 1 hour of fermentation until it reaches about 50 degrees. At this point, the dough will be firm enough to be run through a sheeter to speed up production.

ROSEMARY AND WALNUT SCHIACCIATA

My friends Scott and Laura own a wonderful villa near Orvieto in Umbria, and they have graciously hosted me several times. The small supermarket outside of town has its own craft bakery, where they bake flatbreads and other local specialties. I was there one fall during walnut season, and the baker made *schiacciata*, or "squashed bread," with recently harvested nuts. Although I didn't have the opportunity to meet him and get his recipe, I was inspired to develop this one as a souvenir of my trip.

INGREDIENTS	BAKER'S %	METRIC WEIGHT
FINAL DOUGH		
Tipo OO flour with W value of 250 to 260	100	562 g
Water	68	382 g
Unused Liquid Sourdough Starter (page 182)	20	112 g
Dry instant yeast	0.9	5 g
Salt	2	11 g
Dark honey, such as buckwheat	2	11 g
Extra-virgin olive oil	10	56 g
Walnuts, toasted and coarsely chopped	25	140 g
Fresh rosemary, finely chopped	0.9	5 g
Coarse sea salt for sprinkling		

START TO FINISH:

4½
hours

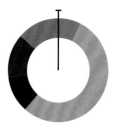

KNEAD
16 minutes

FIRST FERMENTATION
2 hours

REST
15 to 25 minutes

FINAL PROOF
30 minutes

BAKE
25 to 30 minutes

MAKES
one 1,284-gram loaf

1. **MAKE THE FINAL DOUGH**: Combine the flour, water, sourdough starter, yeast, salt, honey, and oil in the bowl of a standing mixer fitted with a dough hook. Give the mixture a few turns with a rubber spatula to form a rough dough. Knead on the lowest speed for 1 minute. Turn to low (2 on a KitchenAid mixer) and knead for 5 minutes. Scrape down the sides of the bowl with a rubber spatula, turn to medium-low (4 on a KitchenAid mixer), and knead until

recipe continues

recipe continued from previous page

smooth and silky, 8 minutes. Add the walnuts and rosemary and knead on low until well incorporated, about 2 minutes.

2. **FIRST FERMENTATION**: Use a dough scraper to transfer the dough to a lightly oiled, clear 4-quart container with a lid. Turn the dough over so all sides are oiled. Cover and let stand at room temperature until doubled in volume, 1 hour. Pat into a 6- by 8-inch rectangle and fold like a business letter. Slide both hands under the dough and flip it over so the folds are underneath. Slip it back into the container, cover, and let stand another hour.

3. **FINAL PROOF**: Oil the bottom and sides of a rimmed 18- by 13-inch baking sheet. Turn the dough onto the oiled sheet, cover, and let rest 15 minutes. With oiled hands, press and stretch the dough evenly to the edges of the pan. If the dough resists, cover and let it stand another 10 minutes to relax before pressing and stretching again.

4. **FINAL PROOF**: Sprinkle with sea salt and allow the schiacciata to sit, uncovered, for 30 minutes.

5. **BAKE**: Preheat the oven to 425 degrees. Bake in the middle of the oven until the loaf is well browned, 25 to 30 minutes. Let cool on the baking sheet for 5 minutes, then lift with a large spatula onto a wire rack to cool completely before cutting into squares.

Note for Professional Bakers

To make a dough that is easier to handle in a production environment, you can use the double hydration technique. The water is divided in two parts: The first part—about baker's 60 percent—creates a dough with a medium-soft consistency (like a baguette dough) and the second part—about baker's 10 percent—is added once the gluten is developed enough to create the desired soft consistency. Add the nuts and rosemary after the second hydration. The dough will be stronger and easier to process.

SCRAP-DOUGH PAVÉ

This bread is inspired by the *pavé Alesian* at Dominique Saibron's Paris bakery. It is a handy all-purpose shape, good for sandwiches and tartines. These breads freeze very well. I recommend underbaking them by about 5 minutes, cooling and freezing them, and then warming them up in a 350-degree oven as needed.

INGREDIENTS	BAKER'S %	METRIC WEIGHT
FINAL DOUGH		
Type 65 or equivalent flour (11 to 11.5% protein)	100	531g
Water	55	293 g
Unused Liquid Sourdough Starter (page 182)	20	106 g
Salt	2	11 g
Dry instant yeast (optional)	0.9	5 g

1. **MAKE THE FINAL DOUGH:** Combine the flour, water, and levain in the bowl of an electric mixer fitted with a dough hook. Mix with a rubber spatula until a rough dough forms.

2. **AUTOLYSE:** Cover and let rest 20 minutes.

3. **MAKE THE FINAL DOUGH:** Add the salt and yeast to the bowl. With the dough hook, mix on low (2 on a KitchenAid mixer) until the dough clears the sides of the bowl, about 10 minutes.

4. **FIRST FERMENTATION:** Use a dough scraper to transfer the dough to a lightly oiled, clear 4-quart container with a lid. Turn the dough over so all sides are oiled. Cover and let stand at room temperature until increased in volume by about 25 percent, about 45 minutes. Turn the dough out onto a lightly floured counter. Pat it into a 6- by 8-inch rectangle and fold like a business letter. Slide both hands under the dough and flip it over so the folds are underneath. Slip it back into the container, cover, and let stand until it increases in volume by about 50 percent, another 1 hour.

recipe continues

3½ to 4

hours

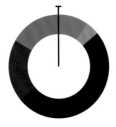

AUTOLYSE
20 minutes

KNEAD
10 minutes

FIRST FERMENTATION
1¾ hours

FINAL PROOF
30 to 40 minutes

BAKE
35 minutes

MAKES
two 473-gram loaves

recipe continued from previous page

5. About 1 hour before baking, place a baking stone on the middle rack of the oven and a cast-iron skillet on the lower rack. Preheat the oven to 450 degrees.

6. **FINAL PROOF**: Cover a baker's peel or rimless baking sheet with parchment and dust with flour. On a lightly floured countertop, gently pat the dough into a 6- by 12-inch rectangle. Cut to divide into two 6-inch squares. Place the dough pieces, top sides down and 3 inches apart, on the parchment. Lift the parchment paper between the loaves, making a pleat and drawing the loaves close together. Alternatively, use baker's linen instead of parchment. Tightly roll up two kitchen towels and slip them under the parchment paper on the sides of the outer loaves to support each square. Lightly dust with flour and drape with plastic wrap. Let rise until pillowy, 30 to 40 minutes.

7. **BAKE**: Uncover the breads, remove the rolled-up towels, and stretch the parchment paper out so that it is flat and the loaves are separated. With a large spatula, flip the breads over. Slide the loaves, still on the parchment, onto the baking stone. Place 1 cup of ice cubes in the skillet to produce steam. Bake until the loaves are golden brown, about 35 minutes. Slide the loaves, still on the parchment, onto a wire rack. Cool completely. Store in a brown paper bag at room temperature for up to 2 days.

Note for Professional Bakers

The length of the first fermentation will depend on the level of maturation of the levain. When working with immature levain, the first fermentation will be longer to compensate for its lack of acidity. For an almost ripe levain, the first fermentation should be shorter to avoid an excess of acidity in the final dough.

SICILIAN BLACK CAKE

I tasted this sweet bread late one morning during my visit to Molini Riggi in Sicily, with a cup of strong espresso after my tour of the mill. It's a Sicilian specialty, explained Marco Riggi, made with the Russello wheat that is grown nearby and milled at Riggi. Blood oranges and pistachios are also important Sicilian crops. The taste of Russello flour (page 40) left a rich impression on my senses. It is so different from the wheat flour that I regularly bake with. It's earthy and nutty with a dark sweetness, reminiscent of buckwheat honey. Substituting whole wheat flour for the Russello will give you an equally delicious bread, although without the particular local flavor of Sicilian wheat. It's a perfect recipe for using leftover sourdough, because the bread doesn't require a lot of lift, and sourdough in any stage of development will add some flavor and moisture.

INGREDIENTS	BAKER'S %	METRIC WEIGHT
FINAL DOUGH		
Russello wheat flour	30	150 g
Tipo OO flour with W value of 250 to 260	70	350 g
Unused Liquid Sourdough Starter (page 182)	25	125 g
Salt	2	10 g
Dry instant yeast	1	5 g
Honey	5	25 g
Eggs	30	150 g (about 3 large)
Milk	20	100 g
Unsalted butter, softened	20	100 g
Blood orange marmalade	7	35 g
Dried figs, chopped	50	250 g
Unsalted pistachio nuts, chopped	20	100 g

recipe continues

START TO FINISH:
6 to 8
hours

KNEAD
5 minutes

FIRST FERMENTATION
3 hours

FINAL PROOF
3 hours

BAKE
1¼ hours

MAKE
one 1.4-kilo cake

recipe continued from previous page

1. **MAKE THE FINAL DOUGH**: Combine the Russello flour, 00 flour, levain, salt, yeast, honey, eggs, milk, butter, marmalade, figs, and pistachios in the bowl of a standing mixer fitted with a paddle. Mix with a rubber spatula until a rough dough forms. Mix on the low speed (2 on a KitchenAid mixer) for 1 minute. Scrape the sides of the bowl with a rubber spatula and mix for 1 minute more. Scrape the dough off the sides and paddle. Mix on medium-low (4 on the KitchenAid) for 3 minutes.

2. **FIRST FERMENTATION**: Use a dough scraper to transfer the dough to a lightly oiled, clear 4-quart container with a lid. Turn the dough over so all sides are oiled. Cover and let stand 3 hours.

3. **FINAL PROOF**: Spray the bottom and sides of a 9-inch round cake pan with nonstick cooking spray. Turn the dough into the pan and use your fingertips to press to the edges of the pan. Cover and let stand until light and well proofed, about 3 hours.

4. **BAKE**: Preheat the oven to 350 degrees. Bake the cake in the middle of the oven until well browned, 1 hour and 15 minutes, tenting with foil after an hour if the bread is getting too brown. Transfer the cake, still in the pan, to a wire rack. Cool in the pan for 5 minutes, invert onto another wire rack, re-invert, and let cool completely. Store in a brown paper bag at room temperature for up to 5 days.

Note for Professional Bakers

For large production, the Sicilian black cake can be mixed in a spiral mixer (recommended mixing time: 5 minutes in first and 1 to 2 minutes in second). The dough can then be scaled in blocks and, after 10 minutes of resting time, divided in a hydraulic dough divider. The dough should then be placed in cake pans for its final proof.

BREAD CONNECTS US

My ears pricked up when Apollonia Poilâne told me that her father, Lionel, believed that bread can connect people and cultures. After so many encounters with different people from different places, all because of bread, I have come to believe this, too.

In 2004, I accepted a consulting job at Pick n Pay, South Africa's biggest supermarket chain. By coincidence, I had just read *We Are All the Same*, a book by Jim Wooten about South African AIDS activist Gail Johnson, who ran a shelter for HIV-positive moms and their kids. Just before departing for Johannesburg, I happened to dine with my friends Mark and Lisa Schwartz, who knew Gail. So I was able to meet Gail the day after my arrival in Johannesburg, and two days later we were baking bread with the residents in the kitchen at the shelter, called Nkosi's Haven. Afterward, she made a surprising leap: "The mums and kids need bread like this. Will you help us open a bakery here for the mums to run?" A conversation with Richard Wilkes, the former CEO of the South African baking supply company Macadams International, led to an affordable plan. Macadams had constructed mobile bakeries inside shipping containers for the South African military and would outfit one for Nkosi's Haven. When the container bakery arrived at Nkosi's Haven, I flew in to train Gail's hand-picked staff of women, who run the bakery to this day.

In February 2012, I flew to Cape Town to attend the opening of a second bakery at the Baphumulele Children's Home in Khayelitsha, the second biggest township in South Africa after Soweto. This facility is an orphanage and community center founded by retired schoolteacher Rosalia Mashale. Rosie and I had met the previous year when I struck up a conversation with her at IBA, the big baking show in Munich, where she was raising money for the home. The Khayelitsha bakery is staffed by formerly unemployed people from the township, and provides income and stability for Rosie's orphanage as well as training and jobs for some of Cape Town's poorest inhabitants. In 2017, I nominated Rosie for a CNN Hero of the Year award, and she became a finalist in this event, which celebrates everyday people who are also extraordinary humanitarians. It was my pleasure to sit in the audience and watch as the evening's hosts broadcast her achievements to the world.

In a career full of surprise encounters and unlikely friendships forged through baking,

these experiences stand out. Until I met Gail and Rosie, I never imagined that the skills I had acquired baking bread would eventually lead me to baking bread with families in South Africa. Baking bread and sharing it with the kids was one of the most unexpected and rewarding experiences of my career.

Bread cuts through the static of life and makes people feel good. Who doesn't enjoy walking into a bakery in the morning when the air is thick with the smell of freshly baked loaves? There is something so essentially human about baking, sharing, and eating bread. It's like a timeless song or a story that doesn't end, and it involves anyone who has ever farmed or milled grain, kneaded a soft dough, or pulled a loaf from the oven. In an often stressful and chaotic world, connecting with bakers through their breads satisfies me, motivates me, and gives me hope.

RESOURCES: INGREDIENTS AND EQUIPMENT

Ingredients

To bake the most authentic breads, you will want to seek out flours similar to the ones used by the bakers profiled here. To find them, look to the following purveyors of high-quality specialty flours:

BUCKWHEAT FLOUR: Central Milling (centralmilling.com) sells organic buckwheat flour. Great River Milling, another quality source for organic flour, sells buckwheat flour as well as rye, corn, and spelt on Amazon.com.

CHESTNUT FLOUR: Several Italian brands are available on Amazon. For domestic organic chestnut flour, there is Ladd Hill Orchards (laddhillchestnuts.com) in Oregon's Willamette Valley.

DEMETER-CERTIFIED BIODYNAMIC FLOUR: If you'd like to try Demeter-certified biodynamically farmed flours like the ones Denise Pölzelbauer and Heinz Weichardt use, look for Isis biodynamic whole wheat flour (isisbiodynamic.com) at Whole Foods.

FRENCH AND FRENCH-STYLE FLOUR: Le Panier (lepanier.com) sells organic Type 55 Francine flour, imported from France. But in general, it is easier to find American-milled French-style flour than it is to find flour imported from France. King Arthur (kingarthurflour.com) sells French-style flour

with a high ash content that is similar to Type 65. For Type 55-, 65-, and 85-style flours, I recommend Central Milling (centralmilling.com): Their all-purpose flour is equivalent to Type 55; their Organic Artisan Baker's Craft flour is like Type 65; their Type 85 equivalent, a high-extraction wheat flour, is labeled Type 85. Heartland Mill (heartlandmill.com), another favorite of craft bakers, sells all-purpose flour that is equivalent to Type 55, as well as Golden Buffalo, a Type 65 equivalent, and Type 65 Turkey flour, another good choice.

GRANO DEL MIRACOLO: Claudio Grossi's heirloom flour blend, milled by Molino Grassi, is available on Amazon.

GRAPESEED FLOUR: Aprèsvin (apresvin.com) sells grapeseed flours made from the seeds of Chardonnay, Reisling, Merlot, and Cabernet grapes.

GRÜNKERN: This flour is available seasonally from Lentz Spelt Farms (lentzspelt.com), a Washington State farm that also sells organic emmer and einkorn flour to consumers.

ITALIAN AND ITALIAN-STYLE FLOUR: Molino Grassi 00 and extra-fancy semolina flours are available in the U.S. from Amazon. Also on Amazon, Mulino Marino organic 0 and 00 flours, and Manitaly 0 flour with a W value of 330 to 350.

RYE FLOUR: King Arthur (kingarthurflour.com) sells dark and white rye flour as well as rye chops. Central Milling (centralmilling.com) sells dark and medium rye flour.

SEEDS AND WHOLE GRAINS: There's no need to mail-order these. Seeds and whole grains from your natural foods store will work well in these recipes.

SICILIAN HERITAGE FLOURS: Senatore Cappelli, Tumminia (also called Timilia), and Maiorca flours are available from Tipici Pugliesi (tipicipugliesi .com), which also sells a number of *grani antichi* flours. Gustiamo (gustiamo.com) is another good source for Sicilian flours. Molini del Ponte (molinidelponte.com) sells a Sicilian flour blend including 30 percent Tumminia on Amazon.

SPELT, EMMER, EINKORN, AND KHORASAN FLOUR: Bob's Red Mill and Arrowhead Mills sell these ancient grain flours at supermarkets across the country. Small Valley Milling (smallvalleymilling.com) sells organic wheat, emmer, einkorn, rye, and corn flour as well as whole wheat, rye, emmer, and einkorn berries. Bluebird Grain Farms (bluebirdgrainfarms.com) sells milled-to-order organic emmer and einkorn flour. Montana Flour & Grains (montanaflour.com) sells organic khorasan and spelt flour. Maine Grains (mainegrains.com) has led the charge in working with local farmers and offering a large variety of heritage wheat, including spelt.

SPROUTED FLOUR: Sprouted wheat flour is available from King Arthur Flour (kingarthurflour.com). Lindley Mills (lindleymills.com) in North Carolina sells organic sprouted wheat flour online. Blue Mountain Organics (bluemountainorganics.com) sells a range of sprouted flours, including rye, spelt, Kamut, and buckwheat.

SALT: My favorite salt is the fine grey sea salt from France. It is available from Brittany Sea Salt on Amazon.

DRY INSTANT YEAST: I like SAF instant yeast, stocked by King Arthur (kingarthurflour.com). Be sure to order the Red Label yeast; Gold label is for high-sugar breads.

Equipment

Here are some resources for the equipment needed to make the breads in this book. Some items (a KitchenAid mixer, a baking stone) are essential, while others (rattan proofing baskets from Germany) are nice to have but not absolutely necessary. A few items—a wood-fired oven, a professional-style spiral mixer, a home mill—are for passionate amateurs.

AMAZON: You can find any baking item you need here, including a pH meter and a Graef manually operated bread slicer.

COOPÉRATIVE VANNERIE DES VILLAINES (VANNERIE.COM): French bannetons and baskets.

HERBERT BIRNBAUM (HERBERT-BIRNBAUM.DE): Beautiful rattan proofing baskets, in all shapes and sizes, made in Germany.

RINGOPLAST (RINGOPLAST.DE): A source for hygieni, dishwasher-safe, plastic bannetons, in a huge variety of sizes.

KING ARTHUR FLOUR (KINGARTHURFLOUR.COM): The King Arthur website sells a wide range of equipment as well as ingredients. A reliable source for the KitchenAid Pro Line stand mixer used to test the recipes in this book, it also stocks bread knives, *lames,* pizza wheels, pastry brushes, bannetons, baker's linen, baking steels, brioche pans, and dough rising containers.

MAINE WOOD HEAT CO. (MAINEWOODHEAT.COM): This company custom-crafts wood-fired ovens for the home, as well as imports and distributes Le Panyol earthenware ovens from France.

PLEASANT HILL GRAIN (PLEASANTHILLGRAIN.COM): An outstanding resource and one-stop shop, with knowledgeable and helpful staff. Baking stones, KoMo and Mockmill home mills, KoMo rattan proofing baskets, bread dough scoring *lames,* bench scrapers, dough stencils, digital scales, baking peels, cast-iron skillets and loaf pans, and Dutch ovens. Pleasant Hill is the exclusive U.S. distributor of the German brand Häussler, offering spiral mixers, which are close to commercial quality and design, and countertop electric stone ovens. It also sells the Brod & Taylor proofer, which will keep your dough at whatever temperature you'd like, in a moist environment. A good source for home mills and flour sifters, it also stocks a good selection of triple-cleaned grain for home milling and sprouting. Pleasant Hill Grain also sells ingredients including barley malt syrup and instant yeast.

MIELE: For information on Miele steam-injected home ovens, look at mieleusa.com

WALDNER BIOTECH (WALDNER-BIOTECH.AT): This company, which makes stone mills for small bakeries (Denise Pölzelbauer has one), also makes a high-quality home mill.

EXTREME WELLNESS SUPPLY: For bakers who want to try hand-milling, (extremewellnesssupply.com) offers a Samap manual stone grain mill grinder.

RESOURCES: BAKERS AND MILLS

Featured Bakers

For readers who would like to experience some of the breads in this book as I first did, here is the contact info of the bakeries featured in this book. Each one of them is worth a visit for unique, extraordinarily crafted loaves.

Marie-Christine Aractingi, Boulangerie Dame Farine
77 avenue de la Corse
13007 Marseille
France
Tel.: 33 4 91 85 05
Damefarine.fr

Vincenzo Benvenuto, Caffetteria del Viale
Viale Regina Mergherita
10 Altamura
Italy
Tel.: 080 3141156

Antonius Beumer and Christa Lutum, Bäckerei Beumer & Lutum
Naumburger Str. 4
12057 Berlin, Neukölln
Germany
Tel.: 030 61 67 55 70
beumer-lutum.de

Pierre-Julien Bouniol, Bella Ciao Boulangerie Utopiste
43 rue des Fourbisseurs
84000 Avignon
France
Tel.: 08 92 97 61 95
facebook.com/boulangeriebellaciao/

Sébastien Bruno and Erwan Blanche, Boulangerie Utopie
20 rue Jean-Pierre Timbaud
75011 Paris
France
Tel.: 09 82 50 74 48
facebook.com/Boulangerie-
Utopie-847556035308522/

Arnaud Delmontel, Maison Arnaud Delmontel
39 rue des Martyrs
75009 Paris
France
(Arnaud has 3 additional Parisian shops, at 45 rue de Douai, 25 rue de Levis, and 57 rue Damremont)
Tel.: 33 (0)1 48 78 29 33
Arnaud-delmontel.com

Florian Domberger, Domberger Brot-Werk
Essener Strasse 11
10555 Berlin
Germany
Tel.: 49 30 23560471
domberger-brot-werk.com

Arnd Erbel, Bäckerei Erbel
Hindenburgpl. 1
91462 Dachsbach
Germany
Tel.: 49 09163 80 96
arnderbel.de

Forno Campo de' Fiori
Piazza Campo de' Fiori 22
00186 Rome
Italy
Tel.: 39 06 6880 6662

Franco Frati, Panificio Franco Frati
Via Raffaello Sanzio 11
43100 Parma
Italy
Tel.: 39 0521 964013

Marianne Ganachaud and Valerie Santrot, Gana
226 rue des Pyrenees
75020 Paris
France
Tel.: 01 43 58 42 62
gana.fr

Jochen Gaues, Bäcker Gaues
Ahnsbecker Strasse 4-6
29331 Lachendorf
Germany
(Jochen operates 14 additional shops—nine in Hamburg, one in Hannover, one in Braunschweig, one in Wolfsburg, one in Burgwedel, and one in Celle)
Tel.: 05145 28 54
baecker-gaues.de

Ottavio Guccione, l'Antico Forno San Michele
Via F.G. Pipitone 61
90144 Palermo
Italy
Tel.: 39 091 346030

Roland Hertzog,
Boulangerie Patisserie Hertzog
28 rue de Colmar
68320 Muntenheim
France
Tel.: 03 89 47 40 91
Boulangerie-patisserie-hertzog.fr

Josef Hinkel, Bäckerei Hinkel
Mittelstrasse 25
40213 Dusseldorf
Germany
Tel.: 49 211 86203421
baeckerei-hinkel.de

Rodolphe Landemaine,
Maison Landemaine
56 rue de Clichy
75009 Paris
France
(This is Rodolphe's original shop;
there are 13 additional locations
around Paris)
Tel.: 01 48 74 37 64
Maisonlandemaine.com

Amber Lambke, Maine Grains
42 Court Street
Skowhegan, ME 04976
Tel.: 207 474 8001
mainegrains.com
Maine Grains has been a leader in
getting local farmers to grow heritage
grain and in milling this grain using a
traditional stone milling process.

Nunzio Ninivaggi, Il Pane di Nunzio
Via Torino 36,
70022 Altamura
Italy
Tel.: 080 3115852
ilpanedinunzio.com

Pierre Nury, Fournil 1869
63410 Loubeyrat
France
Tel.: 33 4 73 86 55 95

Marjo and Tero Peltonen, Tuorilan
Kotileipomo
Kirkkotori 2
06100 Porvoo
Finland
Tel.: 019 650 094
tuorilankotileipomo.fi

Apollonia Poilâne, Poilâne
8 Rue du Cherche-Midi
75006 Paris
France
Tel.: 33 1 45 48 42 59
Poilane.com

Max Poilâne,
Boulangerie Max Poilâne
87 Rue Brancion
75015 Paris
France
Tel.: 33 1 48 28 45 90
Max-poilane.fr

Denise Pölzelbauer,
Denise Bäckerin
Hauptstrasse 23
Brunn an der Pitten
2823 Niederosterreich
Austria
Tel.: 0043 650 80 11 900
baeckerin.at

Rocco Princi
Via Speronari 6
20123 Milan
Italy
Tel.: 39 02 874797
Princi.com

Didier Rosada,
Uptown Bakers
5335 Kilmer Pl.
Hyattsville, MD 20781
Tel.: 301 846 1500
uptownbakers.com

Pierluigi Roscioli,
Antico Forno Roscioli
Via dei Chiavari 34
00186 Rome
Italy
Tel.: 39 06 686 4045
anticofornoroscioli.it

Richard Ruan,
La Boulangerie des Carmes
21 Boulevard Henri Arnauld
49100 Angers
France
Tel.: 33 06 43 2064 14

Dominique Saibron,
Dominique Saibron Paris
77 Avenue du General Leclerc
75014 Paris
France
Tel.: 01 43 35 01 07
dominique-saibron.com

Maurizio Spinello, Forno Santa Rita
C.da Santa Rita
93100 Caltanissetta
Italy
Tel.: 39 339 768 8542
Fornosantarita.com

Heinz Weichardt,
Weichardt-Brot
Mehlitzstrasse 7
10715 Berlin
Germany
49 30 8738099
Weichardt.de

Mills

I gained most of my knowledge of contemporary milling from conversations with the passionate millers at the following mills:

Central Milling

122 E. Center Street
Logan, UT 84321
Tel.: 35-752-6625
centralmilling.com

Nicky Giusto is the fifth generation of Giustos in the bread business. Today he is a managing partner at employee-owned Central Milling, where he is known for cultivating close relationships with farmers who supply the mill with grain. He is also the flour guru to some of America's most innovative and accomplished bakers. Unusual among top mills, Central Milling packages the same flours it sells to professionals in small quantities for home baking. Most of the flours used in the recipes in this book can be found at Central Milling's online store. Central Milling has recently opened a training center for bakers.

Farmer Ground Flour

240 Aiken Road
Trumansburg, NY 14886
Tel.: 607-387-1007
farmergroundflour.com

A U.S. example of farmer/miller collaboration. Millers Greg Russo and Neal Johnston work with organic farmer Thor Oechsner to produce fresh organic flour from grain grown in the Finger Lakes region. Grain is ground to order on a sequence of custom millstones. Some of it is destined for Farmer Ground's colleagues at Wide Awake Bakery. The flour is available to consumers at dozens of markets in the Northeast.

Heartland Mill

124 N. Highway 167
Marienthal, KS 67663
Tel.: 800 232-8533
heartlandmill.com

Former Kansas grain farmer Mark Nightengale has been operating this groundbreaking organic mill since the late 1970s, and continues to innovate. Working with local farmers who thoughtfully grow organic grain, Nightengale meticulously tests his grain and flour both in a lab and by baking test loaves, similar to the French system. Also similar to top French mills, Heartland uses both stone and roller mills. Small bags of flour for home bakers, including flour ground from heirloom Turkey Red wheat, are available from Heartland Mill's online store.

La Milanaise

108 QC-214
Milan, Quebec
Canada
Tel.: 1 450 349 1747
lamilanaise.com

Robert and Lily Beauchemin started milling organic wheat that they grew on their small organic farm 40 years ago. As demand increased, their business grew into a high-tech plant able to process 350 tons of organic Canadian grain a day. La Milanaise has agronomists on staff to support a network of grain farmers in managing organic crops. A testing lab ensures consistency and an on-staff baker offers technical support to professionals. Small bags of La Milanaise flour are available to consumers in markets throughout eastern Canada.

Bellot Minoteries

Geoffret 794000
Saint Martin de Saint Maixent
France
05 49 76 07 87
bellotminoteries.fr

A leading independent mill in France with a full line of organic specialty flours, some of which are available online to consumers.

Bio-Mühle Eiling

Mohnestrasse 98
59581 Warstein-Sichtigvor
Tel.: 02925-2420
Biomuehle-eiling.de

Florian Domberger gets his organic rye flour from this mill, whose building dates back to the 14th century.

Minoterie Suire

Le Feuillou
44190 Boussay
France
Tel.: 02 28 21 21 880
minoterie-suire.com

Family-run for three generations, these days by master miller Bertrand Girardeau, this organic mill supplies flour to some of France's best bakers. Suire is justly famous for its refurbished antique stone mill, as well as its meticulous roller milling. Its state-of-the-art flour testing program, run by Fabrice Guéry, is a model for producing flour of consistent quality.

Molino Grassi
Via Emilia Ovest 347
43126 Parma
Italy
Tel.: 39 0521 662511
Molinograssi.it
A fourth-generation Italian mill that makes flour for both bread and pasta, Molino Grassi has been a leader in organics and heritage wheat flours. Silvio Grassi, along with farmer Claudio Grossi, was instrumental in reviving Grano del Miracolo, an old variety of wheat, local to Parma, that was near extinction but rich in protein, minerals, and antioxidants as well as low in gluten. Molino Grassi flour, including Grano del Miracolo, is available on Amazon, at Eataly stores in the U.S., and at Whole Foods on the East Coast.

Molini Riggi
Via Borremans 116
C.da Busiti
93100 Caltanisetta
Italy
Tel.: 39 0934 555070
moliniriggi.it
Since 1955, the Riggi family has been stone milling Sicilian wheat, including heritage varieties like Senatore Cappelli, Tumminia, and Russello. A short supply chain and personal relationships developed over many years—most of the grain comes from farms within Sicily well known to the Riggi family—assures freshness and quality. As part of a consortium of Sicilian specialty food companies called Gustoso, Riggi will soon be exporting flour to the U.S. for distribution to grocery stores.

Small Valley Milling
917 Small Valley Road
Halifax, PA 17032
Tel.: 717-362-9850
smallvalleymilling.com
A Pennsylvania mill specializing in spelt, Small Valley also sells organic wheat, emmer, einkorn, rye, and corn flour as well as whole wheat, rye, emmer, and einkorn berries. Small quantities are available to home bakers through their website.

Molino Mininni
Via Graviscella 1448
Altamura BA
Italy 70022
Tel.: 390803103625
Molinomininni.com
The Altamura mill where Nunzio Ninivaggi gets his flour, Molino Mininni has a large selection of durum wheat products, from whole semolina flour to semolina remacinata to pasta flour.

Moulin Saint-Joseph
Chemin du Moulin
13450 Grans
France
moulinsaintjoseph.wixsite.com /lemoulin
A lovely old-fashioned mill in Provence, where Marie-Christine Aractangi of Dame Farine buys flour. A store at the mill sells small bags of flour, including Type 170 local rye, whole spelt, buckwheat, and khorasan to visitors.

Moulin Decollogne
4, Rue de l'Ancienne Eglise
77410 Precy-sur-Marne
France
Tel.: 0160019004
decollogne.fr
The organic mill northeast of Paris where Rodolphe Landemaine sources his flour, Moulin Decollogne also sells its flours at retail in French supermarket chain Carrefour.

Rolle-Mühle
Zschopenthal 15
09437 Grunhainichen
Germany
Tel.: 49 3725 34730
rolle-muehle.de
Florian Domberger's source for organic spelt and wheat flour, this hydro-powered mill operates entirely with clean electricity from renewable energy. For visitors, there are tours of the mill and a farm shop where flour as well as butter and yogurt are available for purchase.

ACKNOWLEDGMENTS

This book is the product of my dynamic collaboration partnership with Joerg Lehmann. I couldn't have undertaken such an ambitious project without him by my side. He had dreamed for years about searching out the best European bakers and breads that he might photograph. I had been dreaming about a similar search for unique artisans and their recipes. When we met, it seemed destined. During the past two years, we have traveled together and spoken dozens of times a week, bringing our individual ideas together and taking them in a new direction. On the road, I saw him capture brilliant moments in time—in wheat fields, at bakeries, at mills. I cherish the memory of the many hours we spent together in his Berlin studio, as I watched him capture on camera the essence of each bread. Joerg's curiosity, taste, and perfectionism are evident in every photo. He is now one of the most important people in my life.

On the road and in the studio, Joerg's wife, Lisa, a talented chef and cookbook author, was there to offer her critical eye and styling expertise. Her sense of fun and delightful giggle lightened all the potentially tense moments. She kept us all well fed with her Asian-inflected cooking. As Joerg's long-time collaborator, she is like his second brain, able to suggest ideas and adjustments in perfect alignment with his aesthetic.

I met Didier Rosada at a point in my life when I had been baking for several years without formal training and was in need of a professional mentor. He helped me bring Bread Alone to a new level. Didier began baking at a young age, obtained his Certificat d'Aptitude Professionnel in baking, and had many years of experience at craft bakeries from Brazil to South Korea. He coached the team that won the Coupe du Monde in 2005. He was already well

known in the bread-baking community as a go-to teacher, master technician, and bread scientist. During the writing of this book, I relied on his experience to help me translate professional recipes for serious home bakers. He brought his skill and good humor to our weeklong photo shoot, motivating the team and making the experience fun for everyone while making sure the breads were absolutely beautiful.

It is increasingly rare in the United States to find fathers and sons working together in a family business, especially a business where craft is involved. Seven years ago, my older son, Nels, chose to join the business after getting his M.B.A. from the Stern School of Business at NYU. We didn't have a road map. We didn't even talk about a plan. We only talked about having him come in. Since he came on board he has brought a brilliant vision and new level of discipline, organization, professional passion, and long-term planning to the company. He is working to create a vibrant company culture, introducing events and traditions that bring us closer together. He has developed and is executing an ambitious program for overall sustainability, putting 664 solar panels on the roof of the brand-new bakery he envisioned and quickly made into a reality. Within just a few years, under Nels's leadership, Bread Alone will be producing all of its own power. He is now managing all day-to-day operations of the bakery. Today's reality is that I'm assisting him, he isn't assisting me. I couldn't be more proud or happier about this transition.

Sharon Burns-Leader joined Bread Alone when it was very small. We have worked together through all of the challenges involved in growing the business for thirty years. Today she manages the cafes, runs the old Boiceville bakery where we bake breads made with local heirloom and heritage flours. She has committed herself to supporting the local grain economy and travels throughout the United States and to Scandinavia to learn about the emergence of local grains. She refined and tested some of the trickiest, most complex recipes in this book, bringing her years of experience especially with whole grains and rye breads to bear. I couldn't have written this book without the support of Nels and Sharon, who ran the bakery while I was otherwise occupied. Thanks also to Sarah Cincotti, who assisted Sharon in testing the recipes.

Zach Golper from Bien Cuit recommended Amy Vogler to me when I was looking for a recipe tester. Amy tested every recipe in this book multiple times, photographing her process so I could see where she was encountering difficulties. She was determined to get each bread just right and often made improvements to my work along the way. She is a delight to work with, a recipe tester among recipe testers, and I would work with her again in a second.

Lauren Chattman and I have been writing books together for more than twelve years. This is our fourth collaboration. It takes a very patient and special person to deal with my quirkiness and relentless barrage of big and small ideas that come to me at all hours. Lauren knows how to politely and firmly say to me, "Dan, time to focus."

Bread Alone has been very lucky to be able to count on former County Executive Mike Hein, Ulster Town Supervisor Jim Quigley, New York State Assemblyman Kevin Cahill, and Meghan Taylor and Monique LeGendre from Empire State Development. Bread Alone could never have built our new bakery without their support.

Thanks to Bread Alone's equipment suppliers: Bakon USA, BM Tech, Chris Bernard, Diosna, Heuft, Hoba, Isenhager, Jac, Koma, Kwik Lok, Merrand, Pietroberto, Rheon USA, Revent, Ringoplast, and Rondo.

I owe my early mentors a tremendous debt of gratitude: Pierre Poilâne, Max Poilâne, Lionel Poilâne, Basile Kamir, Bernard Ganachaud, Jean LeFleur, and Pierre Nury introduced me to sourdough baking before I knew what sourdough was, and inspired me to seek out other experts as part of my continuing baker's education.

The following bakers, farmers, and millers generously shared their expertise—on their bread, grain, flour—and tremendous knowledge with me: Craig Adams; Marie-Christine Aractingi; Cesare Agnostini; Chafik Baghdadi; Bernardino and Fabio Bartocci; Vincenzo Benvenuto; Antonius Beumer; Robert Beauchemin; Erwan Blanche; Marco Bocchini; Pierre-Julien Bouniol; Sébastien Bruno; Arnaud Delmontel; Giuseppe DiCarlo; Eugenia Di Cocco; Arnd Erbel; Franco Frati; Jochen Gaues; Bertrand Girardeau; Nicky Giusto; Silvio Grassi; Claudio Grossi; Ottavio Guccione; Josef Hinkel; Neal Johnston; Rodolphe Landemaine; Christa Lutum; Bjorn Meadow; Mark Nightengale; Nunzio Ninivaggi; Marjo and Tero Peltonen; Apollonia Poilâne; Denise Pölzelbauer; Calogero; Marco; and Alessandro Riggi; Pierluigi Roscioli; Richard Ruan; Greg Russo; Dominique Saibron; Maurizio Spinello; Silvia Siletti;; Bruno Texier; Jean Philippe de Tonnac; Heinz Weichardt.

Diosna lent us a spiral mixer for our testing and photo shoot, Pleasant Hill Grain supplied the Haussler mixer, Rofco oven, and KoMo home mill. Cooperative Vannerie and Herbert Birnbaum supplied the bannetons.

Minoterie Suire, Molino Grassi, and Molini Riggi sent flour for our Berlin photo shoot.

Marco Gobetti, Chris Miller, Mark Sorrells, Stephen Jones, Heather Darby, Luc De Vuyst, Dane Cook, and Joao Miguel Rocha took considerable time to explain the science informing grain farming, milling, and sourdough practice.

Nancy Harmon Jenkins is an invaluable resource when it comes to Italian food and culture.

Check out her website, nancyharmonjenkins.com. Nancy introduced me to Onofrio Pepe, my guide in Altamura.

The management team at Bread Alone, Paul Amos, Melissa Beck, Julie Beesmer, Heather Berman-Waner, Teresa Carlucci, Katy Caron, Robby Crafton, Dan Crandell, Charlie DeBellis, David Gardner, Margarito Jiminez, Juan Hermandez, Michael Lewin-Jacus, Ron Limoges, Frank Mackey, Lisa Mason, Andy McDermott, Dan Milroy, Linda Neu, Mike Petty, Mia Pillsworth, Kristen Pratt, Christina Rivera, Angelo Santelli, Halley Santelli, Mike Smetak, Rosa Solis, Karma Tenzin, Sonum Wangdue, and Elizabeth Welch, supported me at all times and in many ways while I was occupied with my research and writing.

Paul Kellar and Ann Finnegan provided legal and financial advice. My sister Nancy Largay has contributed some very helpful and valuable marketing advice over the years. Terry Funk-Antman offered wise words when I needed them.

The team at Penguin Random House was 100 percent onboard and hands-off as Joerg and I traveled through Europe, refining our ideas and our recipe list. Pam Krauss acquired the project and then had the confidence to let us follow our dreams. Lucia Watson provided the perfect balance of guidance and freedom. Ashley Tucker came up with an understated but brilliant book design. Anne Kosmoski, Lindsay Gordon, and Farin Schlussel took charge of marketing and promoting the book. Carrie Bachman joined the publicity team and is helping bring the book to the world. Suzy Swartz handled all of the little details, as well as contributing to the editing of the manuscript.

An informal Living Bread support team was instrumental to the success of this project. My agent, Janis Donnaud, helped me shape my ideas early on and continues to advocate for my work post-publication. I'll always be grateful for the recognition that she gave to my work and her insistence on its value. Florian Domberger not only allowed me to take over his Berlin bakery for a week, but shared his knowledge of German breads and served as a translator and general troubleshooter during and after. Fabrice Guéry amazed everyone including me with his effortless ability to bake beautiful breads for the photo shoot. Jason Tucker, the quality control manager at Bread Alone, took time out of his days to review the recipes and traveled with me to Berlin to bake at the photo shoot, where he learned to drink beer German-style with his new mentors, Didier and Fabrice, while I was sleeping.

Rosie Mashale of Baphumelele and Gail Johnson of Nkosi's Haven both care for hundreds of orphans every day. One of the great and unexpected experiences of my baking life has been working with them to establish bakeries for their communities.

I live eight thousand miles away from Richard and Judy Wilkes in Cape Town, but we couldn't be closer friends. Their friendship and support have been unwavering, whether they are hosting me at their home or visiting me in Woodstock. Along with their daughters Emily and Amy and son-in-law Mike, they've become my second family. Their philanthropic efforts are an inspiration.

While they don't currently work day-to-day in the family business, my extended family and children Liv and Noah; Alex Kasputis; son-in-law Mick Bechtel; daughter-in-law Chloe Leader; Octavia Fleck; and grandchildren Leila, Otto, and Audriana have lent their support to my work. A special thanks to Lynne Gilson for help with recipe testing, and to Katherine Weisberg, Chloe's mom, for her passionate bread research in both LA and in France.

And a very special thanks to Natalka Chas, who takes care of my home and garden so that I always have a peaceful and beautiful place to come home to.

INDEX

Page numbers in *italics* indicate photos, and page numbers in **bold** indicate profiles of individuals.